GW-BASIC®
Made Easy

Bob Albrecht
Don Inman

Osborne **McGraw-Hill**

Berkeley   New York   St. Louis   San Francisco
Auckland   Bogotá   Hamburg   London   Madrid
Mexico City   Milan   Montreal   New Delhi   Panama City
Paris   São Paulo   Singapore   Sydney
Tokyo   Toronto

Osborne **McGraw-Hill**
2600 Tenth Street
Berkeley, California 94710
U.S.A.

For information on translations and book distributors outside of the U.S.A.,
please write to Osborne **McGraw-Hill** at the above address.

A complete list of trademarks appears on page 407. Screens produced with
InSet, from InSet Systems, Inc.

GW-BASIC® **Made Easy**

67890 DOC 9   . . .1

ISBN 0-07-881473-1

The manuscript for this book was prepared and submitted to Osborne/McGraw-Hill
in electronic form. The acquisitions editor for this project was Jeffrey Pepper, the
technical reviewer was Ethan Winer, and the project editor was Nancy Beckus.

Text design by Judy Wohlfrom, using Times Roman for text body and Univers for
display. Typesetting by Marla Wilson.

Cover art by Bay Graphics Design Associates. Color separation and cover supplier,
Phoenix Color Corporation. Screens by Colour Image. Book printed and bound by
R.R. Donnelley & Sons Company, Crawfordsville, Indiana.

CONTENTS

Preface   vii

About This Book   ix

1   Getting Started   1
A Byte of BASIC History   2
A Dollop of DOS   4
Making a GW-BASIC Master Work Disk   5
Write-Protect and Label Your Master Work Disk   13
Make Some GW-BASIC Work Disks   14
Review   17

2   Do It Now — Immediate Operations   19
Load MS-DOS, Set Date and Time   20
Load GW-BASIC   22
Clear the Screen   24
BEEP, Your First GW-BASIC Keyword   25
Another Way to Clear the Screen   27
Turn the Key Line Off or On   28
Print the Date and Time   30
Print Your Name   31
Set the Date   32
Set the Time   34
Arithmetic   36
Shortcuts for Print   39
Leave GW-BASIC and Return to MS-DOS   40
Review   41

3   Introduction to Programming   43

Load GW-BASIC   44
Your First GW-BASIC Program   47
Saving a Program   55
Loading a Program   58
Listing a Program on the Printer   60
Adding a Line to a Program   61
Saving a Program in ASCII Format   63
Deleting Lines from a Program   64
Return to MS-DOS   65
Review   67

4   Number Crunching   69

Arithmetic with Direct Statements   70
Exponents and Floating Point Numbers   73
Types of Numbers   79
Numeric Variables   82
Programming with Variables   89
Program Remarks   93
An Improved Sales Tax Program   95
Formatting the Printed Results   96
Value of Stocks   103
A Future Value — Compound Interest Program   105
Printing to the Printer   109
Review   111

5   Making Programs More Useful   113

The GOTO Loop   114
A Sales Tax Program with a GOTO Loop   122
Value of Stocks with GOTO Loop   123
Future Value — Compound Interest with GOTO Loop   124
A Modified Future Value — Compound Interest Program   127
Future Value — Compound Interest with Counting Loop   130
Input$ to the Rescue   133
Strings and String Variables   136
The INPUT$ String Function   141
Review   143

6   Control Structures: Decisions and Loops   145

The Useful IF Statement   146
The WHILE...WEND Loop   156

The FOR...NEXT Loop   166
Making Music   172
A Multiple-Choice Statement: ON...GOTO   181
The People's Poll   186
Review   188

7   Function Junction   **191**
Built-in Functions   192
User-Defined Functions   212
Wordsworth   223
Review   226

8   Subroutines   **229**
GOSUB and RETURN   230
Divide and Conquer   243
Prefabricated Programs   253
Review   259

9   Arrays   **261**
Arrays   262
Programming with Arrays   268
Rearranging an Array   285
Review   300

10   Sequential Files   **303**
Types of Data Files   304
Unstructured Sequential Files   305
Structured Sequential Files   322
Some Suggestions About Files   331
Review   335

11   Random-Access Files   **337**
Sequential and Random-Access File Storage   338
Creating a Random-Access File   340
Enter Records from the Keyboard to the Japanese.Ran File   351
Use the Japanese.Ran File for Sequential Practice   352
Use Japanese.Ran for Random Practice   357
A Personal Camping Equipment Catalog   359
Scan the Camping.Cat Catalog   368
Review   370

12   Graphics   **371**

Some Facts About High-Resolution (Screen 2)   372
Drawing Lines   372
Roundish Shapes   386
Some Facts About Color Graphics (Screen 1)   389
Selecting Colors   390
PSET in Screen 1   392
LINE in Screen 1   395
Circles in Screen 1   402
Review   404

Index   **409**

PREFACE

BASIC is the most popular programming language in the world. If you have a computer, you probably have BASIC, the People's Computer Language. BASIC is bundled with (or built into) tens of millions of personal computers. Most versions of BASIC in use today are some form of Microsoft BASIC.

This book is a beginners' book about the most widely used version of BASIC, Microsoft's GW-BASIC. GW-BASIC is virtually identical to BASICA, the version distributed by IBM. GW-BASIC will run on any IBM compatible computer. There are probably more than 30 million legal copies of GW-BASIC (or BASICA) in use, and many unauthorized clones exist.

The most personal way to use a computer is to learn a general-purpose programming language, apply it to interesting problems, and produce useful solutions—*your* solutions. With a little help from this book, you can learn how to read and understand programs written in BASIC. You can learn how to express yourself in BASIC. You can learn how to write BASIC programs, *your* programs, that tell the computer what to do and how to do it—and that result in the end product you want.

If you are a beginner, GW-BASIC (or BASICA) is a great way to start. You can use GW-BASIC to write the best software for you. In this book, we try to show you how to write programs that people can read and understand, programs written in *good style*.

If you like programming, consider moving up to the greatest BASIC ever, Microsoft's QuickBASIC. QuickBASIC is fine for beginners or for those who know a little GW-BASIC; QuickBASIC is excellent for people who want to write professional level software. You can transfer everything you learn in this book to using QuickBASIC.

We have been using BASIC since 1964, the year BASIC was created by John Kemeny and Thomas Kurtz at Dartmouth College. We found that BASIC empowered us. BASIC gave us a quick way to explore or solve a problem. As we became older, BASIC became better—and BASIC continues to improve as it is adjusted to meet the needs of its users. We invite you to browse our monthly columns in *One Thousand* magazine: "Play Together, Learn Together" by Bob Albrecht and George Firedrake, and "Better BASIC Tools" by Don Inman. We hope you find the comraderie and satisfaction that we have in personal programming, personal problem-solving, and personal BASIC.

Bob Albrecht
Don Inman
P.O. Box 1635
Sebastapol, CA 95473-1635

ABOUT THIS BOOK

If you have had no previous programming experience, this is just the book for you. All instructions required to learn and use GW-BASIC are included as needed in each chapter. The programming concepts and methods taught in this book can be transferred easily to other versions of BASIC.

Not only does *GW-BASIC Made Easy* introduce you to GW-BASIC, it also offers a different point of view and a different approach to learning than can be found in other programming books. It is geared to the person with no previous programming experience and with very little computer experience.

The text is sprinkled with lots of programming examples that are fun (and even useful). New concepts are introduced within the context of executable programs, and most new programs are thoroughly explained.

The book starts out by familiarizing you with the MS-DOS and GW-BASIC programming environments. You begin by creating a GW-BASIC work disk customized for your own computer system. You will learn how to execute simple commands in the immediate mode, and then use these commands in your first programs.

Next, you will learn how to use GW-BASIC to do some simple arithmetic, first without and then with numeric variables. Examples are drawn from the area of personal finance. You will then use some of GW-BASIC's control structures to make your programs more useful, more efficient, and more easily understood.

There are a number of useful preprogrammed functions in GW-BASIC that make programming quicker and easier. Many of the features you need to write programs quickly are already part of the language. In addition, if you need to perform some procedure or calculation frequently in a program, you can define your own functions.

You will also learn how to use subroutines to divide a large program into smaller, more manageable blocks. You will write separate subroutines to perform each unique task. The main program then calls upon the subroutines as needed.

Arrays allow you to store and access related information easily and efficiently. You will learn why arrays are so powerful, and how to use them for such tasks as sorting lists of numbers or names.

Two chapters introduce you to three different kinds of data files: unstructured sequential files, structured sequential files, and random-access files. You will learn how to store and retrieve information from each kind of file, and how to determine which kind of file is best for different applications.

The book concludes with a chapter on the use of the two most popular graphic modes: You will learn how to locate a position on the screen, draw lines, rectangles, circles, and other shapes. These techniques are applied in drawing various kinds of graphs and charts and in other useful and entertaining endeavors. GW-BASIC is an exceptionally rich and powerful programming language. This book introduces you to its possibilities. In addition, the book will help you develop your own skills in formulating problems and in writing elegant programs.

GW-BASIC Made Easy
Convenience Disk

You may order a disk containing all programs and data files discussed in *GW-BASIC Made Easy*. This disk includes:

- All GW-BASIC programs discussed in the book.

- Variations of many of the programs discussed in the book, showing alternative ways of accomplishing the programming task. These variations do not appear in the book.

- A bonus: several additional programs you can't live without.

Two sizes of disks are available:

5-1/4" disk $10.00
3-1/2" disk $11.00

Each is shipped first class postpaid. Send check or money order to:

> Different Worlds Publications
> 2814 19th Street
> San Francisco, CA 94110

California residents please add applicable sales tax.

Name: _____

Address: _____

City/State: _____ Zip: _____

Teaching BASIC to Kids
A Sharebook by Bob Albrecht and George Firedrake

We would like to share 27 years of experience teaching BASIC to kids. So we are writing a sharebook called, of course, *Teaching BASIC to Kids*.

Teaching BASIC to Kids is written for people who know some BASIC and want to help someone else learn BASIC. Perhaps you are a father or mother teaching BASIC to a daughter or son, or a teacher helping a student. We'll proffer suggestions on how to make the learning task easy—and fun. We are especially interested in using BASIC in mathematics and science. After covering the basics of BASIC, we'll show you many ways to use it as a tool and toy for exploring, learning, and teaching math and science.

The first ten pages are free. To get the first ten pages, send a SELF-ADDRESSED, STAMPED ENVELOPE to:

> BASIC for Kids
> P.O. Box 1635
> Sebastopol, CA 95473-1635

Teaching BASIC to Kids is a sharebook. You may freely copy it and share it with others.

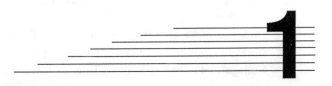

GETTING STARTED

Relax. Make yourself comfortable. In this chapter, you will

- learn a little about the history of BASIC, from its birth in 1964 to its present status as the world's most popular computer language

- be introduced to GW-BASIC, also known as BASICA (on IBM Personal Computers) and Tandy BASIC (the version bundled with the Tandy 1000 series of computers)

- learn how to make GW-BASIC Work Disks that you can use to ease your tasks as you learn to use, understand, and enjoy GW-BASIC

Those of you who are unfamiliar with computers, and the MS-DOS (Microsoft Disk Operating System) commands available to you, will learn everything you need to get started in this chapter; those of you who are already somewhat familiar with MS-DOS may wish simply to scan these sections.

A BYTE OF BASIC HISTORY

On May 1, 1964, at 4:00 A.M., Professor John Kemeny and one of his students simultaneously entered and ran separate BASIC programs on the Dartmouth College Time-Sharing System. Thus was born BASIC, the first computer language designed to be learned and used by just about anyone. On that day, BASIC's creators realized their dream of providing easy computer access to all Dartmouth students and faculty.

Dartmouth professors John G. Kemeny and Thomas E. Kurtz developed the original BASIC language as an instructional tool for training novice programmers. The professors' purpose was to design a language that would be easy to learn, but still useful for any programming task. The success of BASIC (Beginner's All-purpose Symbolic Instruction Code) and its widespread use are due to its simplicity, ease of use, and general-purpose computing power.

The original Dartmouth BASIC was designed to

- be general-purpose in nature and thus useful for writing any type of program

- allow for advanced features to be added later

- provide for user/computer interaction

- provide clear and friendly error messages

- give fast response for small programs

- require no knowledge of hardware

- shield the user from the computer's operating system

One of the authors of this book learned about BASIC soon after its creation, and immediately switched from an earlier language (FORTRAN) to BASIC as the best language for teaching children how to program. He printed cards and buttons with the message SHAFT (Society to Help Abolish FORTRAN Teaching) and traveled the country, spreading the word about BASIC to teachers and students in elementary and secondary schools.

In 1965, BASIC became available outside Dartmouth, initially by means of time-sharing systems. BASIC's use later spread to less expensive dedicated minicomputers. When microcomputers were introduced to the public in the 1970s as personal computers, the computer moved from the realm of the professional programmer into the domain of the creative amateur. The only higher-level language available for these early personal computers was BASIC. BASIC tutorials and programs were regular features of early computer magazines, such as *People's Computer Company* and *Creative Computing.*

A broader base for BASIC was created around 1975, when micro-computers were introduced to the public as personal computers—computers for everyone. In one giant step and a series of short hops, the computer moved into the hands of enthusiastic amateurs, who collectively created a new form of programming called "spaghetti code." BASIC programs were a tangled skein, but the sauce was heady—power over the computer in the hands of people.

Perhaps some of you remember when BASIC really became the people's computer language. In 1975, Ed Roberts, definitely the father of the personal computer, gave us the ALTAIR 8800. Soon thereafter, a kid named Bill Gates gave us ALTAIR BASIC, later called Microsoft BASIC. In its most recent manifestations, Microsoft BASIC is the worldwide de facto standard.

In those days of yore, memory was dear, BASIC was primitive, and BASIC programs were crunched into the smallest possible space—unreadable to anyone who was not a true believer. You still see remnants of this today in computer magazines that publish crunched programs readable by the dedicated user, but incomprehensible to most of us. Fortunately, computers got better, memories got bigger, and BASIC got better and better and better, in answer to the needs of people. You can count on this continuing.

Some form of Microsoft BASIC is built into, or bundled with, most computers used in today's homes, schools, and businesses. The version of Microsoft BASIC covered in this book is the one used on IBM PC compatible computers. It is known by various names, including the following:

- **GW-BASIC** is the generic form of Microsoft BASIC. If you have an IBM PC "clone," you probably already have this version, perhaps on the MS-DOS disk or on a separate disk. For information about GW-BASIC, contact Microsoft Corporation, P.O. Box 97017, Redmond, WA 98073-9717. Phone: (206) 882-8080.

- **BASICA** is virtually the same as GW-BASIC, licensed to and dis-tributed by IBM.

- **Tandy BASIC** is virtually the same as GW-BASIC. It is bundled with the Tandy 1000 series of computers. This is the version of Microsoft BASIC used by the authors in writing this book.

In this book, the term GW-BASIC is used to mean any of the above versions of Microsoft BASIC. GW-BASIC runs under the Microsoft Disk Operating System (MS-DOS) on more than 30 million IBM PC compatible computers, the overwhelming world standard. Most GW-BASIC programs will also run in Microsoft QuickBASIC, the latest and best BASIC for both beginners and professional users. You can begin with GW-BASIC, and then transfer your skills to QuickBASIC. The programming style used in this book is designed to make it easy for you to move on to QuickBASIC.

You can learn to read and understand BASIC programs that are written in good style. Using this book, you can learn to express yourself in BASIC and you can use it to make the computer do what *you* want it to do—the way *you* want it done.

A DOLLOP OF DOS

The authors assume that you have some knowledge of MS-DOS (Microsoft Disk Operating System), or of PC-DOS, the version of MS-DOS licensed to IBM. In particular, we assume that you know how to use the following MS-DOS (or PC-DOS) commands:

DIR	The DIRectory command. Use it to list the names of all files on a disk.
DISKCOPY	Copies everything on a disk to another disk.
COPY	Copies named files, or groups of named files.
FORMAT	Formats a disk. A new, never-before-used disk must be formatted before it can be used. A previously used disk can be recycled, but do so with caution; formatting erases previously stored information from the disk.

It is also assumed that you are using MS-DOS and GW-BASIC from disk drive A. Therefore, when you load MS-DOS into your computer, you will see the famous MS-DOS A> prompt and blinking cursor, as shown here:

A>_

In this case, disk drive A is your *default disk drive*. Information is read from, or written to, drive A (the default drive) unless you designate another disk drive. This book assumes that you will load MS-DOS and GW-BASIC into the computer's memory from disk drive A, the default drive.

However, if your system has a hard disk drive, then you are probably using MS-DOS from your hard disk. You see a C> prompt and blinking cursor, shown here:

```
C>_
```

In this case, your hard disk is the default disk drive. Information is read from, and written to, the hard disk drive (the default drive) unless you designate another drive.

GW-BASIC may reside on the MS-DOS floppy disk, on a separate floppy disk, or on the hard disk. Use the MS-DOS DIR command to locate the GW-BASIC file. You are likely to see one of the following filenames in the printout of the directory:

GWBASIC.EXE   or   BASICA.EXE   or   BASIC.EXE

In this book, the filename GWBASIC.EXE is assumed. If the filename on your disk is different, substitute it for GWBASIC.EXE as you read through this book.

MAKING A GW-BASIC MASTER WORK DISK

There are many GW-BASIC programs in this book. You are encouraged to enter and save them to a disk as you wend your way through this learning experience. You will learn how to save programs and other files to your default disk drive and to a designated drive, such as drive B.

If your computer has a single floppy disk drive (drive A) or two floppy disk drives (drives A and B), consider making a GW-BASIC Work Disk with only two files. Note the following example:

COMMAND.COM   copied from MS-DOS

GWBASIC.EXE   copied from whatever disk contains this file

Remember: The GWBASIC.EXE file might be named differently on the system disks in your possession—for example: BASICA.EXE on an IBM PC disk set, or BASIC.EXE on a disk from a Tandy 1000 system.

As you read this book, store the programs and other files you encounter on your Work Disk. Thus, everything you need will be on one disk. To begin a learning session, put your GW-BASIC Work Disk in disk drive A, turn on the computer, and start learning.

The procedures for making a GW-BASIC Master Work Disk are described in subsequent paragraphs—one procedure for a minimum system with one disk drive (drive A), and one for a system with two floppy disk drives (drives A and B). For either system, it is assumed that disk drive A is the default drive. After making a Master Work Disk, you will then make one or more copies to use, and put the Master Work Disk away in a safe place. Use it only to make working copies.

A System with One Disk Drive (Drive A)

If you are using a minimum system with one disk drive, read this section. If you have a system with two disk drives (A and B), skip this section and move on to the section titled "A System with Two Disk Drives (drives A and B)."

FORMAT A BLANK DISK To make a GW-BASIC Work Disk, first format a blank disk. Use the /S option of the FORMAT command, so that the COMMAND.COM file is automatically copied from the MS-DOS disk to your work disk. First make sure the MS-DOS disk is in drive A; then

Type:

FORMAT A: /S

and press the ENTER key.

You will then see the following, or a similar message:

```
Insert new diskette for drive A:
and press ENTER when ready
```

Remove the MS-DOS disk from drive A, insert a blank disk, and press ENTER. The computer will format the disk, and then copy the COMMAND.COM file to the disk. If you format a 3.5-inch disk, the screen

will look like the following. (For a 5.25-inch disk, the listing of the number
of bytes available on the disk will be different.)

```
A> FORMAT A: /S
Insert new diskette for drive A:
and press ENTER when ready

Format complete
System transferred

   730112  bytes total disk space
    68608  bytes used by system
   661504  bytes available on disk

Format another (Y/N)?_
```

The disk is now formatted. Tell the computer you do not want to format
another disk.

Type:

N

and press the ENTER key.

The MS-DOS prompt and cursor appear as shown here:

```
A>_
```

Next, use the DIR command to verify that the COMMAND.COM file is
on the work disk.

Type:

DIR

and press the ENTER key.

You will see on the screen information similar to the following.

```
A>DIR

 Volume in drive A has no label
 Directory of  A:

COMMAND  COM    23612   7-21-90   3:00p
      1 File(s)    661504 bytes free

A>_
```

If you are using a 5.25-inch disk, the number of bytes free will be much less.

COPY GWBASIC.EXE TO THE WORK DISK   Now copy the file
GWBASIC.EXE to your work disk. Although your computer has only one
disk drive, you can still copy a file from one disk to another. There is only
one *physical* disk drive, but to the computer there are two *logical* disk drives.
A large file is copied in pieces; it is first read from the source disk, then
written to the target disk. You will be prompted when it is time to swap the
source disk for the target disk, or vice versa.

Put the disk containing the GWBASIC.EXE file in disk drive A. This is
the source disk.

Type:

COPY A:GWBASIC.EXE B:

and press the ENTER key.

The computer now reads all or part of the file from the source disk in drive
A. In a few moments, you will see this message, or a similar one:

```
Insert diskette for drive B: and press any key when ready
```

MS-DOS has temporarily renamed the one and only disk drive as logical
drive B. Remove the source disk and insert the target disk, your Master Work
Disk. Press any key. The information previously copied from the source disk
is written to the target disk. Soon you will see this, or a similar message:

```
Insert diskette for drive A: and press any key when ready
```

Remove the target disk and insert the source disk. Press any key to
continue the copying. You will be asked alternately to insert the disk for

drive B (the target disk), and then to insert the disk for drive A (the source disk). When the file copying is complete, you will see the following, or a similar message:

```
1 file(s) copied
Insert diskette for drive A: and press any key when ready
```

If you see the previous message, press a key to get the A> prompt back on the screen. Some of you may just see

```
1 file(s) copied

A>_
```

Make sure that your new GW-BASIC Master Work Disk is in disk drive A. Use the DIR command to verify that both the COMMAND.COM file and the GWBASIC.EXE file are on the disk. You will see information similar to the following:

```
A>DIR

 Volume in drive A has no label
 Directory of A:

COMMAND    COM    23612   7-21-90    3:00p
GWBASIC    EXE    72240   7-21-90    3:00p
        2 File(s)    588800 bytes free

A>_
```

This is your GW-BASIC Master Work Disk. Now skip forward to the section "Write-Protect and Label Your Master Work Disk."

A System with Two Disk Drives (Drives A and B)

If you are using a system with two disk drives (drives A and B), follow the procedures in this section to make a GW-BASIC Master Work Disk.

FORMAT A BLANK DISK   First format a blank disk. Use the /S option of the FORMAT command, so that the COMMAND.COM file is automatically copied from the MS-DOS disk to your work disk. Put the MS-DOS disk in drive A, and a blank disk in drive B.

Type:

FORMAT B: /S

and press the ENTER key.

You will see the following message, or a similar one:

```
Insert a new diskette for drive B:
and press ENTER when ready
```

If you have not already done so, insert a blank disk in drive B. Press ENTER, and formatting begins. The computer will format the disk, and then copy the COMMAND.COM file to it. After formatting a 5.25-inch disk, the screen will look something like this:

```
Format complete
System transferred

   362496  bytes total disk space
    68608  bytes used by system
   293888  bytes available on disk

Format another (Y/N)?_
```

The disk is now formatted. Tell the computer you do not want to format another.

Type:

N

and press the ENTER key.

The MS-DOS prompt and cursor appear as shown here:

```
A>_
```

Next, use the DIR command to verify that the COMMAND.COM file is on the work disk in drive B.

Type:

DIR B:

and press the ENTER key.

You will see on the screen information similar to the following:

```
A>DIR B:

 Volume in drive B has no label
 Directory of  B:

COMMAND   COM   23612    7-21-90    3:00p
         1 File(s)    293888 bytes free

A>_
```

If you are using a 3.5-inch disk, the number of bytes free will be much more.

COPY GWBASIC.EXE TO THE WORK DISK   Now copy the file GWBASIC.EXE to your work disk. Put the disk containing the GWBASIC.EXE file in drive A, and your work disk in drive B.

Type:

COPY A:GWBASIC.EXE B:

and press the ENTER key.

The computer now copies GWBASIC.EXE from the disk in drive A to the disk in drive B. You can watch the two disk drive lights winking and blinking alternately as the file is copied. When the file is copied, you will see the following, or something similar:

```
1 file(s) copied

A>_
```

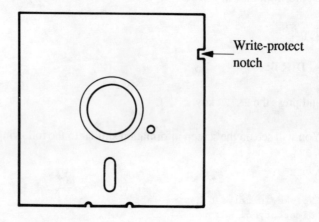

FIGURE 1-1   A write-protect notch on a 5.25-inch disk

Use the DIR command to verify that the work disk in drive B now has two files, COMMAND.COM and GWBASIC.EXE.

Type:

DIR B:

and press the ENTER key.

You will see information similar to the following:

```
A>DIR B:

 Volume in drive B has no label
 Directory of  B:

COMMAND   COM   23612   7-21-90   3:00p

BASIC     EXE   72240   7-21-90   3:00p
        2 File(s)   221184 bytes free

A>_
```

This is your GW-BASIC Master Work Disk.

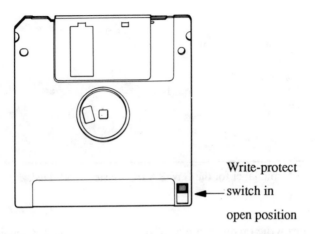

Write-protect
switch in
open position

FIGURE 1-2   A write-protect notch on a 3.5-inch disk

WRITE-PROTECT AND LABEL YOUR MASTER WORK DISK

You will use your GW-BASIC Master Work Disk only to make working copies, each called GW-BASIC Work Disk. Write-protect your Master Work Disk so it cannot be inadvertently erased.

If you are using a 5.25-inch disk, protect it by putting an opaque tab (a write-protect tab) over the write-protect notch on the disk. A write-protect notch is shown in Figure 1-1.

If you are using a 3.5-inch disk, protect it by sliding the write-protect switch to the "no-write" position. When this switch is in the no-write position, you can see through a square hole in the disk. The write-protect switch is shown in Figure 1-2.

If you have not already done so, put a label on your GW-BASIC Master Work Disk. Write on the label a clear description of what is on the disk. If you are using 5.25-inch disks, write the label *before* you put it on the disk. You can damage a 5.25-inch disk by writing on it with a hard-tipped pen. If

```
GW-BASIC                                    1-1-1990
Master Work Disk

COMMAND.COM
GWBASIC.EXE
Use only to make copies
```

FIGURE 1-3   Sample label for the GW-BASIC Master Work Disk

you must write on disks, use a soft-tipped pen. Figure 1-3 shows a sample
label.

Now you are ready to make one or more copies of your Master Work
Disk. These are your working copies; they are not write-protected. Use them
as you learn how to read, understand, and enjoy GW-BASIC. You will save
your programs to these Work Disks.

MAKE SOME GW-BASIC WORK DISKS

Use your GW-BASIC Master Work Disk only to make copies labeled
GW-BASIC Work Disk. Use the copies during a learning session on the
computer. Do not write-protect the working copies; you will save programs
and other files to these Work Disks.

Use the DISKCOPY command to make copies of the Master Work Disk.
The following sections give procedures for a system with only one disk
drive, and for a system with two disk drives. Read the section appropriate for
your system.

A System with One Disk Drive (Drive A)

Although your computer has only one disk drive, you can still copy an entire
disk to another disk, using the MS-DOS DISKCOPY command. There is

only one *physical* drive, but to the computer there are two *logical* drives. Part of a disk is copied at a time. The computer keeps track of which disk is needed at a given time and prompts you when to swap disks.

You will copy *from* the GW-BASIC Master Work Disk (source disk) *to* a GW-BASIC Work Disk (target disk). The DISKCOPY command will copy the contents of the source disk to either a formatted or unformatted target disk. In the description that follows, the contents of the Master Work Disk are copied to an unformatted disk.

Make sure that the MS-DOS disk is in the disk drive, and then do the following:

Type:

DISKCOPY A: B:

and press the ENTER key.

You will then see this message:

```
Insert SOURCE diskette in drive A:
Press any key when ready ...
```

The source disk is your Master Work Disk. Insert this disk in the disk drive and press a key. If you are copying from a 5.25-inch disk, you will see this message:

```
Copying 40 tracks
9 Sectors/Track, 2 side(s)
```

If you are copying from a 3.5-inch disk, you will see a slightly different message, as follows:

```
Copying 80 tracks
9 Sectors/Track, 2 side(s)
```

In a few moments, you will be prompted to insert the target disk, like this:

```
Insert TARGET diskette in drive A:
Press any key when ready ...
```

```
GW-BASIC                                    1-1-1990
Work Disk

COMMAND.COM
GWBASIC.EXE
```

FIGURE 1-4   Sample label for the GW-BASIC Work Disk

Remove the source disk from the disk drive, and insert the target disk. Press a key. In copying to an unformatted target disk, the following message appears:

```
Formatting while copying
```

You may be prompted to again insert the source disk, and then the target disk. When all information on the source disk has been copied to the target disk, you will see the following message:

```
Copy another diskette (Y/N)?_
```

Remove the new Work Disk from the disk drive. If you want to make another copy of the Master Work Disk (a good idea), type **Y**, and press ENTER, and make another copy. When you are finished making copies, respond to the "Copy another?" question by typing **N** and pressing ENTER.

Label your new GW-BASIC Work Disks. (One way to do so is shown in Figure 1-4.)

A System with Two Disk Drives (Drives A and B)

If you are using a system with two 5.25-inch disk drives, or two 3.5-inch disk drives, you can use DISKCOPY to copy the information on your Master Work Disk to an unformatted or formatted disk. In the description that follows, the contents of the Master Work Disk are copied to an unformatted blank disk.

Make sure that the MS-DOS disk is in disk drive A.

Type:

DISKCOPY A: B:

and press the ENTER key.

You will then see the message:

```
Insert SOURCE diskette in drive A:
Insert TARGET diskette in drive B:
Press any key when ready ...
```

Insert your GW-BASIC Master Work Disk in drive A, and a blank disk in drive B. Press a key. In copying to an unformatted target disk, the following message appears:

```
Formatting while copying
```

When all information on the source disk has been copied to the target disk, you will see the following message:

```
Copy another diskette (Y/N)?_
```

Remove the new Work Disk from disk drive B. If you want to make another copy of the Master Work Disk (still in drive A), type **Y** and press ENTER. When you are finished making copies (make at least two), type **N** and press ENTER.

Label your new GW-BASIC Work Disks. Figure 1-4 shows one way to do this.

REVIEW

BASIC began in 1964 at Dartmouth College as the first powerful, easy-to-use programming language. It has since become the world's most popular computer language.

GW-BASIC is the most widely used version of BASIC. It is also known as BASICA (on IBM Personal Computers) and Tandy BASIC (on the Tandy 1000 series of computers). Most GW-BASIC programs will run in Microsoft QuickBASIC, the latest and best version of BASIC for beginners, experts, and everyone in between. You can begin with GW-BASIC, and then transfer your skills to QuickBASIC.

You are encouraged to make one or more GW-BASIC Work Disks to use as you wend your way through this book. In doing so, you will review the use of four MS-DOS commands: DIR, FORMAT, COPY, and DISKCOPY. As you gradually learn to understand the GW-BASIC programs in this book, and to write your own original programs, save them to your Work Disks for later use.

2

DO IT NOW—
IMMEDIATE
OPERATIONS

In this chapter, you will begin learning how to tell the computer to do what you want it to do. You will do this by typing GW-BASIC instructions called *direct statements*. Direct statements are also called *immediate statements*. You will also see them called *direct commands* or *immediate commands*. A direct statement tells the computer to do something immediately. The computer executes (that is, does, obeys, carries out) the statement, and then waits for your next instruction.

In particular, you will

- Load MS-DOS into the computer's memory and set the date and time.

- Load GW-BASIC into the computer's memory.

You will learn how to

- Clear the screen.

- Turn the key line off and on. The key line is the line at the bottom of the GW-BASIC screen.

- Use these GW-BASIC keywords in direct statements: BEEP, CLS, DATE$, KEY, OFF, ON, PRINT, SYSTEM, TIME$.

- Set the date and time from within GW-BASIC.

- Do simple arithmetic using the operators +, −, *, and /.

- Use some shortcuts to save time by reducing the number of keystrokes required to instruct the computer.

- Leave GW-BASIC and return to MS-DOS.

LOAD MS-DOS, SET DATE AND TIME

Begin by loading MS-DOS into your computer. While doing so, set the date and time. You will use the date and time later in this chapter.

In this book, it is assumed that you will use disk drive A most of the time, for the following reasons:

- Some of you may have a system with only one disk drive.

- Using only disk drive A simplifies your learning tasks.

If you have a hard disk system, you may prefer to work in disk drive C. In that case, change all disk drive references throughout this book from disk drive A to disk drive C.

Now insert your MS-DOS disk in disk drive A and start your computer. You will soon see information on the screen similar to the following:

```
Microsoft MS-DOS Version 3.20
(C)Copyright Microsoft Corp 1981, 1986

Current date is Tue  1-01-1990
Enter new date (mm-dd-yy): _
```

Notice the short underline (_) blinking after the colon (:). This is the *cursor*. Whenever you see the cursor, it means the computer is waiting to receive some instruction from you. After typing an instruction, the computer will do nothing until you press the ENTER key. Pressing ENTER tells the computer to go ahead and do what you just told it to do.

Enter the current date. You will use it later in this chapter. Enter the date by typing the number of the month (1 to 12), a hyphen (-), the day of the month (1 to 31), a hyphen (-), and the last two digits of the year. Here is an example:

```
Enter new date (mm-dd-yy): 1-1-90
```

After typing the date, press the ENTER key. You will next see the following (or a similar) message:

```
Current time is 0:01:33.31
Enter new time: _
```

Here again you see the blinking cursor (_) telling you it is your turn to do something. In this case, enter the current time of day.

The computer has a 24-hour clock, so enter the time by typing the hour (0 to 23), a colon (:), the minutes (0 to 59), and, if you wish, another colon (:) and the seconds (0 to 59). For example:

```
Enter new time: 13:30
```

The time shown here (13:30) is 1:30 P.M. Remember, the computer uses a 24-hour clock, so add 12 to the number of hours at or after 1:00 P.M.

After typing the time, press the ENTER key. You will see the disk drive designation (A), the prompt (>), and the blinking cursor, as shown here:

```
A>_
```

where the underscore character (_) is a blinking cursor.

The screen on your computer should now be similar to the screen shown in Figure 2-1. Of course, the date and time will be the date and time that you entered; other information on the screen may also differ.

The screen shown in Figure 2-1 is the MS-DOS Opening Screen. Note the disk drive specification (A), the MS-DOS prompt (>), and the blinking cursor (_). This is called the MS-DOS *command line*. At the MS-DOS command line, you can type a valid MS-DOS command and press the ENTER key. The computer will immediately execute your command. In the next section, you will enter an MS-DOS command to load GW-BASIC into the computer's memory.

Remember: Whenever you see the blinking cursor (_), you know the computer is waiting patiently for you to do something.

```
Microsoft MS-DOS 3.20
(C)Copyright Microsoft Corp 1981, 1986

Current date is Tue  1-01-1980
Enter new date (mm-dd-yy): 1-1-90
Current time is  0:01:33.31
Enter new time: 13:30

A>_
```

FIGURE 2-1   MS-DOS opening screen

LOAD GW-BASIC

You have loaded MS-DOS into your computer's memory. You can see the cursor blinking on the MS-DOS command line, as shown here:

A>_

Now insert the disk containing GW-BASIC in disk drive A. This disk may contain the BASIC file under the names GWBASIC (no hyphen), BASICA, or BASIC. If you are not sure of the name, use the MS-DOS command called DIR (Directory) to determine the proper name. You are likely to see one of the following filenames in a printout or display of the directory:

GWBASIC.EXE or BASICA.EXE or BASIC.EXE

In this book, the filename GWBASIC.EXE is assumed. If the filename on your disk is different, make the appropriate substitution for GWBASIC in

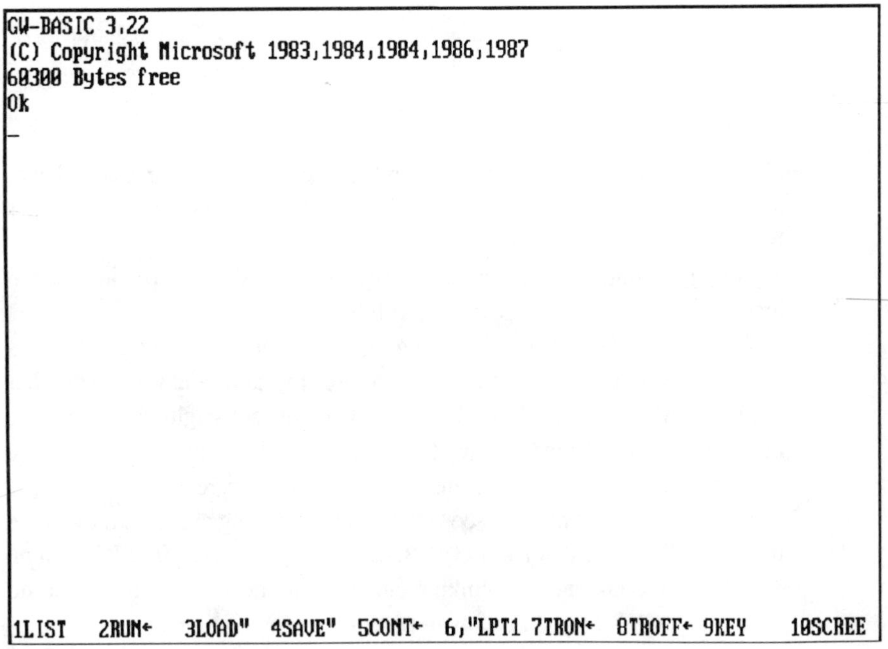

```
GW-BASIC 3.22
(C) Copyright Microsoft 1983,1984,1984,1986,1987
60300 Bytes free
Ok
_




















1LIST    2RUN◄    3LOAD"   4SAVE"   5CONT◄   6,"LPT1 7TRON◄   8TROFF◄ 9KEY      10SCREE
```

FIGURE 2-2   GW-BASIC opening screen

the discussion that follows.

Now let's load GWBASIC.

Type:

GWBASIC

and press the ENTER key.

After you type **GWBASIC**, but before you press the ENTER key, the MS-DOS command line appears as follows:

```
A>GWBASIC_
```

When you press ENTER, the command is executed by MS-DOS. It looks for the GWBASIC.EXE file on the disk in drive A and reads it into the computer's memory. If it can't find the desired file, you will see the following message.

```
A>GWBASIC
Bad command or file name

A>_
```

If this happens, use the DIR command to check the disk directory. Then, make sure that some version of BASIC is on the disk, and note the proper filename.

Note that you do not have to type the file extension (.EXE) in order to load GW-BASIC (or BASICA or BASIC).

GW-BASIC begins with the opening screen shown in Figure 2-2, or a similar screen. At the top of the screen you see the name and version number ("GW-BASIC 3.22"), followed by the Microsoft copyright notice and the number of bytes of memory available for GW-BASIC programs and data. This information may be different on your computer screen.

On the next two lines you see "Ok" and the blinking cursor. You will see these frequently as you learn GW-BASIC. Ok is the GW-BASIC *prompt*. When you see Ok and the blinking cursor, you know it is your turn to do something; GW-BASIC is ready to accept your instructions.

The bottom line on the opening screen is the *key line*. It has brief descriptive labels showing the functions assigned to *function keys* F1 through F10. You will learn how to use these function keys to eliminate keystrokes and save time.

GW-BASIC is now resident in the computer's memory and awaits your instructions.

CLEAR THE SCREEN

It is a good idea to begin each GW-BASIC activity with a clear or almost clear screen. You can clear the screen by holding down the CTRL key and pressing the L key. Do it now.

Hold down the CTRL key and press the L key (CTRL+L).

This clears the screen of all information except the key line at the bottom of the screen and the blinking cursor in the top left corner of the screen, as shown in Figure 2-3.

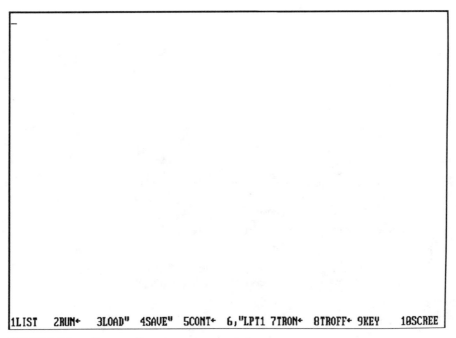

1LIST   2RUN←   3LOAD" 4SAVE" 5CONT← 6,"LPT1 7TRON← 8TROFF← 9KEY   10SCREE

FIGURE 2-3   Screen after CTRL+L command

In this book, the cryptic "CTRL+L" means "hold down the CTRL key and press the L key." Do not type the plus sign (+). Similar abbreviations will be shown for other CTRL key commands when they are introduced later in the book.

Remember: To clear the screen, hold down the CTRL key and press the L key. This command is usually abbreviated CTRL+L.

BEEP, YOUR FIRST GW-BASIC KEYWORD

When you see the cursor blinking all alone at the beginning of a line, you can type a direct statement and press ENTER. The computer will immediately execute your statement, as long as it is a valid GW-BASIC operation. For example, BEEP is a GW-BASIC keyword. You can use it as a direct statement to tell the computer to beep.

Type:

BEEP

and press the ENTER key.

The computer will beep and the top of the screen should look as shown here:

```
BEEP
Ok
_
```

You told the computer to BEEP, so it beeped.

In this book, GW-BASIC keywords, such as BEEP, are shown in uppercase letters. However, you can type **beep** or **Beep** or even **BeeP**. You can type keywords in upper- or lowercase, whichever you prefer.

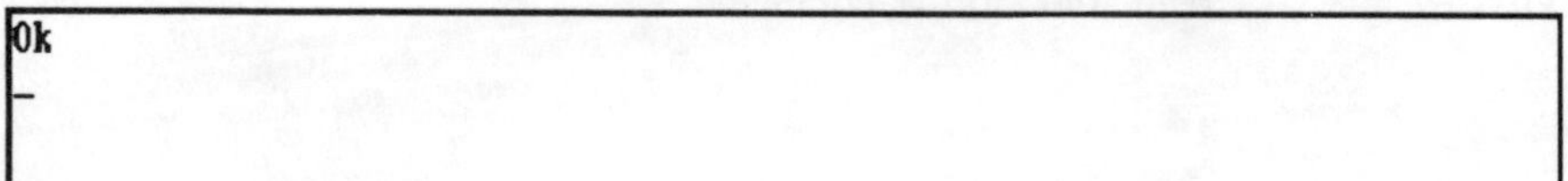

```
Ok
_




















1LIST  2RUN←  3LOAD"  4SAVE"  5CONT←  6,"LPT1  7TRON←  8TROFF←  9KEY    18SCREE
```

FIGURE 2-4   Screen after CLS command

If you type a word that GW-BASIC does not understand, you will then see a syntax error. To see this on your computer, intentionally misspell BEEP.

First, clear the screen (CTRL+L), and then type:

BOOP

and press the ENTER key.

You won't hear a beep. You will see a syntax error message, as follows:

```
BOOP
Syntax error
Ok
_
```

BOOP is not a valid GW-BASIC keyword. So GW-BASIC printed an error message, and then Ok, and then displayed the blinking cursor. It is waiting for your next instruction.

ANOTHER WAY TO CLEAR THE SCREEN

You already know one way to clear the screen, by holding down the CTRL key and pressing the L key. You can also clear the screen by using the keyword CLS as a direct statement. Do this now.

Type:

CLS

and press the ENTER key.

This clears the screen in a slightly different way from using CTRL+L. At the top of the screen, you see Ok and the blinking cursor. The bottom line of the screen is the key line. Figure 2-4 shows the screen after execution of a CLS command (direct statement).

Remember these two ways to clear most of the screen.

- Hold down the CTRL key and press the L key (CTRL+L). This erases everything on the screen except the cursor and the key line.

- Type **CLS** and press the ENTER key. This clears the screen, except for the GW-BASIC prompt (Ok), the cursor, and the key line.

It is a good practice to clear the screen before beginning each example or programming activity.

TURN THE KEY LINE OFF OR ON

You can turn off the key line at the bottom of the screen by using the keywords KEY and OFF. Clear the screen, and then turn off the key line as follows:

Type:

   KEY OFF

and press the ENTER key.

The key line disappears and the top of the screen displays

```
KEY OFF
Ok
_
```

Of course, if you misspell KEY or OFF, or forget to type a space between them, the key line will not disappear. Instead, you will see a syntax error message. For example:

```
KEYOFF
Syntax error
Ok
_
```

The prompt (Ok) and the blinking cursor tell you that everything is all right. The computer is patiently waiting for you to try again.

You can turn the key line on again by using the keywords KEY and ON in a direct statement. Clear the screen, and then turn on the key line, this way:

Type:

KEY ON

and press the ENTER key.

GW-BASIC has many shortcuts designed to reduce the number of keystrokes required to tell the computer to do something. You can use the function keys (F1, F2, F3, and so on) for this purpose. For example, you can use function key F9 to save time turning the key line off or on. The key line itself reminds you of this; near the right end you see "9KEY." This tells you that function key F9 is related to the keyword KEY in some way.

Now try using the F9 key to enter direct statements to turn the key line off, and then on. First, clear the screen. Then press the F9 key. The word "KEY," a space, and the blinking cursor will appear on the screen, this way: KEY _. Next,

Type:

OFF

and press the ENTER key.

The key line disappears, and the top of the screen appears as shown here:

```
KEY OFF
Ok
_
```

Remember: To turn *off* the key line, press the following five keys in left-to-right order:

To turn *on* the key line, press the F9 key, and then type **ON**, and then press the ENTER key. That is, press the following four keys in left-to-right order:

PRINT THE DATE AND TIME

When you first turned on your computer and loaded MS-DOS, you were prompted to set the current date and time. If you did this, the computer now knows the correct date and time. You can use the PRINT keyword to print (that is, display on the screen) the date and time. First, tell the computer to print the date, as follows:

Type:

PRINT DATE$

and press the ENTER key.

Type the word **PRINT**, a space, and then the word **DATE** and a dollar sign, and then press the ENTER key. A possible result is shown below. Of course, the date you see is probably different from the date shown here:

```
PRINT DATE$
04-01-1990
Ok
_
```

You can type the keywords PRINT and DATE$ in upper- or lowercase letters, or a mixture of both. Be sure to spell both keywords correctly and put a space between them. If you misspell either word or omit the space, you will no doubt see the dreaded syntax error message. That's fine; just try again.

Now tell the computer to print the time, as follows:

Type:

PRINT TIME$

and press the ENTER key.

The computer immediately prints the time in hours, minutes, and seconds. For example:

```
PRINT TIME$
09:53:28
Ok
_
```

The computer keeps time on a 24-hour clock. If you tell it to print the time in midafternoon, you might see something like this:

```
PRINT TIME$
15:29:46
Ok
_
```

The time shown is a few seconds before 3:30 P.M.

PRINT YOUR NAME

So far, you have told the computer to beep (BEEP), clear the screen (CTRL+L and CLS), turn off the key line (KEY OFF), turn on the key line (KEY ON), print the date (PRINT DATE$), and print the time (PRINT TIME$). In doing so, you have used eight GW-BASIC keywords: BEEP, CLS, KEY, OFF, ON, PRINT, DATE$, and TIME$.

Now you will learn how to tell the computer to print your name. To do this, you will type the keyword PRINT, a space, and your name enclosed in quotation marks. Then press the ENTER key. George Firedrake did it this way:

George typed:

PRINT "George Firedrake"

and pressed the ENTER key.

The following screen appeared.

```
PRINT "George Firedrake"
George Firedrake
Ok
_
```

Type this command yourself now. Replace "George Firedrake" with your name enclosed in quotation marks.

You have now used the PRINT keyword to display the date, the time, and your name. The PRINT keyword can, in fact, be used to print almost any message. This is what makes PRINT one of the most used and useful keywords in GW-BASIC. You can use the PRINT keyword to tell the computer to print a message, using these steps:

1. Type the keyword PRINT and a space.

2. Type a quotation mark (").

3. Type your name or any desired message.

4. Type another quotation mark (").

5. Press the ENTER key.

The information enclosed in quotation marks is called a *string*. A string can be a name, a message, a telephone number, or any group of characters enclosed in quotation marks. The direct PRINT statement prints the string enclosed in quotation marks, but does not print the quotation marks. You will learn more about strings in the next section and in the next chapter.

SET THE DATE

While loading MS-DOS, you can simply press the ENTER key instead of entering the current date and time. In this case, the computer will use *default* settings, such as 01-01-1980 for the date, and 0:00:00 (midnight) for the time. You can set the date and time while in GW-BASIC. Clear the screen, and then set the date, as in the following.

Type:

DATE$ = "4/1/90"

and press the ENTER key.

After setting the date, verify that it has been set properly by using a direct PRINT statement.

Type:

PRINT DATE$

and press the ENTER key.

If you set the date and print it as described above, the screen will display

```
DATE$ = "4-1-90"
Ok
PRINT DATE$
04-01-1990
Ok
_
```

You can set the date in several ways. Some are shown here:

DATE$ = "4/1/90"

DATE$ = "4-1-1990"

DATE$ = "4/1/1990"

For any of these settings, the date will be printed as 04-01-1990 when you use PRINT DATE$ to print it.

Table 2-1 shows several ways to make a mistake while setting the date. In each case, the computer prints an error message, and then waits patiently for your next try. The error message is shown directly below each incorrect direct statement.

Mistake and Error Message	Comments
DATE$ = 1-1-90 Type mismatch	The date is a string and must be enclosed in quotation marks.
DATE = "1-1-90" Type mismatch	Forgot the dollar sign ($) in DATE$.
DATE$ = "4-31-90" Illegal Function Call	Oops! Too many days in that month.
DATE$ = "13-1-90" Illegal Function Call	Oops! Too many months in that year.
DATE$ = "1 1 90" Illegal Function Call	Need slashes (/) or dashes (-) to separate month, day, and year.

TABLE 2-1   Possible Mistakes and Error Messages in Setting the Date

SET THE TIME

The computer maintains a 24-hour clock. Time is measured from midnight, which is 00:00:00. Table 2-2 shows 24-hour clock times corresponding to selected *ante meridiem* (A.M.) and *post meridiem* (P.M.) times for a conventional 12-hour clock.

You can set the time to exactly 1:00 P.M. as follows:

Type:

   TIME$ = "13"

and press the ENTER key.

The computer automatically sets the minutes and seconds to zero. After setting the time, verify it by means of a direct PRINT statement.

12-Hour Clock	24-Hour Clock	Comments
00:00:01 AM	00:00:01	One second after midnight
00:01:00 AM	00:01:00	One minute after midnight
01:00:00 AM	01:00:00	One hour after midnight
06:00:00 AM	06:00:00	Time to get up
09:00:00 AM	09:00:00	Many companies begin work
10:30:00 AM	10:30:00	Coffee break?
12:00:00 N	12:00:00	High noon
3:00:00 PM	15:00:00	School's out!
7:00:00 PM	19:00:00	Dinner?
11:59:59 PM	23:59:59	One second before midnight

TABLE 2-2   12-Hour Versus 24-Hour Clock Times

Type:

PRINT TIME$

and press the ENTER key.

After executing the above direct statements, the following screen might appear. Of course, the time depends on how much time transpired between execution of the two statements.

```
TIME$ = "13"
Ok
PRINT TIME$
13:00:24
Ok

_
```

Now set the time to exactly 10:30 P.M.

Mistake and Error Message	Comments
TIME$ = 12:00:00 Type mismatch	The time is a string and must be enclosed in quotation marks.
TIME = "8:30" Type mismatch	Forgot the dollar sign ($) in TIME$.
TIME$ = "11:60" Illegal Function Call	Oops! Too many minutes.
TIME$ = "24:00:01" Illegal Function Call	Too many hours. One second after midnight is 00:00:01.
TIME$ = "12-30" Illegal Function Call	In setting time, use colons (:) instead of dashes (-).
TIME$ = "12/30" Illegal Function Call	In setting time, use colons (:) instead of slashes (/).

TABLE 2-3   Possible Mistakes and Error Messages in Setting the Time

Type:

   TIME$ = "22:30"

and press the ENTER key.

Verify your setting by means of a direct PRINT statement.

   Table 2-3 shows several ways to make a mistake while setting the time. In each case, the computer prints an error message, and then waits patiently for your next command. The error message is shown directly below each incorrect direct statement.

ARITHMETIC

If you misplace your $10 solar-powered calculator, relax—you can use your computer as a calculator. Use +, –, *, and / to specify the arithmetic

Operation	Operation Symbol	Example
Addition	+	3 + 4
Subtraction	–	3 – 4
Multiplication	*	3 * 4
Division	/	3 / 4

TABLE 2-4   GW-BASIC Arithmetic Operations

operations of addition, subtraction, multiplication, and division, as shown in Table 2-4.

You use the PRINT statement and the appropriate arithmetic operator to tell the computer to add, subtract, multiply, or divide numbers and display the result. Clear the screen, and then tell the computer to add two numbers, say 3 and 4, and print the result.

Type:

PRINT 3 + 4

and press the ENTER key.

When you press the ENTER key, the computer first adds the numbers (3 plus 4), and then prints the result, as shown here:

```
PRINT 3 + 4
 7
Ok
_
```

Now try the other arithmetic operations: subtraction, multiplication, and division.

To subtract a number from another number,

Type:

PRINT 3 – 4

and press the ENTER key.

To multiply two numbers,

Type:

PRINT 3 ∗ 4

and press the ENTER key.

To divide a number by another number,

Type:

PRINT 3 / 4

and press the ENTER key.

After doing all four of the preceding examples, the screen should look like the following:

```
PRINT 3 + 4              addition (+)
 7
Ok
PRINT 3 - 4              subtraction (–)
-1
Ok
PRINT 3 * 4              multiplication (*)
 12
Ok
PRINT 3 / 4              division (/)
 .75
Ok
_
```

Each of the direct PRINT statements consists of the keyword PRINT followed by a *numerical expression* (3 + 4, 3 – 4, 3 ∗ 4, or 3 / 4). The computer first evaluates the numerical expression (does the arithmetic), and then prints the result, a single number.

Notice how the four numbers shown are printed: the negative number (−1) is printed beginning in the far left position, but the positive numbers are printed with a blank space in front. You will find this is true of any positive or negative numbers which you print. Positive numbers (and zero) are printed with a leading space, while negative numbers are printed with a leading minus sign (−) rather than a leading space.

You will learn much more about GW-BASIC arithmetic in the next two chapters.

SHORTCUTS FOR PRINT

Anything that reduces the amount of typing also reduces the likelihood of a typing mistake. GW-BASIC provides many shortcuts for typing keywords. For example, you already know you can press the F9 function key to type the keyword KEY. Here are some shortcuts for using PRINT.

You can use a question mark (?) as an abbreviation for PRINT. Just type a question mark followed by a space, and then whatever you want to print.

Here are two examples:

Type:

> **? 3 + 4**

and press the ENTER key.

Type:

> **? "George Firedrake"**

and press the ENTER key.

After you do the two preceding PRINT statements (using ? for PRINT), the screen will look like this:

```
? 3 + 4
 7
Ok
? "George Firedrake"
```

```
George Firedrake
Ok
_
```

GW-BASIC provides another handy shortcut that works for many keywords, including PRINT. This shortcut uses the ALT key. You can use the ALT key and the P key to print the keyword PRINT, followed by a space, this way:

Hold down the ALT key and press the P key (ALT+P).

After doing this, you will see the word PRINT, a space, and the blinking cursor, as shown here:

```
PRINT _
```

You can now complete the PRINT statement and press the ENTER key.

Remember: Use ALT+P to print the keyword PRINT. ALT+P is an abbreviation for "Hold down the ALT key and press the P key."

Later in this book, you will use this method to more quickly print other keywords on the screen.

LEAVE GW-BASIC AND RETURN TO MS-DOS

After spending some time with GW-BASIC, you may wish to return to MS-DOS and see the familiar MS-DOS command line (A>_). You can do this by using the SYSTEM command while still in GW-BASIC.

Type:

SYSTEM

and press the ENTER key.

This returns you to MS-DOS with the cursor blinking on the MS-DOS command line, as in the following.

```
SYSTEM
A>_
```

You may now use MS-DOS or, if you wish, return to GW-BASIC.
    To go from MS-DOS to GW-BASIC,

Type:

GWBASIC

and press the ENTER key.

    To go from GW-BASIC to MS-DOS,

Type:

SYSTEM

and press the ENTER key.

    You normally use SYSTEM when you are finished working with
GW-BASIC. Of course, another way to end a work session is to remove the
disk from the disk drive and turn off the computer.

REVIEW

In this chapter you learned how to instruct the computer by means of direct
statements. You type a direct statement and press the ENTER key; the
computer executes the statement immediately. Direct statements are also
called immediate statements, direct commands, or immediate commands.
    You can clear the GW-BASIC screen in one of two ways.

    1. Hold down CTRL and press the L key (CTRL+L).

    2. Use the direct command CLS.

    You use the direct statements KEY OFF and KEY ON to turn the key line
off and on, respectively. To save time and reduce the number of keystrokes,
press the F9 function key to type KEY.

You can set the date and time while entering MS-DOS into the computer's memory. You can also set the date and time from within GW-BASIC. Use direct statements PRINT DATE$ and PRINT TIME$ to print (display) the date and time.

To print your name or any message, write a direct statement consisting of the keyword PRINT, followed by your name or a message enclosed in quotation marks. Information enclosed in quotation marks is called a string.

You can use the computer as a calculator to do arithmetic. The arithmetic operations are addition (+), subtraction (−), multiplication (∗), and division (/). Use a direct PRINT statement consisting of the keyword PRINT followed by the numerical expression you want to evaluate.

There are two shortcuts for PRINT, as follows:

1. Use the question mark (?) as a replacement for PRINT; for example, ? 3 + 4.

2. Use ALT+P to type the word PRINT (hold down the ALT key and press the P key).

To leave GW-BASIC and return to MS-DOS,

Type:

SYSTEM

and press the ENTER key.

3

INTRODUCTION TO PROGRAMMING

In this chapter, you will learn to understand and use simple GW-BASIC programs. A program is a set of instructions that tells the computer what to do and how to do it. You will enter a program into the computer's memory, and then tell the computer to run (execute) the entire program automatically.

When you finish this chapter, you will be able to

- Read, understand, and use programs that include these keywords: BEEP, CLS, DATE$, PRINT, and TIME$.

- Use these keywords: FILES, LIST, LLIST, LOAD, NEW, RUN, and SAVE.

- Use NEW to erase an unwanted program from the computer's memory.

- Enter a program into the computer's memory.

- Use LIST to tell the computer to display on the screen a copy of a program in memory.

- Use LLIST to tell the computer to print on the printer a copy of a program in memory.

- Use RUN to tell the computer to run (execute) a program in memory.

- Make corrections and other changes to a program.

- Use SAVE to save a program to a disk drive.

- Use FILES to print on the screen the names of programs on a disk.

- Use LOAD to load a program from a disk into memory.

- Use the MS-DOS TYPE command to list a program on the screen.

This chapter provides a solid base for your further exploration of GW-BASIC.

LOAD GW-BASIC

Load MS-DOS into your computer. Set the date and time as described in Chapter 2. You will see a screen similar to the one shown here:

```
Microsoft MS-DOS Version 3.20
(C)Copyright Microsoft Corp 1981, 1986

Current date is Tue  1-01-1990
Enter new date (mm-dd-yy): 1-1-90
Current time is  0:01:33:31
Enter new time: 7:15

A>_
```

You have loaded MS-DOS into your computer's memory. You can see the cursor blinking on the MS-DOS command line, as shown here:

```
A>_
```

The disk containing GW-BASIC might be on the same disk as MS-DOS, or on another disk. Make sure that the disk containing GW-BASIC is in disk drive A. The GW-BASIC file may appear under the name GWBASIC (no hyphen), BASICA, or BASIC, followed by the file extension .EXE. If you are not sure of the name, use the MS-DOS DIR command to determine the correct name. You are likely to see one of the following file names in the printout of the directory.

GWBASIC.EXE   or   BASICA.EXE   or   BASIC.EXE

In this book, the file name GWBASIC.EXE is assumed. However, you do not have to type the file extension (.EXE) in order to load GWBASIC (or BASICA or BASIC). If the filename on your disk is different, make appropriate substitution for GWBASIC in the discussion that follows.

Type:

GWBASIC

and press ENTER.

After you type **GWBASIC**, but before you press the ENTER key, the MS-DOS command line appears as follows:

```
A>GWBASIC_
```

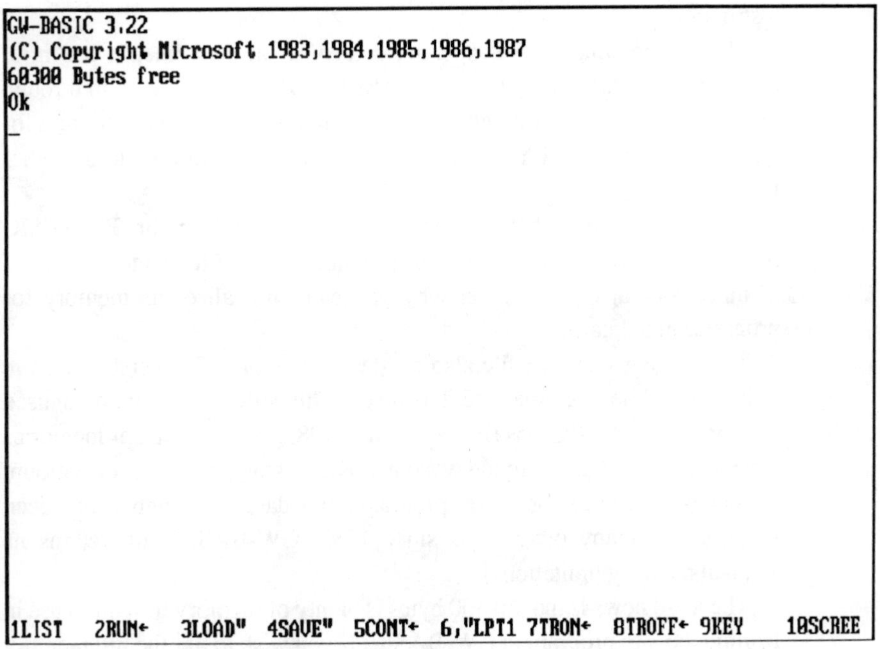

```
GW-BASIC 3.22
(C) Copyright Microsoft 1983,1984,1985,1986,1987
60300 Bytes free
Ok
_





















1LIST   2RUN◄   3LOAD"  4SAVE"  5CONT◄  6,"LPT1 7TRON◄  8TROFF◄ 9KEY     10SCREE
```

FIGURE 3-1   GW-BASIC Opening Screen

When you press ENTER, the command is executed by MS-DOS. It looks for the GWBASIC.EXE file on the disk in drive A and reads it into the computer's memory. If it can't find the desired file, you will see the following message:

```
A>GWBASIC
Bad command or file name

A>_
```

If this happens, use the DIR command to check the disk directory. Make sure that some version of BASIC is on the disk and note the proper filename.

GW-BASIC begins with the opening screen shown in Figure 3-1, or a similar screen. At the top of the screen you see the name and version number ("GW-BASIC 3.22"), followed by the Microsoft copyright notice and the number of bytes of memory available for GW-BASIC programs and data. This information may be different on your computer screen.

On the next two lines you see the GW-BASIC prompt (Ok) and the blinking cursor (_). When you see Ok and the blinking cursor, you know it is your turn to do something; GW-BASIC is ready to accept your instructions.

The bottom line on the opening screen is the key line. It has brief descriptive labels showing the functions assigned to function keys F1 through F10. In Chapter 2, you learned how to use function key F9 as a shortcut for typing the keyword KEY. In this chapter, you will learn how to use other function keys.

In Figure 3-1, note that there are 60,300 bytes free for your GW-BASIC programs and data. Your computer probably has 256K or more bytes of memory. Perhaps you wonder why you can't use all of its memory for programs and data.

The GWBASIC.EXE file also resides in memory. The version used in writing this book occupies 72,240 bytes. This still leaves lots of unused memory! GW-BASIC was first released in 1983, when computer memories were smaller than they are today, so it was necessary to restrict the amount of memory allowed for users' programs and data. Although it has been improved in many other ways since 1983, GW-BASIC still retains its original memory limitation.

The good news is that 60,300 bytes is plenty of memory for you to use in learning how to program in GW-BASIC. If you wish to use the full memory and the full power of your computer, you can move up to the latest and best version of BASIC, Microsoft's elegant and powerful QuickBASIC. You will be pleased to find that you can transfer almost all of your GW-BASIC know-how to QuickBASIC.

YOUR FIRST GW-BASIC PROGRAM

Program? A program is simply a procedure, a set of instructions, or a plan for doing something. You may have already used, or created, or been frustrated by programs written in English. For example:

- a recipe for baking a cake

- instructions for opening a combination lock

- directions on how to get to a friend's house from the airport

- and, of course, those maddening instructions for assembling toys, tricycles, playpens, furniture, and so on—probably at the last minute on Christmas Eve

A GW-BASIC program is a program written using the vocabulary and syntax (rules of grammar) of GW-BASIC. A GW-BASIC program follows this paragraph. This program tells the computer to beep, print the date, print the time, and then print George Firedrake's name. The program uses keywords introduced in Chapter 2: BEEP, PRINT, DATE$, and TIME$.

```
10 BEEP
20 PRINT DATE$                    A GW-BASIC program
30 PRINT TIME$
40 PRINT "George Firedrake"
```

This program has four lines. Each line consists of a line number (10, 20, ...), followed by a statement (BEEP, PRINT DATE$, ...)

```
1st line:  10 BEEP
2nd line:  20 PRINT DATE$
3rd line:  30 PRINT TIME$
4th line:  40 PRINT "George Firedrake"
            ↑
            └── Line number
```

In Chapter 2, you used statements such as BEEP and PRINT DATE$ as immediate statements. You type an immediate statement without a line number and press the ENTER key; the computer executes the statement immediately.

However, when you type a statement with a line number, it is not executed immediately when you press the ENTER key. Instead it is stored in the computer's memory for later execution. After entering all lines of your program, you can tell the computer to run (execute) the entire program. It will do so, unless the program contains something the computer doesn't understand. In this case, the computer prints an error message and, in some cases, displays the line that contains the error. It then waits for you to fix the mistake and tell it what to do next.

The NEW and LIST Keywords

You will soon enter the program into the computer's memory. Before doing so, tell the computer that you will enter a new program. To do this, use the NEW keyword as an immediate statement.

First, clear the screen (CTRL+L). Then

Type:

NEW

and press ENTER.

In this book, keywords such as NEW are always shown in uppercase letters. However, you may type **new**, or **New**, or even **NeW**. The computer will recognize a keyword typed in any mixture of upper- and lowercase letters, as long as you spell it correctly.

After you clear the screen, type **NEW**, and press ENTER, the screen will display

```
NEW
Ok
_
```

The NEW statement clears (erases) the part of the computer's memory used to store a GW-BASIC program. You can verify this by telling the computer to list any program now in memory. The easiest way to do this is to press the F1 function key, and then press the ENTER key. Pressing the F1 function key causes the keyword LIST to appear on the screen, along with the blinking cursor. Pressing ENTER then causes the computer to execute LIST as a direct statement. Do this now, slowly, and watch what happens on the screen.

Press:

    F1

and then press ENTER.

The computer lists any program resident in its memory, and then displays the prompt (Ok) and the cursor (_). Since there is no program in the memory, the screen should look like this:

```
NEW
Ok
LIST                Since no program resides in memory,
Ok                  nothing is listed between LIST and Ok.

_
```

Enter the Program

Clear the screen (CTRL+L) and enter the first line of the program into the computer's memory.

Type:

10 BEEP

and press ENTER.

The screen should look like this:

```
10 BEEP
_
```

There is now a one-line program in the computer's memory. Verify this by telling the computer to list the program.

Press:

    F1

and then press ENTER.

The computer lists the one-line program, this way:

```
LIST                The one-line program is listed
10 BEEP             between LIST and Ok.
Ok
_
```

   If your screen matches what is shown above, your program is correct and
you can now run it. Use the keyword RUN as a direct statement to tell the
computer to run (carry out, execute, do) the program. The easiest way to do
this is to press the F2 key. The computer prints the word RUN on the screen
and immediately executes the program.

    Press the F2 function key.

Of course, this one-line program doesn't do much. It just tells the computer
to beep. You will hear the beep immediately after you press the F2 function
key, and the screen will look like this:

```
10 BEEP
LIST
10 BEEP
Ok
RUN
Ok
_
```

   This BEEP program is successful because there is no error in the program.
But errors do happen. That's all right. GW-BASIC has several ways to help
you find and fix errors.

Fixing a Mistrake

Clear the screen, and then enter the following line 10, which contains an error. (The keyword BEEP is intentionally misspelled as BOOP.) When you enter this line, it will replace the line 10 currently in memory.

Type:

10 BOOP

and press ENTER.

Verify that the above line 10 is now in memory. List the program (press F1, and then press ENTER). You should see the following:

```
LIST
10 BOOP
Ok
_
```

Now run the program (press F2). Instead of hearing a beep, you will see a syntax error message, as shown here:

```
RUN
Syntax error in 10
Ok
10 BOOP_
```

The computer tells you that there is a syntax error in line 10 ("Syntax error in 10"), and then displays line 10 with the cursor blinking to the right of the word it did not understand (BOOP). You can easily correct the error, as shown here:

Do This	See This
1. Press BACKSPACE three times.	10 B_
2. Type **EEP.**	10 BEEP_
3. Press ENTER.	10 BEEP
	_

That's one way. Here's another one, beginning from the error as originally shown (10 BOOP_). Use the arrow keys to move the cursor.

Do This	See This
1. Move cursor to 1st O.	10 B<u>O</u>OP
2. Type **EE**.	10 BE<u>E</u>P
3. Press ENTER.	10 BEEP
	_

After making a correction, list the program to make sure it is all right. Then run it.

Remember: To *list* a program, press F1, and then press ENTER. But to *run* a program, press F2.

You can also list a program by typing the keyword LIST and then pressing ENTER. You can run a program by typing the keyword RUN and then pressing ENTER. Using the function keys saves time and precludes typing mistakes. However, the choice is yours.

Enter the Rest of the Program

Clear the screen and enter the rest of the program (lines 20, 30, and 40), as follows:

Type:

20 PRINT DATE$

and press ENTER.

Type:

30 PRINT TIME$

and press ENTER.

Type:

40 PRINT "George Firedrake"

and press ENTER.

If you typed all three lines without making any mistakes, the screen now appears as shown here:

```
20 PRINT DATE$
30 PRINT TIME$
40 PRINT "George Firedrake"
```

If you do see a mistake, use the arrow keys to position the cursor, fix the mistake, and press the ENTER key. When you press the ENTER key, the corrected line is stored in memory, replacing the previously stored incorrect line. When you are satisfied that everything is all right, clear the screen and list the program. It should look like this:

```
10 BEEP
20 PRINT DATE$
30 PRINT TIME$
40 PRINT "George Firedrake"
```

Run the Program

Press the F2 function key to run the program. If all goes well, you will hear a beep and see information on the screen similar to the following:

```
LIST
10 BEEP
20 PRINT DATE$
30 PRINT TIME$
40 PRINT "George Firedrake"
Ok
RUN
01-01-1990
07:37:05
George Firedrake
Ok
_
```

Of course, when you run the program, the date and time will probably be different from this example. Perhaps you used your own name or another string in line 40. If so, that is what you will see.

If the program did not run properly, list it and fix any errors as shown previously in this chapter. You can also correct or change a line by simply retyping the line, including the line number. Try this now with line 40.

Type:

40 PRINT "Firedrake, George"

and press ENTER.

Then list the program to see the new line 40 that you just entered, as shown here:

```
LIST
10 BEEP
20 PRINT DATE$
30 PRINT TIME$
40 PRINT "Firedrake, George"
Ok
_
```

Next, run this program to see the result of the change. You will hear a beep and see a screen similar to this one:

```
RUN
01-01-1990
07:57:37
Firedrake, George
Ok
_
```

Now change line 40 of the program back to its original appearance (40 PRINT "George Firedrake"); then list and run the program.

SAVING A PROGRAM

You have entered a short GW-BASIC program into the computer's memory, listed the program, and run it. If you save the program to a disk, you can then load it back into memory whenever you wish. Try saving the program to a disk in disk drive A or, if you prefer, to a disk in another disk drive.

Clear the screen and list the program so that the screen looks like this:

```
LIST
10 BEEP
20 PRINT DATE$
30 PRINT TIME$
40 PRINT "George Firedrake"
OK
_
```

In order to save a program, you must give it a name, called a *filename*. A filename can have up to eight characters (letters and numbers). The first character must be a letter. Name this program GWME0301. The letters "GWME" stand for GW-BASIC Made Easy, the title of this book. The numeral "03" refers to this chapter (Chapter 3). The numeral "01" tells you this is the first named program in this chapter. This convention for naming programs continues throughout the book.

Remember that, in this book, it is assumed that you are using disk drive A. That is, you began with MS-DOS in disk drive A, and then loaded GW-BASIC at the MS-DOS command line, as follows:

```
A>GWBASIC
```

In this case, disk drive A is the default disk drive. It is used unless you specify another drive. If you have a hard disk, perhaps you are working from it. (You see a C> instead of an A>.) If so, your hard disk is the default disk drive.

Now save the program to the default disk drive, using the filename GWME0301. To do this, use the keyword SAVE in a direct statement. You can do this using the long way or the short way. Look at both ways before deciding how you want to save the program. First, the long way:

Type:

SAVE "GWME0301"

and press ENTER.

You have probably guessed that the short way involves a function key. You can use the F4 function key to type the keyword SAVE and a quotation mark. Then type in the filename and press ENTER.

Press the F4 key. The keyword SAVE, a quotation mark, and the blinking cursor appear on the screen, as follows:

```
SAVE"_
```

Type:

GWME0301"

and press ENTER.

The completed SAVE statement should appear as shown here:

```
SAVE"GWME0301"
```

You may type the filename in lowercase or a mixture of upper- and lowercase. GW-BASIC recognizes GWME0301, gwme0301, or Gwme0301 as the same filename. Also, you may omit the closing quotation mark at the right side of GWME0301.

Use either the long way or the short way to save the program to the default disk drive. GW-BASIC will add a file extension (.BAS) to the name. Thus, the program is actually stored as GWME0301.BAS. The file extension .BAS denotes a file that is a BASIC program.

Is the program really stored on the disk in the default drive? Use the keyword FILES as a direct statement to find out what is on the disk.

Type:

FILES

and press ENTER.

The computer displays the names of all files on the disk in the default drive (assumed to be drive A). In the next example, three files reside on a 3.5-inch disk in the default drive.

```
FILES
A:\
COMMAND.COM      GWBASIC.EXE     GWME0301.BAS
 586973 Bytes free
Ok
_
```

On disk drive A (A:\), there are three files: COMMAND.COM, GWBASIC.EXE, and GWME0301.BAS. You can see that program GWME0301 is on the disk.

If the disk in the default drive contains many files, you may wish to list the names of only the BASIC programs, the files with a .BAS file extension. In this case, type the FILES statement as follows:

FILES "*.BAS"

This FILES statement tells the computer to list the names of all files that have the file extension .BAS. The asterisk (*) is called a "wild card." It can be used in certain MS-DOS commands, as well as in GW-BASIC. Consult your MS-DOS reference manual for more information on the use of the asterisk as a wild card.

Saving to a Designated Disk Drive

You can save a program to any disk drive by designating the desired drive in the SAVE statement. For example, to save Program GWME0301 to disk drive B, type the SAVE statement as shown here:

SAVE "B:GWME0301"

where **B** is the disk drive designation.

Be sure to include a colon (:) between the disk drive designation (B) and the name of the program (GWME0301). The program is saved to disk drive B with the filename GWME0301.BAS. As before, GW-BASIC adds the file extension .BAS to the name you typed (GWME0301). This denotes a file that is a BASIC program.

You can list the names of the files on any disk drive by using a FILES statement with a disk drive designation. For example, suppose you want to see the names of all files on disk drive B.

Type:

FILES "B:"

and press ENTER.

Remember to enclose the disk drive designation (B:) in quotation marks.

If you want to list only the names of BASIC programs with a .BAS file extension, type the FILES statement as follows:

FILES "B:*.BAS"

The wild card (*) and .BAS extension following the drive designation (B:) tell the computer to list only files on disk drive B that have the .BAS extension.

LOADING A PROGRAM

You can load a program stored on a disk into the computer's memory. To do so, use the keyword LOAD in a direct statement. For example, suppose you want to load Program GWME0301 from the default disk drive. You can do it in two ways, the short way and the long way.

First, the long way.

Type:

LOAD "GWME0301"

and press ENTER.

And now, the short way, using the F3 function key as a shortcut for typing LOAD". Press the F3 key. The keyword LOAD, a quotation mark, and the blinking cursor appear on the screen, as in the following.

```
LOAD"_
```

Type:

GWME0301"

and press ENTER.

After using the short way to load the program, the screen looks like this:

```
LOAD"GWME0301"
Ok
_
```

List the program. Press F1, and then press ENTER. The screen displays:

```
LOAD"GWME0301"
Ok
LIST
10 BEEP
20 PRINT DATE$
30 PRINT TIME$
40 PRINT "George Firedrake"
Ok
_
```

The program is in memory, ready for your use. Note that you do not have to
type the file extension (.BAS) as part of the filename, although it is all right
to do so. The space between LOAD and the first quotation mark (") is
optional. The final quotation mark (after the filename) may be omitted.

Loading from a Designated Disk Drive

You can load a program from any disk drive by designating the desired drive
in the LOAD statement. For example, to load Program GWME0301 from
disk drive B, type the LOAD statement as follows:

LOAD "B:GWME0301"

where **B** is the disk drive designation.

Remember to include a colon (:) between the disk drive letter (B) and the name of the program (GWME0301). The space following LOAD is optional. Perhaps you have noticed that it does not appear when you use the F3 key as a shortcut for typing LOAD".

LISTING A PROGRAM ON THE PRINTER

If you have a printer, you can list a program on the printer. To do so, use the keyword LLIST as a direct statement. An LLIST statement tells the computer to list on the printer the program in memory. One way to do it is shown below. (Remember, there are two *L*'s in LLIST.)

Type:

LLIST

and press ENTER.

Here is another way, using the handy F1 function key to type LIST:

Type:

L

press F1, and then press ENTER.

Use either method. After the program has been listed on the printer, the screen will look like this:

```
LLIST
Ok
_
```

Remember: To list a program on the screen, use LIST; to list a program on the printer, use LLIST.

ADDING A LINE TO A PROGRAM

Perhaps you wonder why the lines in Program GWME0301 are numbered 10, 20, 30, 40 instead of 1, 2, 3, 4. The program could have been written as shown here:

```
1 BEEP
2 PRINT DATE$
3 PRINT TIME$
4 PRINT "George Firedrake"
```

However, it is better to space the line numbers as shown here:

```
10 BEEP
20 PRINT DATE$
30 PRINT TIME$
40 PRINT "George Firedrake"
```

This line number spacing (10, 20, 30, 40) provides room for inserting additional lines. For example, between lines 10 and 20, you can insert up to nine lines (lines 11, 12, 13, 14, 15, 16, 17, 18, and 19). To insert a line between two existing lines, simply type it in, with a line number that is between the two existing line numbers.

Do this now. Insert a CLS statement between lines 10 and 20 of the program. Use line number 15, which is halfway between line 10 and line 20. First list the program on the screen (press F1, and then press ENTER), and then add line 15.

Type:

15 CLS

and press ENTER.

After you press ENTER, the screen will look like the following.

```
LIST
10 BEEP
20 PRINT DATE$
30 PRINT TIME$
40 PRINT "George Firedrake"
Ok
15 CLS
_
```

Now list the program again. You should see line 15 in its proper place between lines 10 and 20, as shown here:

```
LIST
10 BEEP
15 CLS          ←——————  line 15
20 PRINT DATE$
30 PRINT TIME$
40 PRINT "George Firedrake"
Ok
_
```

Line 15 tells the computer to clear the screen. When you run the program, it will cause the computer to beep (line 10), clear the screen (line 15), and then print the date, time, and George's name (lines 20, 30, and 40). Run the program now; press F2. In the top part of the screen, you see the information printed by the program, as shown here:

```
01-01-1990
08:02:37
George Firedrake
Ok
_
```

Now add another line to the program. Make it line 50, so it will be added to the bottom of the program, after the current line 40. As usual, first clear the screen, and then type the line to be added, as follows:

Type:

50 PRINT "Happy New Year!"

and press ENTER.

List the program. You should see line 50 in its proper place, as shown here:

```
LIST
10 BEEP
15 CLS
20 PRINT DATE$
30 PRINT TIME$
40 PRINT "George Firedrake"
50 PRINT "Happy New Year!"
Ok
_
```

Remember: To insert a line into a program, use a line number between two existing line numbers. To append a line to the end of a program, use a line number greater than the largest line number in the program. To append a line at the beginning of a program (as the first line), use a line number less than the smallest line number in the program. To replace a line in the program, type a new line with the same line number as the line you want to replace.

You can also delete (erase) a line of the program. Just type the line number (nothing else) and press ENTER. For example, if you want to delete line 50 of the program, type **50**, and press ENTER. Don't do it now, but remember how to do it. You will delete lines this way later in this chapter.

SAVING A PROGRAM IN ASCII FORMAT

Earlier, you saved Program GWME0301 to a disk. It is saved in *compressed binary format*, a format peculiar to GW-BASIC. This format is very efficient, using a minimum amount of space on the disk.

You can also save a program as an ASCII text file. This method is less efficient; the program occupies more room on the disk. However, there is an advantage: the program can be read by a word processor. You can also use the MS-DOS TYPE command to display an ASCII program on the screen.

To store the current program as Program GWME0302 in ASCII format,

Type:

SAVE "GWME0302", A

and press ENTER.

Of course, you can save time by using the F4 key to type SAVE". Compare this SAVE statement with the SAVE statement used to store Program GWME0301. In the statement illustrated for GWME0302, the letter *A* tells the computer to save the program as an ASCII text file.

```
SAVE "GWME0302", A
```
└────── Save as an ASCII file

Next, use a FILES statement to verify that Program GWME0302 is on the disk. Its filename should appear as GWME0302.BAS. The filename does not tell you that the program is stored as an ASCII file. This presents no problem to GW-BASIC. You can load the program into memory in the same way you load a program stored in the compressed binary format. Just type **LOAD "GWME0302"** and press ENTER.

If you want, you can also store Program GWME0302 as an ASCII text file with a file extension that tells you it is an ASCII file. For example, you can use .ASC as an explicit file extension. Do so now.

Type:

SAVE "GWME0302.ASC", A

and press ENTER.

Program GWME0302 is now stored under the filename GWME0302.ASC. It is also stored under the filename GWME0302.BAS. Use a FILES statement to verify that the program is on the disk under both names.

DELETING LINES FROM A PROGRAM

Now that Program GWME0302 is safely tucked away on a disk, practice deleting program lines from the copy of the program still stored in memory. Don't worry; these lines will not be deleted from the copies of the program that are on the disk. Begin by clearing the screen and listing the program so that the screen looks like the following.

```
LIST
10 BEEP
15 CLS
20 PRINT DATE$
30 PRINT TIME$
40 PRINT "George Firedrake"
50 PRINT "Happy New Year!"
Ok
_
```

Delete line 15 from the program.

Type:

15

and press ENTER.

Now list the program again. Line 15 will not appear in the listing, which will look like the one shown here:

```
LIST
10 BEEP
20 PRINT DATE$
30 PRINT TIME$
40 PRINT "George Firedrake"
50 PRINT "Happy New Year!"
Ok
_
```

Go ahead and practice deleting lines. To delete a line, type only the line number and press ENTER. After deleting a line or two or more, list the program to verify that the lines are no longer in the program.

If you want to delete an entire program, use NEW as a direct statement. Just type **NEW** and press ENTER. This deletes all program lines in the computer's memory.

RETURN TO MS-DOS

Clear the screen, and then use a SYSTEM statement to exit GW-BASIC and return to MS-DOS.

Type:

SYSTEM

and press ENTER.

If you are working out of disk drive A, the screen will look like this:

```
SYSTEM

A>_
```

Use the DIR command to display a list of files on the screen.

Type:

DIR

and press ENTER.

The disk used by the authors contains the following files. You will probably see somewhat different information.

```
COMMAND   COM      23612   7-21-90   3:00p
GWME0302 BAS        107   1-01-90   8:27a
GWME0302 ASC        107   1-01-90   8:47a
GWBASIC  EXE      72240   7-21-90   3:00p
GWME0301 BAS         54   1-01-90   8:44a
        5 File(s)      585728 bytes free
```

The disk now contains the three programs stored while the authors wrote this chapter: GWME0301.BAS, GWME0302.BAS, and GWME0302.ASC. Since GWME0302.BAS and GWME0302.ASC were stored as ASCII text files, you can use the MS-DOS TYPE command to display them on the screen. Do this now. Tell the computer to display the GWME0302.BAS file.

Type:

TYPE GWME0302.BAS

and press ENTER.

The computer reads the program from the disk, displays it on the screen, and waits for your next command, as follows:

```
A>TYPE GWME0302.BAS
10 BEEP
15 CLS
20 PRINT DATE$
30 PRINT TIME$
40 PRINT "George Firedrake"
50 PRINT "Happy New Year!"

A>_
```

You can display the GWME0302.ASC file in the same way. However, you cannot display the GWME0301.BAS file because it is not an ASCII text file. But go ahead and try it; you will see some strange looking characters on the screen.

REVIEW

In this chapter you learned how to enter a GW-BASIC program into the computer's memory. A program consists of one or more lines containing statements that tell the computer what you want it to do. Each line of a program begins with a line number. When you type a line that begins with a line number, the line is stored for later use.

Before entering a program, use a direct NEW statement to erase any old programs in the computer's memory. Enter the new program by typing each line and pressing ENTER. After entering a program, use a LIST statement to list the program to the screen, or a RUN statement to run (execute) the program.

Use the SAVE statement to save a program to a disk, and a LOAD statement to load a program from a disk into memory. Use a FILES statement to list the names of all disk files on the screen.

You can save a program in compressed binary format or as an ASCII text file. A compressed binary file occupies less space on the disk. An ASCII text file occupies more space, but can be read by a word processor.

Function keys can be used as shortcuts in typing statements, as follows.

- Press F1 to type LIST.
- Press F2 to type RUN and immediately run a program.
- Press F3 to type LOAD".
- Press F4 to type SAVE".

Use the SYSTEM statement to exit GW-BASIC and return to MS-DOS. In MS-DOS, you can use the TYPE command to list a program that is stored in ASCII format.

4

NUMBER CRUNCHING

In this chapter, you will learn how to use the computer to do calculations. You will use direct statements for simple calculations, as well as programs for more complex number crunching. You will use the arithmetic operators (+, −, *, /), and the exponentiation operator (^) with numbers and variables that represent numbers. You'll learn about:

- how to use the keywords INPUT, LPRINT, LPRINT USING, PRINT USING, and REM

- how to add, subtract, multiply, and divide in GW-BASIC

- the exponentiation operator and how to use it

- the different numeric types, including integers, single precision numbers, and double precision numbers

- floating point notation

- what numerical variables are and how to assign values to them

- how to use the INPUT statement to acquire a value of a variable

- how to use the PRINT USING and LPRINT USING statements to print formatted numbers and align numbers vertically

ARITHMETIC WITH DIRECT STATEMENTS

In Chapter 2 you learned how to use your computer as a calculator. You used the arithmetic operators +, −, *, and / to specify the operations of addition, subtraction, multiplication, and division, as shown in Table 4-1.

To tell the computer to do arithmetic, use a direct PRINT statement consisting of the keyword PRINT followed by a numerical expression (such as $3 + 4$, or $3 - 4$). The computer evaluates the numerical expression (does the arithmetic), and then prints the result. For example, tell the computer to add the numbers 3 and 4, and then print the result.

Type:

PRINT 3 + 4

It prints:

7

Now try the following examples. Press ENTER after typing a direct PRINT statement. Remember, you can use ALT+P as a shortcut for PRINT. You can also use a question mark (?) as an abbreviation for PRINT, as shown here:

Type:

? 3 − 4

It prints:

−1

EXAMPLE 1   Mariko is 59 inches tall. Convert her height to centimeters. One inch equals 2.54 centimeters.

Type:

PRINT 59 * 2.54

Operation	Operation Symbol	Example
Addition	+	3 + 4
Subtraction	–	3 – 4
Multiplication	*	3 * 4
Division	/	3 / 4

TABLE 4 -1   GW-BASIC Arithmetic Operations

It prints:

149.86

Of course, it is all right to type the PRINT statement as

PRINT 2.54 * 59

EXAMPLE 2   An ancient ruler named Zalabar measured 100 centimeters from the tip of his nose to the end of his outstretched arms. How long is that in inches?

Type:

PRINT 100 / 2.54

It prints:

39.37008

Does that number look familiar? Perhaps you recall that 100 centimeters equals one meter. One meter equals 39.37 inches, a little more than one yard.

EXAMPLE 3   People usually give their height in feet and inches. If you ask Mariko how tall she is, she will probably tell you she is 4 feet, 11 inches tall. It is easy to write a PRINT statement to convert feet and inches to inches.

Type:

PRINT 4 * 12 + 11

It prints:

59

The computer first does the multiplication (4 times 12), and then the addition (plus 11). In evaluating an expression, the computer does multiplications and divisions first, and then additions and subtractions.

EXAMPLE 4   Almost everyone gets a monthly bill from a utility company. Gas is measured in therms, and electricity in kilowatt hours (kwh). Compute the amount of a monthly bill for 53 therms of gas at $0.41 per therm, and 295 kwh of electricity at $0.08 per kwh.

Type:

PRINT 53 * .41 + 295 * .08

It prints:

45.33

In evaluating this expression, the computer does both multiplications, and then adds the two results to get the final result.

EXAMPLE 5   Before he reached his full stature, King Kong was once 37 feet, 8 inches tall. How tall was he in centimeters?

Type:

PRINT (37 * 12 + 9) * 2.54

It prints:

1148.08

Note the use of parentheses. The computer does the arithmetic inside the parentheses first, and then does the rest. Example 6 also uses parentheses.

EXAMPLE 6 At the beginning of an auto trip, the odometer showed 19,832 miles. At the end of the trip it read 20,219 miles. The car used 9.3 gallons of gas. How many miles per gallon did the car get on the trip?

Type:

PRINT (20219 – 19832) / 9.3

It prints:

41.6129

Note that commas were not used in typing the numbers 20219 and 19832. Commas may not be used within a number, although commas (and semicolons) may be used to separate numerical expressions in PRINT commands.

EXPONENTS AND FLOATING POINT NUMBERS

You have been using the arithmetic operators (+, – , *, /) to add, subtract, multiply, and divide numbers. Now you will use another operator, the *exponentiation operator* (^), to compute a power of a number.

The Exponentiation Operator (^)

A room in a house has a floor that is 12 feet square. That is, the floor is square, and each side of the square is 12 feet long. What is the area of the room in square feet? Here are two ways to compute the area.

The first method uses multiplication.

Type:

PRINT 12 * 12

It prints:

144

The second method uses the *exponentiation operator* (^) to compute the square of 12, also called the second power of 12. To type the exponentiation symbol (^), hold down a SHIFT key and press the key that has both the number 6 and the exponentiation symbol (^).

Type:

PRINT 12 ^ 2

It prints:

144

Now suppose the room has a rather lofty ceiling, exactly 12 feet high. A fortuitous coincidence! The room is 12 by 12 by 12. Therefore, the volume of the room is 12 times 12 times 12, or 12 cubed. Another way to say "12 cubed" is "12 to the third power," or "the third power of 12." You can compute the volume in cubic feet in two ways.

Use multiplication (*).

Type:

PRINT 12 * 12 * 12

It prints:

1728

Or, use exponentiation (^).

Type:

PRINT 12 ^ 3

It prints:

1728

In math books, squares and cubes of numbers are indicated by means of superscript numbers. The numbers 12 squared and 12 cubed are shown below in both standard math notation and in GW-BASIC notation.

Math Notation	GW-BASIC Notation	Meaning
12^2	12 ^2	12 squared, or 12 to the second power
12^3	12 ^3	12 cubed, or 12 to the third power

In an expression such as 12 ^ 3, the number 12 is the *base,* and 3 is the *exponent.* The exponent tells how many times the base is to be used as a factor. Here are some examples.

Expression	Base	Exponent	Equivalent Using Multiplication
12 ^ 2	12	2	12 * 12
12 ^ 3	12	3	12 * 12 * 12
5 ^ 4	5	4	5 * 5 * 5 * 5
2 ^ 10	2	10	2 * 2 * 2 * 2 * 2 * 2 * 2 * 2 * 2 * 2

Exponents can be very useful. It is much easier to write 2 ^ 10 (2 to the power 10) than to write 2 * 2 * 2 * 2 * 2 * 2 * 2 * 2 * 2 * 2. Consider, also, the expression of computer memory capacities. People say a computer has 256K, 512K, 640K, or more bytes of memory. *K* is an abbreviation of the metric term *kilo,* which means 1000. A kilogram is 1000 grams; a kilometer is 1000 meters. However, 1K bytes actually means 2 ^ 10 bytes. The following examples use the exponentiation operator (^) to compute the number of bytes in 1K, 512K, and 640K.

Type:

PRINT 2 ^ 10

It prints:

1024

Type:

PRINT 512 * 2 ^ 10

It prints:

524288

Type:

PRINT 640 * 2 ^ 10

It prints:

655360

In evaluating the expression 512 * 2 ^ 10, the computer first computes the tenth power of 2 (2 ^ 10), and then multiplies that result by 512.

Floating Point Numbers

Computer memories are getting bigger. Memories of one, two, or more megabytes are increasingly common. The term "mega" is also borrowed from the metric system. In metric, it means one million. However, in referring to the size of computer memories or hard disk storage capacity, it means 2 ^ 20 (2 to the twentieth power, or the twentieth power of 2).

How many bytes in a megabyte? Use GW-BASIC to find out.

Type:

PRINT 2 ^ 20

It prints:

1048576

One megabyte equals 1,048,576 bytes, not 1,000,000 bytes.
Next, compute the number of bytes in a 20-megabyte hard disk.

Type:

PRINT 20 * 2 ^ 20

It prints:

2.097152E+07

Twenty megabytes equals 20 times 1 megabyte, so 20 megabytes equals 20 times 2 ^ 20.

GW-BASIC prints this large number as a *floating point number*. Read it like this: 2.097152E+07 is 2.097152 times 10 ^ 7 (10 to the seventh power). Floating point notation is very similar to scientific notation, used in math and science books, as shown here:

Floating point notation: 2.097152E+07
Scientific notation: 2.097152×10^7

Floating point notation is simply a shorthand way of expressing large numbers. A floating point number has two parts: a *mantissa* and an *exponent*. The mantissa and exponent are separated by the letter E (for exponent), as shown here:

Floating point number :   2.097152E+07

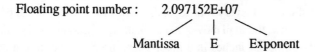

                    Mantissa   E   Exponent

In a floating point number, the exponent is always a power of 10. Here are more examples of large numbers shown in "ordinary" notation, floating point notation, and scientific notation.

Number	Ordinary Notation	Floating Point	Scientific
Population of the earth	5000000000	5E+09	5×10^9
Three trillion	3000000000000	3E+12	3×10^{12}
Miles in one light year	5865696000000	5.865696E+12	5.865696×10^{12}

The national debt of the United States is about three trillion dollars, and the population is about 250 million. You can use floating numbers to compute the debt for each person, as shown in the following example:

Type:

PRINT 3E12 / 250E6

It prints:

12000

The debt for each person in this country is $12,000! Three trillion equals 3 times $10 \wedge 12$. In floating point notation, this is 3E+12. Two hundred fifty million equals 250 times $10 \wedge 6$. In floating point notation, this is *250E+6*. Note that you can write three trillion as *3E12* instead of *3E+12*. Also, 250 million can be written as 250E6 instead of *250E+06*, or *2.5E+08*; all three ways are acceptable.

SMALL NUMBERS As you have seen, GW-BASIC does a good job representing large numbers by means of floating point notation. It is equally adept at representing very small numbers.

A recent experiment has determined that a frightened snail moves at the speed of one inch every four seconds. How fast is that in miles per second? Let's see now, the snail moves at 0.25 inches per second. Divide that number by the number of inches in a mile. There are 5280 feet in a mile, so first compute the number of inches, as follows:

Type:

PRINT 12 * 5280

It prints:

63360

Now divide the snail's speed in inches per second by 63360.

Type:

PRINT 0.25 / 63360

It prints:

3.945707E–06

GW-BASIC prints this very small number as a floating point number with a mantissa (3.945707) and a negative exponent (–06). The mantissa and exponent are separated by the letter *E*. Read it this way: three point nine four five seven zero seven times ten to the minus 6. In math, science, or other high-tech books, you might see this number written in scientific notation as 3.945707×10^{-6}.

Floating point notation	3.945707E–06
Scientific notation:	3.945707×10^{-6}

Hydrogen is universal stuff. It began with the big bang that created the universe. It is here, there, everywhere. The hydrogen atom is very small and light. The mass of the hydrogen atom is about 1.67×10 kilograms.

Floating point notation:	1.67E–27
Scientific notation:	1.67×10^{-27}
Ordinary notation:	.00000000000000000000000000167

As you can see, you can type this number much more quickly in floating point than in ordinary notation, and with less chance for a typing mistake.

TYPES OF NUMBERS

GW-BASIC has several types of numbers: integers, single precision numbers, double precision numbers, and floating point numbers. So far, you have seen three types—integers, single precision numbers, and floating point numbers, examples of which are shown here:

Integers: 3 4 –1 12
Single precision numbers: 2.54 1148.08 655360
Floating point numbers: 2.097152E+07 3E12 250E6

An *integer* is a whole number (that is, a number with no decimal point) in the range −32,768 to 32,767. An integer is stored in two bytes of memory.

A *single precision number* can be an integer or noninteger with up to seven digits. A single precision number is stored in four bytes of memory.

A *floating point number* is a number with a mantissa and an exponent. The mantissa can have up to seven digits. The exponent is in the range −39 to +38. A floating point number is stored in four bytes of memory.

Now explore a number pattern. Clear the screen and do the following:

1. Type:

   PRINT 11 * 11

   It prints:

   121

2. Type:

   PRINT 111 * 111

   It prints:

   12321

3. Type:

   PRINT 1111 * 1111

   It prints:

   1234321

4. Type:

   PRINT 11111 * 1111

   It prints:

   1.234543E+07

The first two results (121 and 12321) can be thought of as integers or single precision numbers. The third result (1234321) is a single precision number. The fourth result (1.234543E+07) is a floating point number. However, it is not the exact answer, which is 123454321. Instead, it is a seven-digit approximation to the true result. Fortunately, there is another number type that you can use to correctly represent numbers with more than seven digits.

Double Precision Numbers

A double precision number can have up to 16 digits. You can specify a number as double precision by appending a number symbol (#) to it.

Type:

PRINT 11111 * 11111#

It prints:

123454321

The number 11111# is a double precision number. Therefore, the expression 11111 * 11111# is evaluated as a double precision result and the answer (123454321) is printed correctly. You can also write the expression in the following manner:

Type:

PRINT 11111# * 11111

It prints:

123454321

If any operand in an expression is double precision, then the computer treats the entire expression as double precision.

Now continue the pattern.

Type:

PRINT 111111 * 111111#

It prints:

12345654321

If you keep going, you will soon see a double precision floating point number, as shown here:

Type:

PRINT 111111111 * 111111111#

It prints:

1.234567898765432D+16

A *double precision floating point number* consists of a mantissa and an exponent separated by the letter *D*. The mantissa can have up to 16 digits. The exponent has the same range as single precision numbers, −39 to +38. A double precision number is stored in eight bytes of memory.

Remember: Integers are whole numbers (no decimal point) in the range −32768 to 32767. An integer is stored in two bytes of memory. Single precision numbers are real numbers (integer or noninteger) with up to seven digits and, possibly, a decimal point. A single precision number can appear as a floating point number consisting of a mantissa, the letter *E*, and an exponent. A double precision number is a real number (integer or noninteger) with up to 16 digits and a decimal point. A double precision number can appear as a double precision floating point number consisting of a mantissa, the letter *D*, and an exponent.

NUMERIC VARIABLES

Imagine that, in the computer's memory, there are many "number boxes." Each number box can hold one number at any one time. A number box can hold, or store, different numbers at different times. Each number box has a name. The next illustration contains number boxes called *a, diameter,* and *Price.* Each number box contains a number.

a [7]   diameter [24]   Price [19.95]

The number 7 is in number box *a;* 24 is in the number box called *diameter;* the number box labeled *Price* contains the number 19.95.

In GW-BASIC, a number box is called a *numeric variable.* The number in a number box is the value of the variable that identifies the box. Therefore,

- The value of the variable *a* is 7.
- The value of the variable *diameter* is 24.
- The value of the variable *Price* is 19.95.

You can create variable names, subject to the following limitations:

- A variable name can be a single letter or any combination of letters and digits (0 to 9) up to 40 characters long.
- The first character must be a letter.
- You cannot use a GW-BASIC keyword (such as BEEP, CLS, or PRINT) as a variable, but a keyword can be part of a variable. For example, "beeper" is all right even though it contains "beep."

Here are seven sample variable names:

a diameter price pi Qty R2D2 TaxRate

Note that letters may be uppercase (A, B, C...) or lowercase (a, b, c...). GW-BASIC does not distinguish between upper- and lowercase. Therefore, *a* and *A* are the same variable; *pi* and *PI* are the same variable; *taxrate* and *TaxRate* are the same variable. Nevertheless, in this book, variable names appear in lowercase, or a mixture of lowercase and uppercase letters. This makes it easy to distinguish variables from keywords (BEEP, CLS, PRINT, and so on), which always appear in uppercase letters.

Types of Numeric Variables

Since GW-BASIC has three types of numbers, it also has three types of variables: *integer variables, single precision variables,* and *double precision variables.* An integer variable can have only integer values. A single precision variable can have single precision numbers as values. A double precision variable can have double precision numbers as values.

An integer variable consists of a variable name followed by a percent sign (%). The percent sign designates the variable as an integer variable.

Integer variables: n% Qty% Year%

A double precision variable consists of a variable name followed by a number symbol (#).

Double precision variables: BigNumber# LotsaBucks# NationalDebt#

A single precision variable consists of a variable name followed by no designator, or by an exclamation point (!).

Single precision variables: x Price Price! pi pi!

Remember: A variable name without a designator (%, !, or #) is automatically a single precision variable. Single precision variables suffice for most programming. Other variables are used when necessary. For example, double precision variables are necessary for problems involving large amounts of money.

Assigning a Value to a Numeric Variable

You can use direct statements to assign a value to a variable and then print the value of that variable. Do it now. Clear the screen and assign the value 7 to the variable *a*.

Type:

    a = 7

and press ENTER.

You will see the following on the screen:

```
a = 7
Ok
_
```

GW-BASIC has now reserved a small part of memory (four bytes) as a single precision variable named *a*, and assigned the number 7 as the value of *a*. When you type **a = 7** and press ENTER, you tell the computer to assign the value 7 to the variable named *a*.

Now use a direct PRINT statement to tell the computer to print the value of *a*.

Type:

PRINT a

It prints:

7

The value of a variable remains the same until you change it. You can verify this by repeating the previous statement.

Type:

PRINT a

It prints:

7

The computer has again printed the value of *a*, which is 7.

Now, assign a different number as the value of *a*, and then print it. Your new number will replace the old value of *a*.

Type:

A = 1.23

Then type:

PRINT a

It prints:

1.23

Assign the value 3.14 to a new variable, *pi*, and print the value of *pi*.

Type:

pi = 3.14

Then type:

PRINT pi

It prints:

3.14

Both *pi* and *a* will maintain their values until changed. Confirm this by printing both variables. You can do this with a single PRINT statement, using a comma (,) between the two variables.

Type:

PRINT pi, a

It prints:

3.14   1.23

You can use variables in arithmetic expressions. Assign values to the variables *a* and *b*, as shown here:

Type:

a = 7

Then type:

b = 5

Now use the variables *a* and *b* in PRINT statements to do arithmetic.

Type:

PRINT a + b

It prints:

12

Type:

PRINT a – b

It prints:

2

Type:

PRINT a * b

It prints:

35

Type:

PRINT a / b

It prints:

1.4

Two bicycles have wheels with diameters of 21 and 24 inches. How far does each bike travel in one turn of the wheels? The distance is the diameter multiplied by *pi* (π), where *pi* is approximately equal to 3.14. First, assign the value 3.14 to *pi*.

Type:

pi = 3.14

Now use *pi* to compute the distance each bike travels in one wheel turn.

Bike #1.   *Bike #2.*

Type: Type:

PRINT pi * 21   **PRINT pi * 24**

It prints: It prints:

65.94   75.36

The answers in the previous examples are in inches. If you want the results in feet, do it this way:

Bike #1.   *Bike #2.*
Type: Type:

PRINT pi * 21 / 12   **PRINT pi * 24 / 12**

It prints: It prints:

5.495001   6.28

The local sales tax rate is 6%. Assign this value to the variable *TaxRate*, as follows:

Type:

TaxRate = .06

The value of *TaxRate* is .06, since 6% is 6/100, or .06 when stated as a decimal. You can also assign the value of *TaxRate* as shown here:

Type:

TaxRate = 6 / 100

You can now use *TaxRate* to compute the amount of sales tax for various amounts of money. Here are two examples.

You purchase an item that costs $169. How much sales tax will you pay on this purchase?

Type:

PRINT 169 * TaxRate

It prints:

10.14

You buy a computer game that costs $29.95. How much is the sales tax?

Type:

PRINT 29.95 * TaxRate

It prints:

1.797

Rounded to the nearest cent, the tax on the $29.95 computer game is $1.80. Later in this chapter, you will learn how to print results that are rounded to the nearest cent.

PROGRAMMING WITH VARIABLES

The computer becomes a much more powerful and useful tool if you create programs that perform calculations using variables. Values of variables can

```
10 CLS
20 TaxRate = 6 / 100
30 INPUT SalesAmount
40 PRINT SalesAmount * TaxRate
```

PROGRAM GWME0401   Sales Tax with INPUT Statement

be entered as needed from the keyboard. The program can then do most of the work automatically.

The INPUT Statement

The INPUT statement provides the means for entering values of variables as needed by a program. In its simplest form, an INPUT statement consists of the keyword INPUT followed by a variable.

Program GWME0401 (Sales Tax with INPUT Statement) illustrates the use of an INPUT statement to acquire the value of the variable *SalesAmount.* Enter this program into the computer's memory, as follows:

1. First, type **NEW** and press ENTER. This erases the part of memory used for GW-BASIC programs. The computer is ready for a new program.

2. Type each line of the program and press ENTER. You can use ALT+P as a shortcut for typing PRINT; you can also use ALT+I as a shortcut for typing INPUT.

After entering the program, list it on the screen.

Remember: To list a program, you can type **LIST** and press ENTER. Or you can use a shortcut; press the F1 function key, and then press ENTER. The program should appear as shown here:

```
LIST
10 CLS
20 TAXRATE = 6 / 100
30 INPUT SALESAMOUNT
40 PRINT SALESAMOUNT * TAXRATE
Ok
_
```

As you can see from the listing of the program, GW-BASIC converts variable names to all uppercase letters, no matter how they were typed. If you type keywords in lowercase letters, they are also converted to uppercase. Nevertheless, in this book, variables are shown in either lowercase, or a mixture of uppercase and lowercase, except in listings. This is done to make programs easier to read.

Now run the program. You can type **RUN** and press ENTER, or you can press the F2 function key. Pressing F2 runs the program immediately; you don't even have to press ENTER.

The program first clears the screen (line 10), and then sets the value of *TaxRate* to .06 (line 20); then executes the INPUT statement in line 30. It prints a question mark on the screen, turns on the blinking cursor, and waits. The top of the screen looks like this:

```
? _
```

The computer is waiting for you to enter a value of *SalesAmount* and press ENTER. If you type **169** and press ENTER, the computer will accept that number as the value of *SalesAmount,* compute and print the sales tax (line 40), and stop, as shown here:

```
? 169
 10.14
Ok
_
```

Run the program again (press F2). This time, enter 29.95 as the value of *SalesAmount.*

```
? 29.95
 1.797
Ok
_
```

Run the program again and enter the number of your choice. Also try entering numbers such as **1, 10,** or **100,** so you can easily verify that the program is running correctly and producing the right answers. Then examine the program; it works as described in Table 4-2.

Program Line	Explanation
10 CLS	Clear the screen.
20 TaxRate = 6 / 100	Divide 6 by 100 and assign the result as the value of *TaxRate*.
30 INPUT SalesAmount	Display a question mark and wait for a number to be entered.
40 PRINT SalesAmount * TaxRate	Compute the amount of sales tax and print it.

TABLE 4-2   The Sales Tax Program Explained

If the sales tax rate in your neighborhood is different from 6%, change line 20 of the program. For example, if the tax rate is 6.5%, replace the current line 20 as follows:

Type:

20 TaxRate = 6.5 / 100

List the program to verify that the change has been made correctly, and then run the modified program.

Remember: To replace a line in a program, type the new line using the number of the line you want to replace. You can also change a line by listing it on the screen, editing the line, and pressing ENTER. To list only line 20, type **LIST 20** and press ENTER.

Save the Program

Save Program GWME0401 to the default disk drive. The easiest way to do this is

1. Press the F4 function key.

2. Type the filename (GWME0401).

3. Press ENTER.

It's as easy as 1-2-3. The SAVE statement will appear as shown here:

```
SAVE"GWME0401
```

Note that a closing quotation mark is not required, unless you want to save the program as an ASCII text file. In that case, type the SAVE statement this way:

```
SAVE"GWME0401", A
```

If you want to save the program to a designated disk drive, include the drive letter followed by a colon (:) as part of the filename, as shown here for disk drive B:

```
SAVE"B:GWME0401    or    SAVE"B:GWME0401", A
```

After saving the program, use a FILES statement to verify that the program is on the disk. Two examples of FILES statements are shown below—one to examine the default disk drive, and the other to see what files are on disk drive B.

To see default disk drive:	**FILES**
To see disk drive B:	**FILES "B"**

PROGRAM REMARKS

It is good practice to put information at the beginning of a program to tell people something about the program. The REM (REMark) statement allows you to do this. Any text that follows REM in a program line is ignored when you run the program. You can use an apostrophe (') as an abbreviation for REM.

Let's add four REM lines to Program GWME0401. If the program is not now in memory, first use one of the following LOAD statements to load it from disk to memory:

To load from the default disk drive:	**LOAD"GWME0401**
To load from disk drive B:	**LOAD"B:GWME0401**

Remember: You can press F3 to type **LOAD"**. Now add the four lines shown here. Just type each line and press ENTER.

```
1 REM ** Sales Tax with INPUT Statement **
2 ' GW-BASIC Made Easy, Chapter 4.  File: GWME0401.BAS
3 ' Written on a rainy day in January
9 '
```

List the program. You should see the original program, plus the above four lines, all in line number order, as shown here:

```
LIST
1 REM ** Sales Tax with INPUT Statement **
2 ' GW-BASIC Made Easy, Chapter 4.  File: GWME0401.BAS
3 ' Written on a rainy day in January
9 '
10 CLS
20 TAXRATE = 6 / 100
30 INPUT SALESAMOUNT
40 PRINT SALESAMOUNT * TAXRATE
```

Line 1 is a REM statement that briefly describes the program. Line 2 uses an apostrophe (') instead of the word REM. It tells where the program originated (GW-BASIC Made Easy, Chapter 4) and gives the filename (GWME0401.BAS) under which it is stored on a disk. The full filename, including the .BAS extension, is shown. Line 3 is optional. You can put whatever comments you want in these first few lines. You might want to include the date the program was written or the date of the last time you modified the program. Line 9 serves as a blank line spacer, separating this

---

```
1 REM ** Sales Tax with Enhanced INPUT Statement **
2 ' GW-BASIC Made Easy, Chapter  4.  File: GWME0402.BAS
9 '
10 CLS
20 TaxRate = 6 / 100
30 INPUT "Amount of Sale"; SalesAmount
40 PRINT SalesAmount * TaxRate
```

PROGRAM GWME0402   Sales Tax with Enhanced INPUT Statement

block of descriptive information from the rest of the program, which does the actual work. You can put five more lines (4, 5, 6, 7, and 8) between line 3 and line 9.

The information in REM statements is for people; the computer ignores it. Run the program to verify this. From now on, most programs will have REM statements that will help you identify and understand the programs.

AN IMPROVED SALES TAX PROGRAM

The INPUT statement tells the computer to put a question mark on the screen and wait for a number to be entered. This is useful, but it would be more useful if the computer identified what sort of input it wanted. There is an easy way to do this.

Program GWME0402 (Sales Tax with Enhanced INPUT Statement) is an improved version of the sales tax program. It features an "enhanced" INPUT statement.

Run the program. Two sample runs are shown here:

Run #1. Run #2.

```
Amount of Sale? 169          Amount of Sale? 29.95
 10.14                        1.797
Ok                           Ok

 —                            —
```

The statement

INPUT "Amount of sale"; SalesAmount

tells the computer to do the following:

1. Print the message "Amount of sale."

2. Print a question mark.

3. Wait for a number to be entered and assign it as the value of *SalesAmount*.

```
1 REM ** Sales Tax with Enhanced INPUT & PRINT Statements **
2 ' GW-BASIC Made Easy, Chapter 4.  File: GWME0403.BAS
9 '
10 CLS
20 TaxRate = 6 / 100
30 INPUT "Amount of Sale"; SalesAmount
40 PRINT "Amount of sales tax is"; SalesAmount * TaxRate
```

PROGRAM GWME0403   Sales Tax with Enhanced INPUT & PRINT
                        Statements

Note that the message to be displayed is enclosed in quotation marks and
followed by a semicolon. This is an example of a string, previously described
in Chapter 2.

Now change the program so that it identifies the result as the amount of
sales tax, as shown in Program GWME0403.BAS (Sales Tax with Enhanced
INPUT & PRINT Statements). Be sure to type all punctuation, including
quotation marks ("").

Save this program under the filename GWME0403, and then run it. A
sample run is shown here:

```
Amount of Sale? 29.95
Amount of sales tax is 1.797
Ok
_
```

FORMATTING THE PRINTED RESULTS

The next version of the sales tax program GWME0404 (Expanded Sales Tax
Program) is considerably expanded. It prints the amount of sale entered from
the keyboard, the amount of the sales tax, and the total amount of the sale,
including sales tax. The TAB function is used to line the numbers up
vertically. Blank lines are added to make the program easier to read. These
blank lines will not appear when you list the program.

Note several new things in this program.

```
1 REM ** Expanded Sales Tax Program **
2 ' GW-BASIC Made Easy, Chapter 4.  File: GWME0404.BAS

10 CLS
20 TaxRate = 6 / 100

30 INPUT "Amount of sale"; SalesAmount

40 SalesTax = SalesAmount * TaxRate
50 TotalAmount = SalesAmount + SalesTax

60 PRINT
70 PRINT "Amount of sale is"; TAB(30); SalesAmount

80 PRINT "Amount of sales tax is"; TAB(30); SalesTax

90 PRINT "Total amount is"; TAB(30); TotalAmount
```

PROGRAM GWME0404   Expanded Sales Tax Program

- Line 40 computes the sales tax and assigns it as the value of SalesTax

- Line 50 computes the total amount of the sale and assigns it as the value of *TotalAmount*.

- Line 60 is an "empty" PRINT statement. It causes a blank line to be printed. You can control and improve the appearance of printed results by using PRINT statements appropriately.

- In lines 70, 80, and 90, the TAB function tells the computer to move the cursor to the column specified in parentheses. "TAB(30)" moves the cursor to column 30.

Enter and save this program with the name GWME0404, and run it. A sample run is shown here:

```
Amount of sale? 1

Amount of sale is           1
Amount of sales tax is      .06
Total amount is             1.06
```

Note: From now on, the GW-BASIC prompt (Ok) and the cursor (_) will be omitted when showing the results of running a program.

The PRINT USING Statement

Although the values of *SalesAmount*, *SalesTax*, and *TotalAmount* are all printed beginning in column 30, the decimal points do not line up correctly. To solve this problem, use a variation of the print statement called PRINT USING. The PRINT USING statement lets you specify the appearance and positioning of numbers. It also provides the means for rounding numbers to a given number of decimal places.

The following statement tells the computer to print the value of *SalesAmount* with up to five digits before the decimal point, and two digits following the decimal point, rounded, if necessary:

```
PRINT USING "#####.##"; SalesAmount
```

```
1 REM ** Expanded Sales Tax Program with PRINT USING **
2 ' GW-BASIC Made Easy, Chapter 4.  File: GWME0405.BAS

10 CLS
20 TaxRate = 6 / 100

30 INPUT "Amount of sale"; SalesAmount

40 SalesTax = SalesAmount * TaxRate
50 TotalAmount = SalesAmount + SalesTax

60 PRINT
70 PRINT "Amount of sale is"; TAB(30);
75 PRINT USING "#####.##"; SalesAmount

80 PRINT "Amount of sales tax is"; TAB(30);
85 PRINT USING "#####.##"; SalesTax

90 PRINT "Total amount is"; TAB(30);
95 PRINT USING "#####.##"; TotalAmount
```

PROGRAM GWME0405   Expanded Sales Tax Program with PRINT USING

Program GWME0405 (Expanded Sales Tax Program with PRINT USING), uses three PRINT USING statements, in lines 75, 85, and 95.

Enter and save this program with the name GWME0405, and run it. Since all three numbers are printed with the same PRINT USING format string ("#####.##"), they line up vertically along the decimal point, as shown in the following two runs:

```
Amount of sale? 1

Amount of sale is              1.00
Amount of sales tax is         0.06
Total amount is                1.06


Amount of sale? 29.95

Amount of sale is             29.95
Amount of sales tax is         1.80
Total amount is               31.75
```

The following pair of statements prints one line on the screen:

```
70 PRINT "Amount of sale is"; TAB(30);
75 PRINT USING "#####.##"; SalesAmount
```

Line 70 prints the string "Amount of sale is," and then tabs over to column 30. The semicolon at the end of line 70 holds the cursor at column 30, so that the information printed by line 75 will begin there. Line 75 prints the value of *SalesAmount* as specified by the format string, "#####.##". For example:

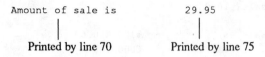

```
    Amount of sale is            29.95
```

Printed by line 70	Printed by line 75

Lines 80 and 85 also work together to produce one line of print, as do lines 90 and 95.

Note that all numbers are shown with two decimal places, as specified by the format string ("#####.##") in the PRINT USING statements. The format string limits the printed number to, at most, five digits before the decimal point. If a printed number is more than 99999.99, a percent sign (%) is

```
1 REM ** Sales Tax with Double Precision Variables **
2 ' GW-BASIC Made Easy, Chapter 4.  File: GWME0406.BAS

10 CLS
20 TaxRate# = 6 / 100#

30 INPUT "Amount of sale"; SalesAmount#

40 SalesTax# = SalesAmount# * TaxRate#
50 TotalAmount# = SalesAmount# + SalesTax#

60 PRINT
70 PRINT "Amount of sale is"; TAB(30);
75 PRINT USING "############.##"; SalesAmount#

80 PRINT "Amount of sales tax is"; TAB(30);
85 PRINT USING "############.##"; SalesTax#

90 PRINT "Total amount is"; TAB(30);
95 PRINT USING "############.##"; TotalAmount#
```

PROGRAM GWME0406   Sales Tax with Double Precision Variables

printed in front of the number, as shown here:

```
Amount of sale? 1000000

Amount of sale is            %1000000.00
Amount of sales tax is       60000.00
Total amount is              %1060000.00
```

This problem has an easy solution. Use double precision variables and format strings that allow more digits before the decimal point, as illustrated by Program GWME0406 (Sales Tax with Double Precision Variables).

Let's enter and save Program GWME0406, and then run it for a really big sales amount, one billion dollars (1000000000), as the following shows.

```
Amount of sale? 1000000000

Amount of sale is              1000000000.00
Amount of sales tax is           60000000.00
Total amount is                1060000000.00
```

In Program GWME0406, note the following things:

- The double precision variables *TaxRate#*, *SalesAmount#*, *SalesTax#*, and *TotalAmount#*.

- In line 20, a double precision number (100#) is used to ensure that the value of *TaxRate#* will be as precise as possible. Numbers in GW-BASIC are stored as *binary* (base 2) *numbers*. The decimal number .06 cannot be stored exactly as a binary number; a small "round-off error" occurs. This error is much less if the computation is done using a double precision number. A complete description of round-off error is beyond the scope of this book.

- The format string ("############.##") in PRINT USING statements allows up to 12 digits before the decimal point.

More Features of PRINT USING

The PRINT USING format statement has many variations. Among the most useful of these are printing dollar signs ($) before numbers, and automatically putting commas in very large numbers. These features are shown in lines 75, 85, and 95 of Program GWME0407 (Sales Tax with Dollars and Commas in Printout).

Edit Program GWME0406 to create Program GWME0407, save the modified program, and run it. Here is a sample run. Note the dollar sign ($) before each number, and the commas imbedded in the part of the number to the left of the decimal point.

```
Amount of sale? 1000000000

Amount of sale is            $1,000,000,000.00
Amount of sales tax is          $60,000,000.00
Total amount is              $1,060,000,000.00
```

```
1 REM ** Sales Tax with Dollar Signs & Commas in Printout **
2 ' GW- BASIC Made Easy, Chapter 4.  File: GWME0407.BAS

10 CLS
20 TaxRate# = 6 / 100#

30 INPUT "Amount of sale"; SalesAmount#

40 SalesTax# = SalesAmount# * TaxRate#
50 TotalAmount# = SalesAmount# + SalesTax#

60 PRINT
70 PRINT "Amount of sale is"; TAB(30);
75 PRINT USING "$$###,###,###,###.##"; SalesAmount#

80 PRINT "Amount of sales tax is"; TAB(30);
85 PRINT USING "$$###,###,###,###.##"; SalesTax#

90 PRINT "Total amount is"; TAB(30);
95 PRINT USING "$$###,###,###,###.##"; TotalAmount#
```

PROGRAM GWME0407   Sales Tax with Dollars and Commas in Printout

The format string "$$###,###,###,###.##" tells the computer to print a number as follows:

- The double dollar sign ($$) causes a dollar sign to be printed to the left of the number.

- The 12 number signs (#) separated by commas allow up to 12 digits of the number to be printed, with commas inserted every three digits. If fewer than 12 digits are printed, spaces are printed instead, in this case to the left of the dollar sign.

- The decimal point causes a decimal point to be printed in the number.

- The two number signs to the right of the decimal point cause two digits to be printed to the right of the decimal point. If necessary, the number being printed is rounded to two places.

```
1 REM ** Value of Stocks **
2 ' GW-BASIC Made Easy, Chapter 4.  File: GWME0408.BAS

10 CLS

20 INPUT "Number of shares"; NumberOfShares#
30 INPUT "Price per share "; PricePerShare#

40 Value# = NumberOfShares# * PricePerShare#

50 PRINT
60 PRINT "The value is ";
70 PRINT USING "$$############,.##"; Value#
```

PROGRAM GWME0408   Value of Stocks

VALUE OF STOCKS

If you own stocks, you might find the next program useful. It computes and prints the value of a block of stock shares, given the number of shares and the price per share.

Enter and save Program GWME0408 (Value of Stocks), and then run it. A sample run is shown here:

```
Number of shares? 1200
Price per share? 37.50

The value is       $45,000.00
```

The format string "$$############,.##" is equivalent to the format string "$$###,###,###,###.##" used previously in Program GWME0407. In either case, commas are printed every three digits in the part of the number to the left of the decimal point.

Remember: A number sign (#) at the end of a variable name defines the variable as a double precision variable.

```
1 REM ** Future Value of Money -- Compound Interest **
2 ' GW-BASIC Made Easy, Chapter 4.  File: GWME0409.BAS

100 REM ** Clear the screen **
110 CLS

200 REM ** Get principal, interest rate, number of periods **
210 INPUT "Principal amount invested ($)"; Principal#
220 INPUT "Interest rate per period (%) "; Rate#
230 INPUT "Number of interest periods   "; Periods#

300 REM ** Compute future value **
310 Rate# = Rate# / 100
320 FutureValue# = Principal# * (1 + Rate#) ^ Periods#

400 REM ** Print the future value **
410 PRINT
420 PRINT "At maturity, the value will be ";
430 PRINT USING "$$############,.##"; FutureValue#
```

PROGRAM GWME0409   Future Value of Money — Compound Interest

Program GWME0408 uses the following double precision variables:

- *NumberOfShares#*

- *PricePerShare#*

- *Value#*

A double precision variable provides about 16 digits of precision. Try the program with very large numbers. What happens when the value of *Value#* is bigger than the limit imposed by the PRINT USING format string? Try it and find out. Also try other format strings, perhaps one that allows printout of even larger numbers. The format string in the program permits printout of amounts up to $999,999,999,999.99.

A FUTURE VALUE—COMPOUND INTEREST PROGRAM

Let's suppose you keep your money in a bank account that pays regular interest, compounded periodically. Program GWME0409 computes the value of money (principal) invested at a particular interest rate per period, compounded for a given number of periods.

Examine the following runs and think about how you would write the program. The first sample is for $1 invested at 1% interest, compounded for one period. This is used to test the program. The answer should be $1.01.

```
Principal amount invested ($)? 1
Interest rate per period (%) ? 1
Number of interest periods   ? 1

At maturity, the value will be              $1.01
```

Now suppose you have a balance of $500 on a credit card that charges 1.5% interest per month, and you put off paying it for 12 months.

```
Principal amount invested ($)? -500
Interest rate per period (%) ? 1.5
Number of interest periods   ? 12
At maturity, the value will be         -$597.81
```

The "investment" is entered as −500 as a reminder that you owe $500 and that you are therefore paying the interest. The result is −$597.81.

You might find it helpful to write an outline of the program in REM statements first. The next listing shows a possible outline.

```
1 REM ** Future Value of Money -- Compound Interest **
2 ' GW-BASIC Made Easy, Chapter 4.  File: GWME0409.BAS

100 REM ** Clear the screen **

200 REM ** Get principal, interest rate, number of periods **

300 REM ** Compute the future value **

400 REM ** Print the future value **
```

Once you have an outline for your program, you can expand it as shown in Program GWME0409.

The program has five blocks. Each block begins with a REM statement that tells what the block does. The first block (1 REM) gives the name of the program, where it was first published, and the file name of the program as stored on a disk.

The second block (100 REM) clears the screen; if there were any other program set-up to be done, this block would include those instructions as well.

The third block (200 REM) uses INPUT statements to get values for the three variables used to compute the amount of interest and future value. All variables are double precision—useful for handling large values.

- *Principal#* is the amount invested, in dollars and cents.

- *Rate#* is the interest rate per interest period. Enter 1 for 1%, 1.5 for 1.5%, and so on.

- *Period#* is the number of periods over which the interest is compounded. For example, if the interest is compounded monthly for one year, enter 12 as the value of *Period#*.

The fourth block (300 REM) calculates the future value. The interest rate is first converted to a decimal fraction (line 310), which is used in the formula to compute the future value. Note the use of the exponentiation operator (^). In a math book, you might see a compound interest formula such as the one shown here.

$$A = P(1 + r)^n$$

where P is the principal, placed at an interest rate r for n periods, producing an amount A (future value).

In GW-BASIC, the formula would be written like this:

$$A = P * (1 + r) \wedge n$$

In this book, more descriptive variables are used in order to make programs easier for you to understand. The variable *Principal#* is more descriptive than the letter P.

```
1 REM ** Future Value of Money -- Compound Interest #2 **
2 ' GW-BASIC Made Easy, Chapter 4.  File: GWME0410.BAS
3 ' Compute future value of money invested at a yearly
4 ' interest rate and compounded one or more times a year.

100 REM ** Clear the screen **
110 CLS

200 REM ** Get principal, interest rate, number of periods **
210 INPUT "Principal amount invested ($)"; Principal#
220 INPUT "Interest rate per year (%)   "; YearlyRate#
230 INPUT "Interest periods per year    "; PeriodsPerYear#
240 INPUT "Number of interest periods   "; Periods#

300 REM ** Compute future value **
310 Rate# = YearlyRate# / PeriodsPerYear# / 100
320 FutureValue# = Principal# * (1 + Rate#) ^ Periods#

400 REM ** Print the future value **
410 PRINT
420 PRINT "At maturity, the value will be ";
430 PRINT USING "$$#############,.##; FutureValue#
```

PROGRAM GWME0410   Future Value of Money — Compound Interest #2

The fifth and final block (400 REM) prints the value of the future value, preceded by the string "At maturity, the value will be." The format string "$$#############,.##" causes the number to be printed with a dollar sign and commas every three digits.

A variation of the program is shown next as GWME0410 (Future Value of Money — Compound Interest #2). It asks for the principal, the yearly interest rate, the number of times per year the interest is compounded, and the number of interest periods. Here are four sample runs to illustrate the usefulness of this program.

The sample runs are for an investment of $1000 at 12% per year. Sample run #1 is compounded annually. Sample run #2 is compounded monthly. Sample run #3 is compounded weekly and sample run #4 is compounded daily.

```
Principal amount invested ($)? 1000
Interest rate per year (%)    ? 12
Interest periods per year     ? 1
Number of interest periods    ? 1

At maturity, the value will be          $1,120.00
```

Sample run #2:

```
Principal amount invested ($)? 1000
Interest rate per year (%)    ? 12
Interest periods per year     ? 12
Number of interest periods    ? 12

At maturity, the value will be          $1,126.82
```

Sample run #3:

```
Principal amount invested ($)? 1000
Interest rate per year (%)    ? 12
Interest periods per year     ? 52
Number of interest periods    ? 52

At maturity, the value will be          $1,127.34
```

Sample run #4:

```
Principal amount invested ($)? 1000
Interest rate per year (%)    ? 12
Interest periods per year     ? 365
Number of interest periods    ? 365

At maturity, the value will be          $1,127.48
```

Suppose the interest is compounded hourly, 24 hours a day, for a year. Use a direct PRINT statement to compute the number of interest periods:

Type:

PRINT 24 * 365

It prints:

8760

Now use this value when you run the program. Also try compounding every minute, and compounding every second for a year. Use a direct PRINT statement to compute the number of interest periods. Do you gain much by compounding more frequently?

PRINTING TO THE PRINTER

In Chapter 3, you learned how to use the LLIST statement to list a program to the printer. You can also use LPRINT or LPRINT USING in a program to print information to the printer. In Program GWME0410, change block 1 and add block 500, as shown here:

```
1 REM ** Future Value of Money -- Compound Interest #3 **
2 ' GW-BASIC Made Easy, Chapter 4.  File: GWME0411.BAS
3 ' Compute future value of money invested at a yearly
4 ' interest rate and compounded one or more times a year.
5 ' Output is to both screen & printer.
  .
  .
  .
500 REM ** Print all values to the printer **
510 LPRINT "Principal amount invested"; TAB(32);
515 LPRINT USING "$$###########,.##"; Principal#
520 LPRINT "Interest rate per year (%)"; TAB(34);
525 LPRINT USING "###########,.##"; YearlyRate#
540 LPRINT "Interest periods per year"; TAB(34);
545 LPRINT USING "###########,.##"; Periods#
550 LPRINT "Number of interest periods"; TAB(34);
555 LPRINT USING "###########,.##"; Periods#
560 LPRINT
570 LPRINT "At maturity, the value will be"; TAB(32);
575 LPRINT USING "$$###########,.##"; FutureValue#
580 LPRINT : LPRINT : LPRINT
590 END
```

Notice that the double dollar signs ($$) are not used in the LPRINT USING statements for the values of the variables *YearlyRate#* and *Periods#*.

```
1 REM ** Future Value of Money -- Compound Interest #3 **
2 ' GW-BASIC Made Easy, Chapter 4.  File: GWME0411.BAS
3 ' Compute future value of money invested at a yearly
4 ' interest rate and compounded one or more times a year.
5 ' Output is to both screen & printer.

100 REM ** Clear the screen **
110 CLS

200 REM ** Get principal, interest rate, number of periods **
210 INPUT "Principal amount invested ($)"; Principal#
220 INPUT "Interest rate per year (%)   "; YearlyRate#
230 INPUT "Interest periods per year    "; PeriodsPerYear#
240 INPUT "Number of interest periods   "; Periods#

300 REM ** Compute future value **
310 Rate# = YearlyRate# / PeriodsPerYear# / 100
320 FutureValue# = Principal# * (1 + Rate#) ^ Periods#

400 REM ** Print the future value **
410 PRINT
420 PRINT "At maturity, the value will be";
430 PRINT USING "$$############,.##"; FutureValue#

500 REM ** Print all values to the printer **
510 LPRINT "Principal amount invested"; TAB(32);
515 LPRINT USING "$$############,.##"; Principal#
520 LPRINT "Interest rate per year (%)"; TAB(34);
525 LPRINT USING "############,.##"; YearlyRate#
540 LPRINT "Interest periods per year"; TAB(34);
545 LPRINT USING "############,.##"; Periods#
550 LPRINT "Number of interest periods"; TAB(34);
555 LPRINT USING "############,.##"; Periods#
560 LPRINT
570 LPRINT "At maturity, the value will be"; TAB(32);
575 LPRINT USING "$$############,.##"; FutureValue#
580 LPRINT : LPRINT : LPRINT
590 END
```

PROGRAM GWME0411   Future Value of Money — Compound Interest #3

Since the double dollar signs cause a space and a dollar sign to be printed, the TAB value is changed from 32 to 34 for the formatted printing of

"Interest rate per year," "Interest periods per year," and "Number of interest periods."

Save the modified program under the filename GWME0411, and then run it. The information will appear on the screen as before, and also on the printer, as shown here:

```
Principal amount invested ($)          $1,000.00
Interest rate per year (%)                 12.00
Interest periods per year                  12.00
Number of interest periods                 12.00

At maturity, the value will be         $1,126.82
```

Remember:

- To list a program on the printer, use LLIST.

- To print strings and numbers to the printer from within a program, use LPRINT or LPRINT USING.

REVIEW

Use the arithmetic operators $(+, -, *, /)$ and the exponentiation operator $(\char`\^)$ to make calculations. You can do this with direct statements or by means of a program. GW-BASIC provides three types of numbers you can use for number crunching:

- An *integer* is a whole number in the range of −32,768 to 32,767. An integer does not have a decimal point. You can use a percent sign (%) to designate a number as an integer.

- A *single precision number* is an integer or noninteger with up to seven digits and a decimal point. If a number is too large to be represented in seven digits, it is expressed as a floating point number with a mantissa and an exponent, separated by the letter *E*. You can use an exclamation point (!) to designate a number as a single precision number.

- A *double precision number* is an integer or noninteger with up to 16 digits and a decimal point. If a number is too large to be represented in 16 digits, it is expressed as a double precision floating point number with a mantissa and exponent, separated by the letter *D*. You can use a number sign (#) to designate a number as a double precision number.

A *numeric variable* is the label, or name, of a "number box" in which a number can be stored. A variable name can be any combination of letters and digits up to 40 characters long. The first character must be a letter. GW-BASIC does not distinguish between uppercase and lowercase letters in variable names: for example, *pi, Pi,* and *PI* are the same. Use %, !, or # to designate variables as integer, single precision, or double precision, respectively. GW-BASIC assumes that an undesignated variable is single precision. Use the INPUT statement to acquire values of variables. You can include a string in the INPUT statement to identify the information required.

Use PRINT and PRINT USING statements to display information on the screen. Use LPRINT and LPRINT USING statements to print information on the printer.

Include REM statements in programs to make them easier to read and understand. You can use an apostrophe (') as an abbreviation for REM. You can even use REM statements to write an outline of a program before writing the complete program. This will save you lots of time.

5

MAKING PROGRAMS MORE USEFUL

In this chapter, you will learn how to create programs that "loop back" and automatically repeat. You can modify programs from the preceding chapter to make them run automatically. You will also learn about another kind of variable: a string variable. In particular, you will learn

- how to use the GOTO statement and GOTO loops

- how to use CTRL+BREAK to stop a program

- how to use SCROLL LOCK (or HOLD on Tandy computers) to "freeze" and "unfreeze" the screen

- how to make loops that count automatically

- what string variables are and how to assign values

- how to use the INPUT$ string function to acquire the value of a single key press or a predetermined number of key presses

THE GOTO LOOP

The programs you have seen so far are executed once when you type **RUN** and press ENTER, or when you simply press the F2 function key. The program runs from the top (smallest line number) to the bottom (largest line number), and then stops. Now you will learn how to make programs that "loop back" and repeat, so that all or part of the program is executed repeatedly. This feature can be very useful, especially when you need to execute the same process more than once to produce the desired result.

One way to make all or part of a program repeat is to use a GOTO statement to tell the computer to go to a previous line and continue from there. In this book, this program structure is called a *GOTO loop*. A GOTO loop repeats until you interrupt by pressing keys on the keyboard.

Simple GOTO Loops

Tell the computer you are going to enter a new program (type **NEW**, and then press ENTER). Enter the following program, which illustrates a simple GOTO loop. When you run this program, it will run and run and run, until you tell it to stop. To stop the program, hold down the CTRL key and press the BREAK key. (This key combination is called CTRL+BREAK.)

```
10 PRINT "Hold down CTRL and press BREAK to stop me"
20 GOTO 10
```

Run the program. The screen quickly fills with the message printed by line 10, "Hold down CTRL and press BREAK to stop me." When you tire of watching this message repeated endlessly, stop the computer, as directed by the message. You will then see a screen similar to the one in Figure 5-1. (Note that the key line is omitted.)

Run the program again (press F2). The screen quickly fills with the message in the PRINT statement (line 10). Look at the next-to-last line on the screen (above the key line): it flickers. The flicker is caused by rapid scrolling of the message up the screen. When a new message is printed (by line 10) at the bottom of the screen, previous copies of the message are pushed up one line and the top line disappears. This happens so fast that you cannot see the scrolling, unless you have ultrafast superhero eyes. Only the flicker tells you something is happening.

```
Hold down CTRL and press BREAK to stop me.
Hold down CTRL and press BREAK to stop me.
Hold down CTRL and press BREAK to stop me.
Hold down CTRL and press BREAK to stop me.
Hold down CTRL and press BREAK to stop me.
Hold down CTRL and press BREAK to stop me.
Hold down CTRL and press BREAK to stop me.
Hold down CTRL and press BREAK to stop me.
Hold down CTRL and press BREAK to stop me.
Hold down CTRL and press BREAK to stop me.
Hold down CTRL and press BREAK to stop me.
Hold down CTRL and press BREAK to stop me.
Hold down CTRL and press BREAK to stop me.
Hold down CTRL and press BREAK to stop me.
Hold down CTRL and press BREAK to stop me.
Hold down CTRL and press BREAK to stop me.
Hold down CTRL and press BREAK to stop me.
Hold down CTRL and press BREAK to stop me.
Hold down CTRL and press BREAK to stop me.
Hold down CTRL and press BREAK to stop me.
Hold down CTRL and press BREAK to stop me.

Break in 10
Ok

_
```

FIGURE 5-1   To stop a GOTO loop, do what it says on the screen

Remember: To stop a GOTO loop, hold down CTRL and press BREAK
(CTRL+BREAK).

When you interrupt a program by pressing CTRL+BREAK, the computer
stops doing what it was doing and tells you that it stopped because you
pressed CTRL+BREAK. You will see:

```
Break in line 10
Ok

_
```

The message "Break in line 10" tells you the computer stopped just after
doing line 10 of the program. The GW-BASIC prompt (Ok) and the blinking
cursor tell you the computer is ready for your next instruction.

The statement

20 GOTO 10

tells the computer to go to line 10 and continue from there. When you run
the program, it begins with line 10, and then goes to line 20, which tells it to
go to line 10. It goes to line 10, does that, and then goes to line 20, which
sends it back to line 10. It does line 10, and then line 20, which sends it back
to line 10. And so on. This continuing process is illustrated here:

```
Run
 ↓
10 PRINT "Hold down CTRL and press BREAK to stop me"  ◄─┐
 ↓                                                      │
20 GOTO 10  ────────────────────────────────────────────┘
```

In the early days of computers in the classroom, BASIC was used for
almost everything. Stories similar to the following were told: A teacher sees
a student talking to another student at an inappropriate time. The teacher
solemnly pronounces, "Tomorrow, your extra homework is to hand in 100
copies of the message, 'I will not talk out of turn in class.' " There were many
groans from classmates, but only a knowing smile on the face of the student,
who was learning BASIC. During recess, she wrote and ran the following
program:

```
10 LPRINT "I will not talk out of turn in class."
20 GOTO 10
```

If you have a printer, enter and run this program. The LPRINT statement
(line 10) prints information on the printer. When you have printed 100 copies
of the message in the LPRINT statement, or even sooner, stop the computer;
hold down CTRL and press BREAK.

The program that follows is another example of a GOTO loop. This
program repeatedly prints the time until you interrupt it.

```
10 PRINT TIME$
20 GOTO 10
```

If you watch as the program runs, you will immediately see the seconds change. Of course, the minutes and hours may also change, but more slowly. Notice the lines on the screen scrolling as new information is printed on the line just above the key line.

GW-BASIC has a keyword called TIMER that keeps track of the number of seconds since midnight. Enter and run the following program to see TIMER in action:

```
10 PRINT TIMER
20 GOTO 10
```

If you run this program at about 8:05 A.M., let it run for a few seconds and stop it, you will see something similar to this in the bottom part of the screen (the key line is omitted):

```
29119.51
29119.51
29119.57
29119.57
29117.57
29117.62
29117.62
29119.68
29119.68
29119.68

Break in 10
Ok
_
```

The computer prints the value of TIMER with up to two decimal places. However, the printed value may not be precise to one hundredth of a second, unless you are using a very fast computer. In the above example, note that the value changes by about .05 or .06 second. You can count on the value of TIMER being precise to one-tenth of a second or better. Later in this book, you will use TIMER to construct time delays, and to compute and print the amount of time it takes the computer to do something.

FREEZING AND UNFREEZING THE SCREEN   Sometimes it is useful to "freeze" the screen, so that you can study the results of an executing program without actually stopping the program. After freezing the screen and examining it, you can "unfreeze" the screen and let the program continue. The keys described here work for some computers; for others you may have to use a different method to freeze the screen.

To freeze the screen, use the SCROLL LOCK key.

Press:

    SCROLL LOCK

Use the same key to unfreeze the screen.

Press:

    SCROLL LOCK

On some Tandy 1000 computers, use the HOLD key to freeze and unfreeze the screen.

This same technique (SCROLL LOCK or HOLD) is used throughout this chapter. If neither SCROLL LOCK nor HOLD works for you, consult the user's manual for your computer.

Use the following program to practice freezing and unfreezing the screen. This program prints the value of TIMER repeatedly. Because of the comma (,) at the end of line 10, the values will be printed five to a line, in standard print positions across the screen.

```
10 PRINT TIMER,  ◄──── Comma
20 GOTO 10
```

Enter and run the program. Press SCROLL LOCK (or HOLD) to freeze the screen. Press SCROLL LOCK (or HOLD) again to unfreeze the screen. Figure 5-2 shows a sample frozen screen.

Longer GOTO Loops

The GOTO loops you have seen so far are very simple. Each loop consists of two lines. The first line, with the smaller line number, is the top of the loop. The second line, the one with the GOTO statement, is the bottom of the loop.

31545.96	31545.96	31545.96	31546.01	31546.01
31546.01	31546.01	31546.07	31546.07	31546.07
31546.12	31546.12	31546.12	31546.12	31546.12
31546.18	31546.18	31546.18	31546.18	31546.23
31546.23	31546.23	31546.23	31546.29	31546.29
31546.29	31546.29	31546.34	31546.34	31546.34
31546.34	31546.4	31546.4	31546.4	31546.4
31546.45	31546.45	31546.45	31546.45	31546.45
31546.51	31546.51	31546.51	31546.51	31546.56
31546.56	31546.56	31546.56	31546.62	31546.62
31546.62	31546.62	31546.67	31546.67	31546.67
31546.67	31546.73	31546.73	31546.73	31546.73
31546.78	31546.78	31546.78	31546.78	31546.84
31546.84	31546.84	31546.84	31546.89	31546.89
31546.89	31546.89	31546.95	31546.95	31546.95
31546.95	31547	31547	31547	31547
31550.9	31550.96	31550.96	31550.96	31550.96
31551.01	31551.01	31551.01	31551.01	31551.07
31551.07	31551.07	31551.07	31551.12	31551.12
31551.12	31551.12	31551.18	31551.18	31551.18
31551.18	31551.23	31551.23	31551.23	31551.23
31551.29	31551.29	31551.29	31551.29	31551.29
31551.34	31551.34	31551.34	31551.34	31551.4

FIGURE 5-2   Values of TIMER while screen is "frozen"

Let's look at a modified version of one of the programs:

```
10 PRINT TIME$      'Top of GOTO loop
20 GOTO 10          'Bottom of GOTO loop
```

Note that a comment has been added to each line. The comment following the apostrophe in each line is treated like a REM statement—it is ignored by the computer. These comments are added to make the program easier for you to understand. Here is another example:

```
10 PRINT TIMER,     'Top of GOTO loop
20 GOTO 10          'Bottom of GOTO loop
```

A GOTO loop can contain any number of lines. In the following program, a three-line GOTO loop is used to tell the computer to print the numbers 1,

2, 3, and so on, until you interrupt by using CTRL+BREAK.

```
10 CLS

20 number = 1

30 PRINT number,         'Top of GOTO loop
40 number = number + 1
50 GOTO 30               'Bottom of GOTO loop
```

Enter and run this program. The computer rapidly prints the numbers 1, 2, 3, and so on. Since the first two lines of the program (10 and 20) are outside the GOTO loop, they are executed only once. The lines of the GOTO loop (lines 30, 40, and 50) are repeated until you stop the program.

Since the PRINT statement in line 30 ends with a comma,

```
30 PRINT number,
```

the values of *number* are printed five to a line, as shown here:

```
1            2            3            4            5
6            7            8            9            10
11           12           13           14           15
16           17           18           19           20
21           22           23           24           25
26           27           28           29           30
31           32           33           34           35
36           37           38           39           40
41           42           43
Break in 30
Ok
_
```

The program first clears the screen (10 CLS), and assigns the value 1 to the numeric variable *number* (20 *number* = 1). The statements in the GOTO loop are then repeated until you stop the program. Each time through the loop, the computer prints the current value of *number* (30 PRINT *number*,), increases the value of *number* by 1 (40 *number* = *number* + 1), and then goes back to line 30 and continues from there (50 GOTO 30).

The statement

40 number = number + 1

tells the computer to add 1 to the current value of *number* and assign the resulting value to *number*. This new value replaces the old value of *number*.

Variations of this program follow. Since the programs are very similar, you can edit the original program to get the first variation, edit that program to get the second variation, and so on.

Variation #1: Print the odd positive integers (1, 3, 5, and so on).

```
10 CLS

20 number = 1

30 PRINT number,        'Top of GOTO loop
40 number = number + 2
50 GOTO 30              'Bottom of GOTO loop
```

Variation #2: Print the even positive integers (2, 4, 6, and so on).

```
10 CLS

20 number = 2

30 PRINT number,        'Top of GOTO loop
40 number = number + 2
50 GOTO 30              'Bottom of GOTO loop
```

Variation #3: Count by tens (10, 20, 30, and so on).

```
10 CLS

20 number = 10

30 PRINT number,        'Top of GOTO loop
40 number = number + 10
50 GOTO 30              'Bottom of GOTO loop
```

Enter and run each program. Press SCROLL LOCK (or HOLD) to freeze the screen. Press SCROLL LOCK (or HOLD) again to unfreeze the screen. Press CTRL+BREAK to stop the program.

```
1 REM ** Sales Tax with GOTO Loop **
2 ' GW-BASIC Made Easy, Chapter 5.  File: GWME0501.BAS
3 ' Edit Program GWME0407.BAS to get this program

10 CLS
20 TaxRate# = 6 / 100#

30 INPUT "Amount of sale"; SalesAmount#        'Top of loop

40 SalesTax# = SalesAmount# * TaxRate#
50 TotalAmount# = SalesAmount# + SalesTax#

60 PRINT
70 PRINT "Amount of sale is"; TAB(30);
75 PRINT USING "$$###,###,###,###.##"; SalesAmount#

80 PRINT "Amount of sales tax is"; TAB(30);
85 PRINT USING "$$###,###,###,###.##"; SalesTax#

90 PRINT "Total amount is"; TAB(30);
95 PRINT USING "$$###,###,###,###.##"; TotalAmount#

100 PRINT
110 GOTO 30                                    'Bottom of loop
```

PROGRAM GWME0501   Sales Tax with GOTO Loop

A SALES TAX PROGRAM WITH A GOTO LOOP

You can easily modify the sales tax programs of Chapter 4, "Number Crunching," to make them even more convenient. For example, through the use of a GOTO loop, the sales tax for different sales amounts can be calculated more easily. Program GWME0501 (Sales Tax with GOTO Loop) is a modification of Program GWME0407 (Sales Tax with Dollar Signs & Commas in Printout).

The following sample run of Program GWME0501 shows the results from two different sales amounts.

```
Amount of sale? 29.95

Amount of sale is                        $29.95
Amount of sales tax is                    $1.80
Total amount is                          $31.75

Amount of sale? 1000000000

Amount of sale is              $1,000,000,000.00
Amount of sales tax is            $60,000,000.00
Total amount is                $1,060,000,000.00

Amount of sale? _
```

The computer is waiting at the top of the GOTO loop (line 30) for someone to enter another sales amount. Instead, press CTRL+BREAK to stop the program. You will see the following:

```
Amount of sale?
Break in 30
Ok
_
```

VALUE OF STOCKS WITH GOTO LOOP

If your portfolio contains several stocks, you can use the next program to compute the value of each block of shares. First, look at the following sample run and think about how you might write the program.

```
Number of shares? 100
Price per share ? 37.125

The value is        $3,712.50

Number of shares? 1000000
Price per share ? .01

The value is        $10,000.00

Number of shares? _
```

You can modify Program GWME0408 (Value of Stocks) to get the Program GWME0502 (Value of Stocks with GOTO Loop).

```
1 REM ** Value of Stocks with GOTO Loop **
2 ' GW-BASIC Made Easy, Chapter 5.  File: GWME0502.BAS
3 ' Edit Program GWME0408.BAS to get this program

10 CLS

20 INPUT "Number of shares"; NumberOfShares#    'Top of loop
30 INPUT "Price per share "; PricePerShare#

40 Value# = NumberOfShares# * PricePerShare#

50 PRINT
60 PRINT "The value is ";
70 PRINT USING "$$############,.##"; Value#

80 PRINT
90 GOTO 20                                     'Bottom of loop
```

PROGRAM GWME0502   Value of Stocks with GOTO Loop

FUTURE VALUE—COMPOUND INTEREST WITH GOTO LOOP

If your money is invested in a bank or other account that pays interest compounded regularly, you can use the next program, GWME0503, to calculate the future value of your investment. This program is a modification of Program GWME0410 (Future Value of Money — Compound Interest) in Chapter 4. Here is a REM outline of the program.

```
1 REM ** Future Value -- Compound Interest with GOTO Loop **
2 ' GW-BASIC Made Easy, Chapter 5.  File: GWME0503.BAS
3 ' Edit Program GWME0410.BAS to get this program

100 REM ** Clear the screen **

200 REM ** Get principal, interest rate, number of periods **

300 REM ** Compute future value **
```

```
400 REM ** Print the future value **

500 REM ** Print line space & go to top of loop **
```

Think about how you would modify Program GWME0410 to get Program GWME0503. Load Program GWME0410 from the disk into memory (you did save it, didn't you?). Make your changes, and then compare it with Program GWME0503 (Future Value — Compound Interest with GOTO Loop).

Note that the GOTO statement in line 520 sends the computer back to the INPUT statement in line 210, not to the REM statement in line 200.

```
1 REM ** Future Value -- Compound Interest with GOTO Loop **
2 ' GW-BASIC Made Easy, Chapter 5.  File: GWME0503.BAS
3 ' Compute future value of money invested at a yearly
4 ' interest rate and compounded one or more times a year.

100 REM ** Clear the screen **
110 CLS

200 REM ** Get principal, interest rate, number of periods **
210 INPUT "Principal amount invested ($)"; Principal#      'Top
220 INPUT "Interest rate per year (%)   "; YearlyRate#
230 INPUT "Interest periods per year    "; PeriodsPerYear#
240 INPUT "Number of interest periods   "; Periods#

300 REM ** Compute future value **
310 Rate# = YearlyRate# / PeriodsPerYear# / 100
320 FutureValue# = Principal# * (1 + Rate#) ^ Periods#

400 REM ** Print the future value **
410 PRINT
420 PRINT "At maturity, the value will be ";
430 PRINT USING "$$############,.##"; FutureValue#

500 REM ** Print line space & go to top of loop **
510 PRINT
520 GOTO 210                                        'Bottom
```

PROGRAM GWME0503   Future Value — Compound Interest with GOTO Loop

Remember: REM statements can be omitted without changing the execution of the program. In this book, a GOTO statement will always go to the line number of an executable statement, never to a REM statement.

Perhaps you are thinking of putting your money in Erosion Savings and Loan for 6 percent per year, compounded monthly. How long will it take to double your money? The following run of Program GWME0503 shows the future value of an original investment (principal) of $1000 for 60 months (5 years), 120 months (10 years), and 180 months (15 years).

```
Principal amount invested ($)? 1000
Interest rate per year (%)    ? 6
Interest periods per year     ? 12
Number of interest periods    ? 60

At maturity, the value will be          $1,348.85

Principal amount invested ($)? 1000
Interest rate per year (%)    ? 6
Interest periods per year     ? 12
Number of interest periods    ? 120

At maturity, the value will be          $1,819.40

Principal amount invested ($)? 1000
Interest rate per year (%)    ? 6
Interest periods per year     ? 12
Number of interest periods    ? 180

At maturity, the value will be          $2,454.10

Principal amount invested ($)? _
```

Your investment doubles at some point between 120 and 180 months (between 10 and 15 years).

Since the computer is waiting for another principal amount, try 130 months, 140 months, and so on.

```
Principal amount invested ($)? 1000
Interest rate per year (%)    ? 6
Interest periods per year     ? 12
Number of interest periods    ? 130

At maturity, the value will be          $1,912.44
```

```
Principal amount invested ($)? 1000
Interest rate per year (%)   ? 6
Interest periods per year    ? 12
Number of interest periods   ? 140

At maturity, the value will be          $2,010.24

Principal amount invested ($)? _
```

It appears that your investment doubles sometime between 130 and 140 months. If you want to find the number of months most precisely, try some numbers between 130 and 140 as the number of interest periods.

If you are willing to accept more risk, you might find a place to invest your nest egg at, say, 12 percent. As shown here, you can double your money in about 6 years (72 months).

```
Principal amount invested ($)? 1000
Interest rate per year (%)   ? 12
Interest periods per year    ? 12
Number of interest periods   ? 36

At maturity, the value will be          $1,430.77

Principal amount invested ($)? 1000
Interest rate per year (%)   ? 12
Interest periods per year    ? 12
Number of interest periods   ? 72

At maturity, the value will be          $2,047.10

Principal amount invested ($)? _
```

To pin down the time more precisely, try numbers between 36 and 72 for the number of interest periods. Do you think the doubling time is closer to 36 months or closer to 72 months?

A MODIFIED FUTURE VALUE—COMPOUND INTEREST PROGRAM

Program GWME0504 offers a more convenient way to experiment with the number of interest periods needed to reach a predetermined future value. In

```
1 REM ** Modified Future Value -- Compound Interest Program **
2 ' GW-BASIC Made Easy, Chapter 5.  File: GWME0504.BAS
3 ' Compute future value of money invested at a yearly
4 ' interest rate and compounded one or more times a year.

100 REM ** Clear the screen, print date & time **
110 CLS
120 PRINT "The date is "; DATE$
130 PRINT "The time is "; TIME$
140 PRINT

200 REM ** Get principal, interest rate, periods per year **
210 INPUT "Principal amount invested ($)"; Principal#
220 INPUT "Interest rate per year (%)    "; YearlyRate#
230 INPUT "Interest periods per year     "; PeriodsPerYear#

300 REM ** Compute rate per interest period **
310 Rate# = YearlyRate# / PeriodsPerYear# / 100

400 REM ** Get total number of interest periods **
410 PRINT                                              'Top
420 INPUT "Number of interest periods   "; Periods#

500 REM ** Compute & print the future value **
510 FutureValue# = Principal# * (1 + Rate#) ^ Periods#
520 PRINT "At maturity, the value will be ";
530 PRINT USING "$$###########,.##"; FutureValue#

600 REM ** Go to top of loop **
610 GOTO 410                                           'Bottom
```

PROGRAM GWME0504   Modified Future Value — Compound Interest
                       Program

---

using this program, you enter the amount of the investment, interest rate per
year, and number of interest periods per year all only once; then you enter
the total number of interest periods as many times as you want. Here is a
REM outline of the program. An arrow from block 600 to block 400 shows
the GOTO loop. Blocks 400, 500, and 600 are part of the loop.

```
1 REM ** Modified Future Value -- Compound Interest Program **
2 ' GW-BASIC Made Easy, Chapter 5.  File: GWME0504.BAS
3 ' Compute future value of money invested at a yearly
4 ' interest rate and compounded one or more times a year

100 REM ** Clear the screen, print date & time **

200 REM ** Get principal, interest rate, periods per year **

300 REM ** Compute rate per interest period **

400 REM ** Get total number of interest periods **

500 REM ** Compute & print the future value **

600 REM ** Go to top of loop **
```

A sample run of Program GWME0504 is shown here:

```
The date is 01-01-1990
The time is 13:07:20

Principal amount invested ($)? 1000
Interest rate per year (%)    ? 12
Interest periods per year     ? 12

Number of interest periods    ? 36
At maturity, the value will be       $1,430.77

Number of interest periods    ? 72
At maturity, the value will be       $2,047.10

Number of interest periods    ? 70
At maturity, the value will be       $2,006.76

Number of interest periods    ? 69
At maturity, the value will be       $1,986.89

Number of interest periods    ? _
```

Study the sample run and the REM outline. Much of the overall program design is finished once you decide how you want the output to look and have written an outline of the program. Now try completing the program; one possible version is Program GWME0504 (Modified Future Value— Compound Interest).

FUTURE VALUE—COMPOUND INTEREST WITH COUNTING LOOP

The next program has a *counting loop*. Using a counting loop, you can compute and print the future value for the number of interest periods equal to 1, 2, 3, 4, 5, and so on, until you interrupt. Here is a REM outline of Program GWME0505.

```
1 REM ** Future Value--Compound Interest with Counting Loop **
2 ' GW-BASIC Made Easy, Chapter 5. File: GWME0505.BAS
3 ' Compute future value of money invested at a yearly
4 ' interest rate and compounded one or more times a year.

100 REM ** Clear the screen, print date & time **

200 REM ** Get principal, interest rate, periods per year **

300 REM ** Compute rate per interest period **

400 REM ** Set number of interest periods to 1 **

500 REM ** Compute & print the future value **

600 REM ** Increment number of interest periods **

700 REM ** Go to top of loop **
```

A sample run is shown below for a principal amount of $1000, yearly interest rate of 12 percent, compounded monthly (12 times). The number of interest periods per year has been typed, but ENTER has not been pressed. Note the cursor following the number 12.

```
The date is 01-01-1990
The time is   :56:16

Principal amount invested ($)? 1000
Interest rate per year (%)    ? 12
Interest periods per year     ? 12_
```

If you now press ENTER, and then quickly press SCROLL LOCK (or HOLD), you might see the following, or something similar.

```
The date is 01-01-1990
The time is 01:57:42

Principal amount invested ($)? 1000
Interest rate per year (%)    ? 12
Interest periods per year     ? 12

In 1 periods, the value will be      $1,010.00

In 2 periods, the value will be      $1,020.10

In 3 periods, the value will be      $1,030.30

In 4 periods, the value will be      $1,040.60

In 5 periods, the value will be      $1,051.01

In 6 periods, the value will be      $1,061.52
```

Now press SCROLL LOCK (or HOLD) again. Watch the screen and try to press SCROLL LOCK (or HOLD) soon after the future value passes 2000, as shown in the partial screen here:

```
In 68 periods, the value will be      $1,967.22

In 69 periods, the value will be      $1,986.89

In 70 periods, the value will be      $2,006.76

In 71 periods, the value will be      $2,026.83

In 72 periods, the value will be      $2,047.10
```

Together, the REM outline and the sample run give you lots of information on how to write the program. You can modify the REM outline to obtain Program GWME0505 (Future Value—Compound Interest with Counting Loop).

In Program GWME0505's counting loop, block 400 sets the value of *Periods#* to 1. The GOTO loop begins at line 510 (the top of the loop) and ends at line 710 (the bottom of the loop). Each time through the loop, block 500 uses the current value of *Periods#* to compute and print the future value. Line 610 increases the value of *Periods#* by 1 for use the next time through the loop.

```
1 REM ** Future Value -- Compound Interest with Counting Loop **
2 ' GW-BASIC Made Easy, Chapter 5.  File: GWME0505.BAS
3 ' Compute future value of money invested at a yearly
4 ' interest rate and compounded one or more times a year.

100 REM ** Clear the screen, print date & time **
110 CLS
120 PRINT "The date is "; DATE$
130 PRINT "The time is "; TIME$
140 PRINT

200 REM ** Get principal, interest rate, periods per year **
210 INPUT "Principal amount invested ($)"; Principal#
220 INPUT "Interest rate per year (%)   "; YearlyRate#
230 INPUT "Interest periods per year    "; PeriodsPerYear#
240 PRINT

300 REM ** Compute rate per interest period **
310 Rate# = YearlyRate# / PeriodsPerYear# / 100

400 REM ** Set number of interest periods to 1 **
410 Periods# = 1

500 REM ** Compute & print the future value **
510 FutureValue# = Principal# * (1 + Rate#) ^ Periods#    'Top
520 PRINT "In"; Periods#; "periods, the value will be ";
530 PRINT USING "$$############,.##"; FutureValue#
540 PRINT

600 REM ** Increment number of interest periods **
610 Periods# = Periods# + 1

700 REM ** Go to top of loop **
710 GOTO 510                                            'Bottom
```

PROGRAM GWME0505   Future Value — Compound Interest with Counting Loop

The statement

520 PRINT "In"; Periods#; "periods, the value will be ";

prints the string "In", and then the value of *Periods#*, and then the string "periods, the value will be ". The semicolon at the end of the statement holds the cursor so that the information printed by line 530 will be on the same line. For example, if the value of *Periods#* is 7, line 520 prints

```
In 7 periods, the value will be
```

If you have a printer, modify Program GWME0505 so that the information produced by the GOTO loop is printed on the printer. You can do this by changing the PRINT statements in block 500 to LPRINT statements, as shown here:

```
500 REM ** Compute & print the future value **
510 FutureValue# = Principal# * (1 + Rate#) ^ Periods# 'Top
520 LPRINT "In"; Periods#; "periods, the value will be ";
530 LPRINT USING "$$###########,.##"; FutureValue#
540 LPRINT
```

You may also want to change block 100 so that the date and time are also printed on the printer. While you are making these changes, consider adding LPRINT statements in block 200 to print on the printer the values of *Principal#*, *YearlyRate#*, and *PeriodsPerYear#*.

INPUT$ TO THE RESCUE

Program GWME0506 is a slightly modified version of Program GWME0505. It contains a string variable called *anykey$*, and the INPUT$ function in block 700, as follows:

```
700 REM ** Wait for a key press, then go to top of loop **
710 anykey$ = INPUT$(1)
720 GOTO 510
```

```
1 REM ** Future Value -- Compound Interest with Modified GOTO Loop **
2 ' GW-BASIC Made Easy, Chapter 5.  File: GWME0506.BAS
3 ' Compute future value of money invested at a yearly
4 ' interest rate and compounded one or more times a year.

100 REM ** Clear the screen, print date & time **
110 CLS
120 PRINT "The date is "; DATE$
130 PRINT "The time is "; TIME$
140 PRINT

200 REM ** Get principal, interest rate, periods per year **
210 INPUT "Principal amount invested ($)"; Principal#
220 INPUT "Interest rate per year (%)   "; YearlyRate#
230 INPUT "Interest periods per year    "; PeriodsPerYear#
240 PRINT

300 REM ** Compute rate per interest period **
310 Rate# = YearlyRate# / PeriodsPerYear# / 100

400 REM ** Set number of interest periods to 1 **
410 Periods# = 1

500 REM ** Compute & print the future value **
510 FutureValue# = Principal# * (1 + Rate#) ^ Periods#    'Top
520 PRINT "In"; Periods#; "periods, the value will be ";
530 PRINT USING "$$############,.##"; FutureValue#
540 PRINT

600 REM ** Increment number of interest periods **
610 Periods# = Periods# + 1

700 REM ** Wait for a key press, then go to top of loop **
710 anykey$ = INPUT$(1)
720 GOTO 510                                            'Bottom
```

PROGRAM GWME0506   Future Value — Compound Interest with Modified
GOTO Loop

The statement

```
710 anykey$ = INPUT$(1)
```

tells the computer to wait for a key press. Almost any key will do. When you press a key, the string value of the key is stored as the value of *anykey$*, and the computer goes on to line 720, which, of course, sends it to the top of the loop. You will learn more about *anykey$* and INPUT$ in the next section. But first take a look at Program GWME0506 (Future Value—Compound Interest with Modified GOTO Loop).

Note that Program GWME0506 is the same as Program GWME0505, except for block 1 (lines 1 through 4) and block 700 (lines 700, 710, and 720). Here is a sample run of Program GWME0506. It begins this way:

```
The date is 01-01-1990
The time is 14:31:41

Principal amount invested ($)? 1000
Interest rate per year (%)    ? 12
Interest periods per year     ? 12

In 1 period, the value will be        $1,010.00
```

The computer is waiting at line 710 for you to press a key. Press a key—the space bar is a good choice—and the program continues as follows:

```
In 2 periods, the value will be        $1,020.10
```

Press a key several more times. Each time you press a key, the computer goes again through the GOTO loop. After a few presses, you will see:

```
The date is 01-01-1990
The time is 14:31:41

Principal amount invested ($)? 1000
Interest rate per year (%)    ? 12
Interest periods per year     ? 12

In 1 period, the value will be        $1,010.00

In 2 periods, the value will be        $1,020.10
```

```
In 3 periods, the value will be        $1,030.30

In 4 periods, the value will be        $1,040.60

In 5 periods, the value will be        $1,051.01

In 6 periods, the value will be        $1,061.52

In 7 periods, the value will be        $1,072.14
```

Now press a key and hold it down. The computer rapidly computes and prints more information. Release the key to stop. How many months to triple your money?

Note: This method of interrupting a program is easier to use than pressing SCROLL LOCK or HOLD. It allows you to more efficiently control the stream of output from the program.

STRINGS AND STRING VARIABLES

A string is a group of characters, one after another in, well, a string. A string can be

- a name: Mariko

- a telephone number: 707-555-1212

- a message: Trust your psychic tailwind

- a date: 1/1/1990

- a time: 3:30:57

- gibberish: 123Bz#m%@

You have seen strings enclosed in quotation marks:

```
DATE$ = "1/1/1990"
TIME$ = "8:30:57"
PRINT "George Firedrake"
```

The quotation marks enclose the string, but are not part of the string.

A string can be the value of a *string variable*. You can think of a string variable as a labeled box that can hold, or store, a string:

DATE$ | 1/1/1990 | TIME$ | 8:30:57 |

FirstName$ | George | Message$ | Take a dragon to lunch |

A string variable is specified by a name followed by a dollar sign ($). The name can be any combination of letters and numbers, but the first character must be a letter. Here are some examples of string variables:

Naym$ Address$ City$ State$

TIME$ DATE$ Word$ Agent007$

Two of these variables, *TIME$* and *DATE$*, are already familiar to you. They are string variables; they are also GW-BASIC keywords.

Note: Most keywords may not be used as variables. For example, you may not use Name$ as a string variable, because NAME is a GW-BASIC keyword. However, note the use of *Naym$*, above, as a string variable name that sounds and looks like Name$.

In this book, string variables are shown in lowercase letters, or a mixture of lowercase and uppercase letters (except DATE$ and TIME$). However, when you list a program, GW-BASIC will print all variables in uppercase.

You can assign a value to a string variable in the same way that you assign a value to a numeric variable. For example, assign a value to the string variable *Naym$*, as follows:

Type:

Naym$ = "George Firedrake"

and press ENTER.

Verify that George's full name is now the value of *Naym$*.

Type:

PRINT Naym$

and press ENTER.

It prints:

George Firedrake

Assign a value to the string variable *PhoneNumber$*, and then verify it.

Type:

PhoneNumber$ = "707-555-1212"

and press ENTER.

Type:

PRINT PhoneNumber$

and press ENTER.

It prints:

707-555-1212

Enter and run the following short program:

```
10 CLS
20 FirstName$ = "George"
30 LastName$ = "Firedrake"
40 PRINT FirstName$, LastName$          'Note comma
50 PRINT FirstName$; LastName$          'Note semicolon
60 PRINT FirstName$; " "; Lastname$     'Put in a space
70 PRINT FirstName$ + " " + LastName$   'Use + to join strings
80 PRINT LastName$; ", "; FirstName$    'Reverse order
90 PRINT LastName$ + ", " + FirstName$  'Another way to do it
```

Study the program and the following output of the program to learn more about strings, commas, and semicolons in PRINT statements, and about the use of a plus sign (+) to concatenate (join) strings.

```
George          Firedrake
GeorgeFiredrake
George Firedrake
```

```
George Firedrake
Firedrake, George
Firedrake, George
```

Using INPUT with String Variables

You can use INPUT to acquire a value for a string variable. In the following short program, an INPUT statement is used to acquire a value for the string variable *Strng$*. This variable is used in lieu of String$, which is a GW-BASIC keyword (STRING$).

```
10 CLS
20 INPUT Strng$
30 PRINT Strng$
40 PRINT
50 GOTO 20
```

Enter and run the program. It clears the screen, prints a question mark, displays the cursor, and waits for you to enter a value for the string variable *Strng$*, as shown here:

```
? _
```

Enter George Firedrake's name.

Type:

George Firedrake

and press ENTER.

The computer accepts George's name as the value of *Strng$*, prints the value of *Strng$*, and then loops back to the INPUT statement and waits for a new value of *Strng$*. The screen looks like this:

```
? George Firedrake
George Firedrake

? _
```

Now enter George's name in reverse order: last name, a comma, and then first name.

Type:

Firedrake, George

and press ENTER.

Oops! Trouble. You will see the following on the screen:

```
? Firedrake, George
?Redo from start
? _
```

Remember: If a string contains a comma, you must enclose the entire string in quotation marks. Enter George's name in reverse order, enclosed in quotation marks.

Type:

"Firedrake, George"

and press ENTER.

This time the computer should accept the string containing a comma. The screen will look like this:

```
? "Firedrake, George"
Firedrake, George

? _
```

Here is another example showing entry of a string containing a comma, with and without quotation marks:

```
? January 1, 1990
?Redo from start
? "January 1, 1990"
January 1, 1990

? _
```

ng$. When you are finished, use

ING FUNCTION

ng program to demonstrate the use of the INPUT$ function.

```
  PRINT "Press a key"              'Top of loop
 0 anykey$ = INPUT$(1)
40 PRINT "You pressed "; anykey$
50 PRINT
60 GOTO 20                        'Bottom of loop
```

Enter and run the program. It begins this way:

```
Press a key
_
```

Note the blinking cursor. The computer is executing line 30. It is waiting for you to press a key. You can press almost any single key; the computer will accept it as the value of INPUT$(1), assign it as the value of *anykey$,* and then go on to line 40.

When executed, line 40 tells you what key you pressed, if you pressed a "printable" key. Letter keys and number keys will result in a printout. SHIFT by itself is ignored, but SHIFT plus another key counts as one key. Use SHIFT and a letter key to enter an uppercase letter as the value of INPUT$(1). Here is an annotated sample run:

```
Press a key
You pressed a

Press a key
You pressed A            SHIFT+A was pressed

Press a key
You pressed 8

Press a key
You pressed *            SHIFT+8 was pressed
```

```
Press a key
You pressed                    The space bar was pressed

Press a key
_
```

Your turn now. Press some keys. What happens if you press ENTER? Try it and find out. Press a function key (F1, F2, F3, and so on). Try CTRL+A, or CTRL plus another letter key (hold down CTRL and press a letter key). Use CTRL+BREAK to stop the program.

The string function

INPUT$(1)

tells the computer to wait for entry of one character from the keyboard. SHIFT plus another key counts as one character; so does CTRL plus another key. Pressing a function key is the same as pressing each character printed by the function key. Unlike the INPUT *statement,* the INPUT$ *function* does not print a question mark.

The statement

30 anykey$ = INPUT$(1)

tells the computer to assign the value of INPUT$(1) to the string variable *anykey$*. This, of course, will be the character entered from the keyboard.

You can use INPUT$ to acquire two, three, or more characters from the keyboard. Just put the number of characters you want in parentheses, following the keyword INPUT$. For example, to get two characters, write the function as INPUT$(2). To try this out, modify lines 20 and 30 of the program, this way:

```
20 PRINT "Press two keys"
30 anykey$ = INPUT$(2)
```

When you run the modified program, remember to enter two characters when the computer prints "Press two keys."

REVIEW

Use a GOTO statement to go to a previous line and continue from there. In this way, you construct a GOTO loop that repeats until you interrupt by using CTRL+BREAK. You can easily modify programs from Chapter 4, "Number Crunching," so that they operate more automatically under control of a GOTO loop.

If a program is running continuously and printing lots of information on the screen, press SCROLL LOCK to "freeze" the screen. This suspends operation of the program. Press SCROLL LOCK again to "unfreeze" the screen and let the program continue.

String variables are variables that represent strings. They can be used, for example, to store names, addresses, and telephone numbers. You can assign a value to a string (for example, PhoneNumber$ = "707-555-1212"), or use an INPUT statement to acquire a value of a string (such as INPUT *Strng$*). INPUT$ is a string function. Use it to acquire a single character from the keyboard (without pressing ENTER) or a predetermined number of characters.

6

CONTROL STRUCTURES: DECISIONS AND LOOPS

GW-BASIC has several *control structures* you can use to make your programs more useful. In this chapter you will learn how to use the decision-making statements: IF and ON...GOTO. You will also learn how to use two loop structures: WHILE...WEND and FOR...NEXT. You will apply these new control structures to previously seen applications, such as computing the value of stocks, and to new applications, such as printing in colors and making sound effects. In particular, you will learn how to

- use the IF statement as an automatic decision-making tool

- use WHILE...WEND loops to automatically repeat a set of statements while a certain condition is true

- construct precise time delay loops

- use FOR...NEXT loops to execute a set of statements for a sequence of values of a numeric variable

- use the COLOR statement to print text in 16 colors

- use the SOUND statement to make sounds and effects

- use the INKEY$ function for fingertip control of a program

- use the ON...GOTO statement for multiple-choice decision making

This chapter introduces the following GW-BASIC keywords:

CHR$	COLOR	ELSE	END	FIX	FOR
IF	INKEY$	LOCATE	NEXT	ON	SGN
SOUND	STEP	THEN	TO	WEND	WHILE

THE USEFUL IF STATEMENT

The IF statement tells the computer to make a simple decision. It tells the computer to do a certain operation *if* a given condition is *true*. However, *if* the condition is *false* (not true), the operation is not done. Here is a simple IF statement:

```
420 IF number = 0 THEN PRINT z$
```

This IF statement tells the computer:

- If the value of the numeric variable *number* is equal to zero, then print the value of the string variable *z$*.

- If the value of the numeric variable *number* is not equal to zero, then don't print the value of the string variable *z$*.

Here is another way to think about it:

- If the value of *number* is equal to zero, execute the statement following the keyword THEN.

- If the value of *number* is not equal to zero, don't execute the statement following the keyword THEN.

And yet another way:

This is the condition

↓

```
420 IF number = 0 THEN PRINT z$
```

↑

Do this if the condition is true

Don't do this if the condition is false

In the above IF statement, the condition is *number* = *zero*. Consider these possibilities:

- Suppose the value of *number* is 3.14. In this case, the condition is false, and the computer does not print the value of *z$*.

- Suppose the value of *number* is zero. Now the condition is true. The computer prints the value of *z$*.

- Suppose the value of *number* is −7. The condition is false. The computer does not print the value of *z$*.

The above IF statement is in the form:

IF condition THEN statement

In this form, the *statement* can be any GW-BASIC statement. The *condition* is usually a comparison between a variable and a value, between two variables, or between two complicated expressions. Table 6-1 shows some comparison symbols in both math and GW-BASIC notation.

Comparison	Math Symbol	GW-BASIC Symbol
is equal to	$=$	$=$
is less than	$<$	$<$
is greater than	$>$	$>$
is less than or equal to	$\leq$	$<=$
is greater than or equal to	$\geq$	$>=$
is not equal to	$\neq$	$< >$

TABLE 6-1   Comparison Symbols, Math and GW-BASIC

```
1 REM ** Negative, Zero, or Positive #1 **
2 ' GW-BASIC Made Easy, Chapter 6.  File: GWME0601.BAS

100 REM ** Assign messages to string variables **
110 n$ = "negative"
120 z$ = "zero"
130 p$ = "positive"

200 REM ** Tell what to do **
210 CLS : KEY OFF
220 PRINT "Enter a number and I will tell you whether"
230 PRINT "your number is negative, zero, or positive."

300 REM ** Ask for a number **
310 PRINT                          'Top of loop
320 INPUT "Number, please"; number

400 REM ** Tell about the number **
410 IF number < 0 THEN PRINT n$
420 IF number = 0 THEN PRINT z$
430 IF number > 0 THEN PRINT p$

500 REM ** Go to top of loop **
510 GOTO 310                             'Bottom of loop
```

PROGRAM GWME0601   Negative, Zero, or Positive #1

Negative, Zero, or Positive Program

Program GWME0601 (Negative, Zero, or Positive #1) tests a number
entered from the keyboard to determine whether the number is negative,
zero, or positive. Here is a REM outline of the program:

```
1 REM ** Negative, Zero, or Positive #1 **
2 ' GW-BASIC Made Easy, Chapter 6.  File: GWME0601.BAS

100 REM ** Assign messages to string variables **

200 REM ** Tell what to do **
```

```
300 REM ** Ask for a number **

400 REM ** Tell about the number **

500 REM ** Go to top of loop **
```

The program uses three IF statements. Look for them in lines 410, 420, and 430.

Enter and run the program. A sample run is shown in Figure 6-1.

First, the messages printed by the program are assigned to string variables in block 100 near the beginning of the program, as shown here:

```
100 REM ** Assign messages to string variables **
110 n$ = "negative"
120 z$ = "zero"
130 p$ = "positive"
```

If you want a less succinct message, rewrite lines 110, 120, and 130 using the messages of your choice.

```
Enter a number and I will tell you whether
your number is negative, zero, or positive.

Number, please? 0
zero

Number, please? 3.14
positive

Number, please? -7
negative

Number, please? _
```

FIGURE 6-1 Sample run of Program GWME0601

The program will next "tell what to do," as follows:

```
200 REM ** Tell what to do **
210 CLS : KEY OFF
220 PRINT "Enter a number and I will tell you whether"
230 PRINT "your number is negative, zero, or positive."
```

Line 210 contains two statements separated by a colon. The first statement (CLS) clears the screen, except for the key line at the bottom. The second statement (KEY OFF) turns off the key line. If you want the key line left on, delete the KEY OFF statement from line 210.

The rest of the program is a GOTO loop that acquires a number entered from the keyboard, then tells whether the number is negative, zero, or positive. The GOTO loop in blocks 300 through 500 is shown here:

```
300 REM ** Ask for a number **
310 PRINT                            'Top of loop
320 INPUT "Number, please"; number

400 REM ** Tell about the number **
410 IF number < 0 THEN PRINT n$
420 IF number = 0 THEN PRINT z$
430 IF number > 0 THEN PRINT p$

500 REM ** Go to top of loop **
510 GOTO 310                         'Bottom of loop
```

If you enter a negative number, line 410 causes the value of *n$* ("negative") to be printed. If you enter zero (0), line 420 is activated; the value of *z$* ("zero") is printed. If your number is positive, line 430 prints the value of *p$* ("positive").

Line 510 then sends control back to the top of the loop. Use CTRL+BREAK to stop the program.

Value of Stocks Program

You can use an IF statement to provide an exit from a GOTO loop. You can end the next program by entering zero (0) as the number of shares. It then

```
The date is 01-01-1990
The time is 19:04:22

Number of shares? 1
Price per share ? 1.375
The value of these shares is                 $1.38

Number of shares? 1000
Price per share ? 29.75
The value of these shares is             $29,750.00

Number of shares? 200
Price per share ? 67.125
The value of these shares is             $13,425.00

Number of shares? 0

Total value of all stocks is              43,176.38
Ok

_
```

FIGURE 6-2   Sample run of Program GWME0602

prints the total value of all shares previously entered. Figure 6-2 shows the output of a sample run.

First, examine the sample run. You will enter the number of shares and price per share for a block of stock. The computer then calculates and prints the value of that block of stock. It also adds the value of the block to a running total for all blocks of shares entered, but does not print the total each time. After you enter the data for all your stocks, you can then enter zero (0) when the computer asks for the number of shares. It will then print the total value of all shares previously entered, and the program will end.

A REM outline of Program GWME0602 is shown here:

```
1 REM ** Value of Stocks with Total Value of All Stocks **
2 ' GW-BASIC Made Easy, Chapter 6.  File: GWME0602.BAS

100 REM ** Set up the screen **

200 REM ** Print the date and time **
```

```
300 REM ** Set total value of all shares to zero **

400 REM ** Get number of shares and price per share **
405 ' If number of shares equals zero, then exit loop

500 REM ** Compute value and add to total value **

600 REM ** Print value of shares & go to top of loop **

700 REM ** Print total of all stocks and end program **
```

Before looking at the complete program, try your hand at writing your version of the program. Study both the sample run and the REM outline. Much of the overall design is done once you decide how you want the printed information to look and write a REM outline.

One version is shown of Program GWME0602 (Value of Stocks with Total Value of All Stocks). The program begins by clearing the screen and turning off the key line. Then it prints the date and time, probably useful in an application where information can vary rapidly with time. Before asking for data to be entered from the keyboard, the program sets the total value of all shares to zero, as in the following:

```
300 REM ** Set total value of all shares to zero **
310 TotalValue# = 0
```

Note that *TotalValue#* is a double precision variable, used to accommodate you high rollers (or should that be deep plungers?).

The program is now ready to acquire and process stock data. This is done by means of a GOTO loop that begins in block 400.

```
400 REM ** Get number of shares and price per share **
405 ' If number of shares is zero, then exit loop
410 INPUT "Number of shares"; NumberOfShares#        'Top
420 IF NumberOfShares# = 0 THEN GOTO 710             'Exit if 0
430 INPUT "Price per share "; PricePerShare#
```

Line 410 acquires a value of *NumberOfShares#* entered from the keyboard. If this value is zero, line 420 sends the computer down to line 710. If the

```
1 REM ** Value of Stocks with Total Value of All Stocks **
2 ' GW-BASIC Made Easy, Chapter 6.  File: GWME0602.BAS

100 REM ** Set up the screen **
110 CLS : KEY OFF

200 REM ** Print the date and time **
210 PRINT "The date is "; DATE$
220 PRINT "The time is "; TIME$
230 PRINT

300 REM ** Set total value of all shares to zero **
310 TotalValue# = 0

400 REM ** Get number of shares and price per share **
405 ' If number of shares is zero, then exit loop
410 INPUT "Number of shares"; NumberOfShares#       'Top
420 IF NumberOfShares# = 0 THEN GOTO 710            'Exit if 0
430 INPUT "Price per share "; PricePerShare#

500 REM ** Compute value and add to total value **
510 Value# = NumberOfShares# * PricePerShare#
520 TotalValue# = TotalValue# + Value#

600 REM ** Print value of shares & go to top of loop **
610 PRINT "The value of these shares is";
620 PRINT USING "$$############,.##"; Value#
630 PRINT : GOTO 410                                'Bottom

700 REM ** Print total of all stocks and end program **
710 PRINT
720 PRINT "Total value of all stocks is";
730 PRINT USING "$$############,.##"; TotalValue#
740 END
```

PROGRAM GWME0602   Value of Stocks with Total Value of All Stocks

value is not zero, this doesn't happen. Instead, the computer continues in line number order. Line 420 can be written in a somewhat shortened form, with GOTO omitted, as shown in the following.

```
420 IF NumberOfShares = 0 THEN 710
```

Block 500 computes the value of one block of stock and adds it to the current total value, thus keeping a running total of all stocks entered. The new total value is computed in line 520.

```
500 REM ** Compute value and add to total value **
510 Value# = NumberOfShares# * PricePerShare#
520 TotalValue# = TotalValue# + Value#
```

Block 600 prints the value of the block of stock just entered, and then loops back to the top of the GOTO loop.

```
600 REM ** Print value of shares & go to top of loop **
610 PRINT "The value of these shares is"; TAB(35);
620 PRINT USING "$$############,.##"; Value#
630 PRINT : GOTO 410                                    'Bottom
```

```
The date is 01-01-1990
The time is 19:06:38

Number of shares? 1
Price per share ? 1.375
The value of these shares is              $1.38

Number of shares? 1
Price per share ? 1.375
The value of these shares is              $1.38

Number of shares? 0

Total value of all stocks is              $2.75
Ok
_
```

FIGURE 6-3   Second sample run of Program GWME0602

```
The date is 01-01-1990
The time is 19:10:32

Number of shares? 1
Price per share ? 1.375
The value of these shares is              $1.38

Number of shares? 1
Price per share ? 1.375
The value of these shares is              $1.38

Number of shares? 0

Total value of all stocks is              $2.76
Ok

_
```

FIGURE 6-4   Third sample run of Program GWME0602

If you enter zero as the number of shares, line 420 sends control to line 710, where the program prints the total value of all shares and ends. Here is block 700:

```
700 REM ** Print total of all stocks and end program **
710 PRINT
720 PRINT "Total value of all stocks is"; TAB(35);
730 PRINT USING "$$############,.##"; TotalValue#
799 END
```

It is possible for the total value to differ slightly from the sum of the individual values of blocks of shares, as shown in Figure 6-3. This happens because the PRINT USING statement rounds the printed values, but they are not rounded inside the computer. In Figure 6-3, the computed value of each block of stock is actually 1.375 inside the computer. They are added inside the computer to produce a total: 1.375 + 1.375 = 2.75. When printed, the 1.375 values are rounded to 1.38.

You can partially solve this problem by rewriting block 500 as shown in the following.

```
500 REM ** Compute value and add to total value **
510 Value# = NumberOfShares# * PricePerShare#
520 Value# = INT(100 * Value# + .5) / 100        'Round to cents
530 TotalValue# = TotalValue# + Value#
```

Line 520 rounds the value of *Value#* to two decimal places. After making this change, verify the sample run shown in Figure 6-4. Here, the values seem to add correctly to the total value. Of course, the total value is really high by a penny.

Try both versions of the program with many blocks of stocks, and pick the version you like the best.

THE WHILE...WEND LOOP

You have already used GOTO loops to repeat a group of statements. Now learn about another loop structure, called a WHILE...WEND loop. A WHILE...WEND loop repeats a set of statements *while* a condition is *true*. A WHILE...WEND loop begins with a WHILE statement (lowest line number), ends with a WEND statement (highest line number), and can have any number of statements in between. The WHILE statement must contain an expression that serves as a condition, which can be true or false. If the condition is true, the loop continues; if the condition is false, the loop ends, and the program continues with the line following the WEND statement (if there is a line).

In the following WHILE...WEND loop, the condition in the WHILE statement is the number one (1). This "condition" is always true. Therefore, the loop continues until press CTRL+BREAK.

```
10 WHILE 1
20   PRINT "Press CTRL+BREAK to stop me"
30 WEND
```

Enter and run the program listed above. The screen quickly fills with the message "Press CTRL+BREAK to stop me" as the statement inside the WHILE...WEND loop (line 20) is repeated. Press CTRL+BREAK to stop the program. The bottom part of the screen will look like the following (key line omitted).

```
Press CTRL+BREAK to stop me
Press CTRL+BREAK to stop me
Press CTRL+BREAK to stop me
Press CTRL+BREAK to stop me
Press CTRL+BREAK to stop me

Break in 20
Ok

_
```

Any number other than zero (0) serves as a true condition in the WHILE statement. The most standard number used to mean true is negative one (−1), shown in the following WHILE...WEND loop:

```
10 WHILE -1
20   PRINT "Press CTRL+BREAK to stop me"
30 WEND
```

Now change line 10 so that the program looks like this:

```
10 WHILE 0
20   PRINT "Press CTRL+BREAK to stop me"
30 WEND
```

Here the condition in the WHILE statement is the number zero (0). This condition is always false. The statement inside the loop (line 20) is not executed, not even once. You can verify this by running the program, as shown here:

```
RUN
Ok

_
```

Note: Line 20 is indented. This line is inside the WHILE...WEND loop. That is, line 20 is between the beginning of the loop (line 10) and the end of the loop (line 30). It is always good practice to indent lines in a WHILE...WEND loop, although it is not necessary to do so. When you indent lines, your programs are easier to read and understand; this will become more important later on when your programs become longer and more complex.

Counting Up

The condition in the WHILE statement is usually an expression that can be either true or false. The following program prints the integers from 1 to 10. The condition in the WHILE statement is true while the value of *number* is less than or equal to 10, but false for any value greater than 10.

```
10 CLS

20 number = 1

30 WHILE number <= 10
40   PRINT number,
50   number = number + 1
60 WEND
```

Enter and run the program. The screen should look like this:

```
1          2          3          4          5
6          7          8          9          10
Ok
_
```

Counting Down

You can also use a WHILE...WEND loop to count down. Here is a short "Count Down...Blast Off!" program.

```
10 CLS

20 number = 10

30 WHILE number >= 0
40   PRINT number
50   number = number - 1
60 WEND

70 PRINT "Blastoff!!!"
80 PRINT "Everything is A"
```

```
10
9
8
7
6
5
4
3
2
1
0
Blastoff!!!
Everything is A
Ok

_
```

FIGURE 6-5   Output of Count Down...Blast Off! program

Line 20 sets the value of *number* to 10. The lines inside the WHILE...WEND loop are repeated as long as the value of *number* is greater than or equal to zero (WHILE *number* >= 0). Since line 50 counts down the value of *number*, eventually it reaches zero, and then goes negative. The loop ends without printing the negative value.

Enter and run the program. The output is shown in Figure 6-5.

Two Ways to Count to Ten

Program GWME0603 (Count to Ten Method #1) is a variation of an earlier program. Line 80 has been added to print the value of the variable number after the WHILE...WEND loop is completed.

Enter and run the program. The WHILE...WEND loop (lines 30 through 60) prints the integers from 1 to 10. Upon exit from the loop, line 80 prints the final value of *number,* which was not printed by the WHILE...WEND loop. Note that, inside the loop, the value of *number* is increased by one after the current value is printed. Here is a run of the program.

```
1 REM ** Count to Ten Method #1 **
2 ' GW-BASIC Made Easy, Chapter 6.  File: GWME0603.BAS

10 CLS

20 number = 1

30 WHILE number <= 10
40   PRINT number,
50   number = number + 1
60 WEND

70 PRINT
80 PRINT "On exit from WHILE...WEND, number is"; number
```

PROGRAM GWME0603   Count to Ten Method #1

```
1             2             3             4             5
6             7             8             9             10
On exit from WHILE...WEND, number is 11
Ok

_
```

In programming, there's always another way to do something. Program GWME0604 (Count to Ten Method #2) shows another way to count to ten. Enter and run the program. The numbers printed by the WEND...WHILE loop are exactly the same as those printed by Program GWME0603. Notice, however, that the number printed by line 80 is different.

```
1             2             3             4             5
6             7             8             9             10
On exit from WHILE...WEND, number is 10
Ok

_
```

Compare the two programs. The differences are in line 20, which sets the value of *number* before entering the WHILE...WEND loop, and in lines 30, 40, and 50 of the loop. To help you compare these differences, corresponding lines of both programs are shown here, side by side.

```
From program GWME0603:        From program GWME0604:

20 number = 1                 20 number = 0

30 WHILE number <= 10         30 WHILE number < 10
40   PRINT number,            40   number = number + 1
50   number = number + 1      50   PRINT number,
60 WEND                       60 WEND
```

Remember the two counting methods you have learned here. In many applications, it may be important to control the value of a variable used for counting (like *number*) upon exit from a counting loop.

A Time Delay Loop

Some applications require precise timing of events. For example, suppose you are writing a "flash card" program. You want to put a question on the screen for, say, 10 seconds, then erase it and ask for the answer. Perhaps you also want to limit the time for entering the answer. You can use the TIMER function in a WHILE...WEND loop to construct a time delay, as shown by

---

```
1 REM ** Count to Ten Method #2 **
2 ' GW-BASIC Made Easy, Chapter 6.  File: GWME0604.BAS

10 CLS

20 number = 0

30 WHILE number < 10
40   number = number + 1
50   PRINT number,
60 WEND

70 PRINT
80 PRINT "On exit from WHILE...WEND, number is"; number
```

PROGRAM GWME0604   Count to Ten Method #2

the following short program. This program causes the computer to beep one time per second.

```
10 CLS
20 PRINT "You will hear a beep every second"

30 BEEP                          'Top of GOTO loop

40 start = TIMER
50 WHILE TIMER < start + 1      'One second time delay
60 WEND

70 GOTO 30                       'Bottom of GOTO loop
```

Enter and run the program. At the top of the screen you will see the message, "You will hear a beep every second." Indeed, you do hear the computer beep...beep...beep... as the seconds pass. This happens because lines 40 through 60 cause a one-second time delay.

In line 40, the value of *start* is set equal to the current value of TIMER. TIMER, of course, keeps ticking away, keeping track of the number of seconds since midnight. The value of TIMER is precise to better than a tenth of a second. Therefore, the value of TIMER is increasing. The WHILE...WEND loop goes round and round as long as TIMER is less than the value of start plus one second.

Caution: At midnight, TIMER is reset to zero. If you try this program at less than one second before midnight, it won't work.

You can shorten the time delay loop by putting the entire WHILE...WEND loop on one line, as shown next. Line 50 consists of two statements, separated by a colon (:).

```
10 CLS
20 PRINT "You will hear a beep every second"

30 BEEP                              'Top of GOTO loop

40 start = TIMER
50 WHILE TIMER < start + 1 : WEND    'One second time delay

60 GOTO 30                           'Bottom of GOTO loop
```

Now shorten this program even more by combining lines 40 and 50 into a single line.

```
10 CLS
20 PRINT "You will hear a beep every second"

30 BEEP                                  'Top of loop

40 start=TIMER: WHILE TIMER<start + 1: WEND   '1 second delay

50 GOTO 30                               'Bottom of loop
```

You can easily change the amount of delay. For example, if you want a 10-second delay, change the WHILE statement, as follows:

```
WHILE TIMER < start + 10
```

Program GWME0605, Time Delay Using a WHILE...WEND Loop, illustrates a variable time delay. The amount of delay is assigned to the variable called, appropriately, *delay*. If you want a different time delay, change line 20. You can also change line 20 so that the amount of delay is acquired by an INPUT statement. For example:

```
20 INPUT "Amount of time delay (seconds)"; delay
```

```
1 REM ** Time Delay Using a WHILE...WEND Loop **
2 ' GW-BASIC Made Easy, Chapter 6.  File: GWME0605.BAS

10 CLS

20 delay = 10

30 PRINT "You will hear a beep every"; delay; "seconds"

40 BEEP                                          'Loop top

50 start = TIMER: WHILE TIMER < start + delay: WEND    'Delay

60 GOTO 40                                       'Loop bottom
```

PROGRAM GWME0605   Time Delay Using a WHILE...WEND Loop

```
1 REM ** Countdown...Blastoff! with Spaceship Liftoff **
2 ' GW-BASIC Made Easy, Chapter 6.  File: GWME0606.BAS

100 REM ** Clear screen & turn off key line **
110 CLS : KEY OFF

200 REM ** Countdown **
210 number = 10
220 WHILE number >= 0
230   BEEP: PRINT number
240   number = number - 1
250   start = TIMER: WHILE TIMER < start + 1: WEND   '1 second
260 WEND
270 PRINT "Blastoff!!!"
280 start = TIMER: WHILE TIMER < start + 2: WEND      '2 seconds

300 REM ** Show bird on the launch pad **
310 CLS
320 LOCATE 18, 36: PRINT "   *";
330 LOCATE 19, 36: PRINT "  *U*";
340 LOCATE 20, 36: PRINT "  *S*";
350 LOCATE 21, 36: PRINT "  *A*";
360 LOCATE 22, 36: PRINT " *****";
370 LOCATE 23, 36: PRINT "*******";
390 start = TIMER: WHILE TIMER < start + 2: WEND      '2 seconds

400 REM ** Launch the bird **
410 LOCATE 24, 36: PRINT "  !!!"
420 start = TIMER: WHILE TIMER < start + 1: WEND    '1 second
430 LOCATE 24, 36: PRINT "  !!!"
440 start = TIMER: WHILE TIMER < start + .5: WEND   '.5 second
450 LOCATE 24, 36: PRINT "  !!!"
460 start = TIMER: WHILE TIMER < start + .25: WEND  '.25 second
470 n = 1: WHILE n < 26: PRINT : n = n + 1: WEND    '25 prints

500 REM ** Announce a successful launch **
510 LOCATE 12, 5
520 PRINT "All systems are go.  Everything is AOK."
```

PROGRAM GWME0606   Count Down...Blast Off! with Spaceship Lift Off

Count Down...Blast Off! with Spaceship Lift Off

Program GWME0606 (Count Down...Blast Off! with Spaceship Lift Off) has several time delays. It also introduces the LOCATE statement, which lets you print anywhere on the screen. The program begins this way:

```
1 REM ** Countdown...Blastoff! with Spaceship Liftoff **
2 ' GW-BASIC Made Easy, Chapter 6.  File: GWME0606.BAS

100 REM ** Clear screen & turn off key line **
110 CLS : KEY OFF
```

Block 100 clears the screen and turns off the key line, thus presenting a completely empty screen. Next, block 200 produces a countdown from 10 seconds to zero seconds, with a beep every second:

```
200 REM ** Countdown **
210 number = 10
220 WHILE number >= 0
230   BEEP: PRINT number
240   number = number - 1
250   start = TIMER: WHILE TIMER < start + 1: WEND   '1 second
260 WEND
270 PRINT "Blastoff!!!"
280 start = TIMER: WHILE TIMER < start + 2: WEND     '2 seconds
```

Block 200 features a WHILE...WEND loop that is inside a larger WHILE...WEND loop. The outer loop consists of lines 220 through 260. The inner loop is part of line 250.

The next block, block 300, shows the spaceship (the "bird" in astronaut's jargon) on the launch pad. Note the use of LOCATE in statements in lines 320 through 370.

```
300 REM ** Show bird on the launch pad **
310 CLS
320 LOCATE 18, 36: PRINT "   *";
330 LOCATE 19, 36: PRINT "  *U*";
340 LOCATE 20, 36: PRINT "  *S*";
350 LOCATE 21, 36: PRINT "  *A*";
360 LOCATE 22, 36: PRINT " *****";
370 LOCATE 23, 36: PRINT "*******";
390 start = TIMER: WHILE TIMER < start + 2: WEND    '2 seconds
```

Lines 320 through 370 each contain two statements, separated by a colon (:). The first statement is a LOCATE statement; the second statement is a PRINT statement. The LOCATE statement positions the cursor on the screen; the PRINT statement prints at that place.

The statement

LOCATE 18, 36

positions the cursor at row 18, column 36 on the screen. (This is the "nosecone" of the bird.)

Remember: The screen has 25 rows (or lines), numbered 1 to 25, and 80 columns, numbered 1 to 80.

Soon after the bird appears on the pad, you see the launch begin—at first slowly, then more rapidly as the launch vehicle accelerates. This is done by block 400, shown here:

```
400 REM ** Launch the bird **
410 LOCATE 24, 36: PRINT "  !!!"
420 start = TIMER: WHILE TIMER < start + 1: WEND     '1 second
430 LOCATE 24, 36: PRINT "  !!!"
440 start = TIMER: WHILE TIMER < start + .5: WEND    '.5 second
450 LOCATE 24, 36: PRINT "  !!!"
460 start = TIMER: WHILE TIMER < start + .25: WEND '.25 second
470 n = 1: WHILE n < 26: PRINT : n = n + 1: WEND     '25 prints
```

Note the decreasing time delays in lines 420, 440, and 460. These are intended to give the feeling of acceleration as the bird lifts off the pad. This could be carried on for several more lines to provide a smooth increase in speed, but let's save that concept for later. Instead, line 470 prints 25 empty PRINT statements, thus rapidly boosting the bird beyond the top of the screen. All that is left to do is announce a successful launch, as shown here:

```
500 REM ** Announce a successful launch **
510 LOCATE 12, 5
520 PRINT "All systems are go.  Everything is AOK."
```

THE FOR…NEXT LOOP

Counting loops occur frequently in programs. So GW-BASIC has a loop structure designed to make counting easy. It is called the FOR…NEXT loop.

The following short program contains a short FOR...NEXT loop in lines 20 through 40.

```
10 CLS

20 FOR number = 1 TO 10
30    PRINT number,
40 NEXT number

50 PRINT
60 PRINT "On exit from FOR...NEXT, number is"; number
```

Enter and run the program. The FOR...NEXT loop generates and prints the integers from 1 to 10. Line 50 prints the value of *number* upon exit from the FOR...NEXT loop. Here is a run:

```
 1              2              3              4              5
 6              7              8              9              10
On exit from FOR...NEXT, number is 11
Ok
_
```

The above FOR...NEXT loop tells the computer to count from 1 to 10, as illustrated here:

Count from here   To here

$$20 \quad FOR \quad number \quad = \quad 1 \quad TO \quad 10$$

As the computer counts from 1 to 10, each value is assigned to the variable *number*. This value is printed by the PRINT statement in line 30, which is inside the FOR...NEXT loop.

A FOR...NEXT loop begins with a FOR statement, ends with a NEXT statement, and can have any number of statements in between. In the FOR statement, a numeric variable must follow the keyword FOR.

$$20 \quad FOR \quad number \quad = \quad 1 \quad TO \quad 10$$

Numeric variable

FOR Statement	Sequence of Values
FOR number = 1 TO 10	1, 2, 3, 4, 5, 6, 7, 8, 9, 10
FOR k = 1 TO 6	1, 2, 3, 4, 5, 6
FOR x = 0 TO 7	0, 1, 2, 3, 4, 5, 6, 7
FOR n = -1 TO 1	-1, 0, 1

TABLE 6-2   The FOR Statement Defines a Sequence of Values

The same numeric variable follows the keyword NEXT:

```
40 NEXT number
```
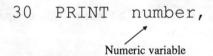
Numeric variable

This numeric variable can be used in statements between the FOR and NEXT statements as in the following.

```
30  PRINT number,
```
Numeric variable

A FOR statement defines a sequence of values for the variable that follows the keyword FOR. Some examples are shown in Table 6-2.

A Colorful FOR...NEXT Loop

The "normal" screen colors are white letters on a black screen. You can use the COLOR statement to tell the computer to print in any of 16 colors, including black (COLOR 0) and the standard white (COLOR 7). Of course, if you print in black on a black screen, you won't see it. Program GWME0607, A Colorful FOR...NEXT Loop, prints one line in each of the 15 colors from 1 to 15, and tells you the color number in which it prints.

Run the program. If you have a color system, you will see 15 vivid colors. A black and white output is shown in Figure 6-6.

```
1 REM ** A Colorful FOR...NEXT Loop **
2 ' GW-BASIC Made Easy, Chapter 6.  File: GWME0607.BAS

10 CLS

20 FOR kolor = 1 TO 15
30   COLOR kolor
40   PRINT "This is color number"; kolor
50 NEXT kolor

60 COLOR 7             'Normal screen color
70 PRINT
80 PRINT "This is the 'normal' screen color"
```

PROGRAM GWME0607   A Colorful FOR...NEXT Loop

```
This is color number 1
This is color number 2
This is color number 3
This is color number 4
This is color number 5
This is color number 6
This is color number 7
This is color number 8
This is color number 9
This is color number 10
This is color number 11
This is color number 12
This is color number 13
This is color number 14
This is color number 15

This is the 'normal' screen color
Ok

_
```

FIGURE 6-6   Output of Program GWME0607

Most of the work is done by the FOR...NEXT loop shown here:

```
20 FOR kolor = 1 TO 15
30    COLOR kolor
40    PRINT "This is color number"; kolor
50 NEXT kolor
```

Since COLOR is a keyword, a sound-alike word (*kolor*) is used as the numeric variable for the sequence of color numbers, 1 through 15. This variable appears in all four lines of the FOR...NEXT loop.

The statement

COLOR kolor

tells the computer to set the color for printed information to the color specified by the value of the numeric variable *kolor*. The information printed by line 40 appears in this color. (A table of colors and color numbers is

Color	Number (Nonblinking)	Number (Blinking)
black	0	16
blue	1	17
green	2	18
cyan	3	19
red	4	20
magenta	5	21
brown	6	22
white	7	23
gray	8	24
light blue	9	25
light green	10	26
light cyan	11	27
light red	12	28
light magenta	13	29
yellow	14	30
bright white	15	31

TABLE 6-3   Colors and Color Numbers

shown in Table 6-3.) On exiting from the FOR...NEXT loop, the program assigns the color to the standard color for text, as follows:

```
60 COLOR 7            'Normal screen color
70 PRINT
80 PRINT "This is the 'normal' screen color"
```

Color numbers from 0 to 15 designate nonblinking colors. Color number 0 is black and was not included in the kolor sequence. (Black characters on a black screen are invisible.) Color numbers from 16 to 31 designate blinking colors. If you would like to see blinking colors, change the FOR statement to the following:

```
20 FOR kolor = 17 TO 31
```

After making this change, run the program again to see the blinking colors. Both blinking and nonblinking color numbers are shown in Table 6-3.

Note: You can use COLOR as a direct statement anytime to return the screen to its standard color. Just type **COLOR 7** and press ENTER.

Counting Down with a FOR...NEXT Loop

The FOR...NEXT loops you have seen so far count up, from a lower to a higher number. You can also count down, from a higher number to a lower number. To do so, include a STEP clause, as shown in the following short program:

```
10 CLS

20 FOR number = 10 TO 0 STEP -1
30   PRINT number,
40 NEXT number
```

Enter and run the program. The output is shown in Figure 6-7.

You can use a FOR...NEXT loop to replace block 200 in Program GWME0606, Count Down...Blast Off! with Spaceship Lift Off. Here is one way to do it:

```
200 REM ** Countdown **
210 FOR number = 10 TO 0 STEP -1
```

10	9	8	7	6
5	4	3	2	1
0				

Ok

_

FIGURE 6-7   Output of Count Down Program

```
220    BEEP: PRINT number
230     start = TIMER: WHILE TIMER < start + 1: WEND    '1 second
240 NEXT number
250 PRINT "Blastoff!!!"
260 start = TIMER: WHILE TIMER < start + 2: WEND     '2 seconds
```

Replace block 200 in the original program with this countdown block. Note that this version, using a FOR...NEXT loop, is two lines shorter than the original block 200. Therefore, delete lines 270 and 280 before running the modified program.

MAKING MUSIC

You can use a BEEP statement to make the computer beep. Every beep sounds the same, and lasts for the same length of time. You can make more interesting sounds by using SOUND statements.

The SOUND statement lets you control the *frequency* (or *pitch*) of the sound, as well as its *duration* (the length of time the sound is heard). For example, the following SOUND statement causes the computer to play the note middle C for 18 *ticks*, or about one second (18.2 ticks equal one second):

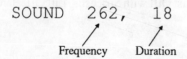

SOUND   262,   18

　　　　　Frequency   Duration

Note	Frequency	Note	Frequency
C	130.81	C	523.25
D	146.83	D	587.33
E	164.81	E	659.26
F	174.61	F	698.46
G	196.00	G	783.99
A	220.00	A	880.00
B	246.94	B	987.77
C	261.63	C	1046.50
D	293.66	D	1174.70
E	329.63	E	1318.50
F	349.23	F	1396.90
G	392.00	G	1568.00
A	440.00	A	1760.00
B	493.88	B	1975.50

TABLE 6-4   Frequencies for Musical Notes

Use this SOUND statement as a direct statement.

Type:

SOUND 262, 18

and press ENTER.

You will hear middle C for about one second.

Now enter and run the following program, which plays two tones alternately until you interrupt with CTRL+BREAK.

```
10 CLS

20 WHILE 1
30    SOUND 262, 9
40    SOUND 440, 9
50 WEND
```

```
1 REM ** SOUND Demonstrator **
2 ' GW-BASIC Made Easy, Chapter 6.  File:: GWME0608.BAS

10 CLS

20 WHILE 1
30   INPUT "Frequency"; frequency
40   IF frequency = 0 THEN END      'Program can end here
50   INPUT "Duration "; duration
60   PRINT
70   SOUND frequency, duration
80 WEND
```

PROGRAM GWME0608   Sound Demonstrator

In the preceding program, the statement

SOUND 262, 9

tells the computer to sound a tone of frequency 262 Hertz (Hz) — or cycles per second — for 9 ticks, or about one-half second. That tone is middle C. The statement

SOUND 440, 9

tells the computer to sound a tone of frequency 440 Hz for a duration of 9 ticks, or about one-half second. That tone is the note A above middle C.

Table 6-4 lists the frequencies of musical notes for four octaves in the scale of C.

Try adding another SOUND statement inside the FOR...NEXT loop. Choose any frequency to play, but it must be a number from 37 to 32,767. You probably will not be able to hear the very high notes. The duration may be a number from 0 to 65,535, and need not be an integer. Try a very short duration such as 0.25 or 0.125.

You can hear any of the notes in Table 6-4, or other frequencies of your choice, by enter and running Program GWME0608, SOUND Demonstrator. To end the program, enter zero (0) as the frequency. An annotated run is shown in Table 6-5.

`Frequency? 262` `Duration ? 18`	Middle C for about one second.
`Frequency? 294` `Duration ? 36`	D for about two seconds.
`Frequency? 330` `Duration ? 54`	E for about three seconds.

`Frequency? 0`
`Ok`
`_`
	Enter zero to quit

TABLE 6-5   Annotated Run of Program GWME0608

Sound Effects

Have you ever wondered how they make all those strange sounds in arcade games? Try the following program:

```
10 CLS

20 FOR frequency = 100 TO 300
30    SOUND frequency, .125
40 NEXT frequency

50 GOTO 20
```

In this program, the FOR...NEXT loop makes a sequence of very short sounds, starting at 100 Hz and ending at 300 Hz. Thus you hear a rapidly rising pitch. Now change line 20 so that the pitch falls from 300 to 100 Hz, as shown here:

```
10 CLS

20 FOR frequency = 300 TO 100 STEP -1
30    SOUND frequency, .125
40 NEXT frequency

50 GOTO 20
```

```
1 REM ** Siren Song **
2 ' GW-BASIC Made Easy, Chapter 6.   File: GWME0609.BAS

10 CLS

20 duration = .125

30 FOR frequency = 523 TO 1046           'Ascending pitch
40   SOUND frequency, duration
50 NEXT frequency

60 FOR frequency = 1046 TO 523 STEP -1   'Descending pitch
70   SOUND frequency, duration
80 NEXT frequency

90 GOTO 20
```

PROGRAM GWME0609   Siren Song

Run this program to hear a familiar arcade game sound. You hear a sound with a rapidly falling pitch. The frequency lowers quickly from 300 Hz to 100 Hz in steps of −1 Hz. The sequence of values is

```
300, 299, 298, ..., 100
```

Now put both ideas together into Program GWME0609 (Siren Song). As the name suggests, it makes a sound like a siren. The sound goes up, down, up, down, and so on, until you press CTRL+BREAK.

You can make the pitch rise and fall at different rates by changing lines 20, 30, and 60. For example, to make the pitch rise and fall more quickly, change lines 30 and 60 as shown here:

```
30 FOR frequency = 523 TO 1046 STEP 2    'Ascending pitch
60 FOR frequency = 1046 TO 523 STEP -2   'Descending pitch
```

Also try using STEP 3 and STEP −3 in lines 30 and 60. Try various combinations of STEP size and duration. With a little experimentation, you can find the ultimate ululation.

```
1 REM ** INKEY$ Demonstrator **
2 ' GW-BASIC Made Easy, Chapter 6.  File: GWME0610.BAS

10 CLS

20 anykey$ = ""                    'anykey$ = empty string

30 WHILE anykey$ = ""              'Loop while no key press
40   PRINT "Press a key to stop me"
50   anykey$ = INKEY$              'anykey$ remembers key
60 WEND

70 PRINT
80 PRINT "You pressed "; anykey$    'Some keys don't print
```

PROGRAM GWME0610   INKEY$ Demonstrator

Use INKEY$ for Fingertip Control

INKEY$ is a string function. It scans the keyboard to see if a key has been pressed. If no key has been pressed, the value of INKEY$ becomes the empty string (" "). If a key has been pressed, the value of INKEY$ becomes a one- or two-character string. You can use this value to "detect" which key or key combination was pressed.

Try the following program. It continues while the value of INKEY$ is the empty string (" "). That is, it continues as long as you *don't* press a key.

```
10 WHILE INKEY$ = ""
20   PRINT "Press a key to stop me"
30 WEND
```

Enter and run the program. The screen quickly fills with the message "Press a key to stop me." If you don't press a key, the condition INKEY$ = " " is true, and the WHILE...WEND loop continues. Press a key, and the condition becomes false; the loop ends.

Use Program GWME0610 (INKEY$ Demonstrator) to learn more about INKEY$. Run this program several times. Each time, use a different key or key combination to stop the program. If you press the number 7 key, you will see this near the bottom of the screen:

```
Press a key to stop me
Press a key to stop me
Press a key to stop me
Press a key to stop me
Press a key to stop me

You pressed 7
Ok

_
```

Instead of pressing any key to interrupt, you can write a WHILE...WEND loop that requires a preselected key as the interrupt key. The following WHILE...WEND loop is ended by pressing the ESC key.

```
10 WHILE INKEY$ <> CHR$(27)
20   PRINT "Press the ESC key to stop me"
30 WEND
```

Run this program. Press several keys other than the ESC key—the program continues to run. You must press the ESC key to stop the program.

The statement

WHILE INKEY$ < > CHR$(27)

tells the computer to continue executing the WHILE...WEND loop while the value of INKEY$ is not equal to the character whose ASCII code is 27. CHR$ is a string function whose value is the character whose ASCII code number is enclosed in parentheses. For example, CHR$(32) is a space; CHR$(65) is the uppercase letter A; CHR$(1) is a tiny face.

More Sound Effects

Use Program GWME0611 (Sound Effects Experimenter) to experiment with FOR...NEXT loops and find effects to your liking.

```
1 REM ** Sound Effects Experimenter **
2 ' GW-BASIC Made Easy, Chapter 6.  File: GWME0611.BAS

100 REM ** Set up **
110 CLS : KEY OFF

200 REM ** Get parameters for experiment **
210 LOCATE 1, 1: INPUT "Beginning frequency"; BeginFreq
220 LOCATE 3, 1: INPUT "Ending frequency   "; FinalFreq
230 LOCATE 5, 1: INPUT "Frequency step size"; StepSize
250 LOCATE 7, 1: INPUT "Duration each sound"; duration

300 REM ** Make the sound **
310 FOR frequency = BeginFreq TO FinalFreq STEP StepSize
320   SOUND frequency, duration
330 NEXT frequency

400 REM ** Go repeat the sound, unless ESC was pressed **
405 ' If ESC was pressed, go get data for a new sound
410 IF INKEY$ <> CHR$(27) THEN 310     'CHR$(27) is ESC key
420 GOTO 110
```

PROGRAM GWME0611   Sound Effects Experimenter

Run the program. To get a rising pitch, enter a smaller number for the beginning frequency, a larger number for the ending frequency, and a positive step size, as shown in this sample run:

```
Beginning frequency? 523

Ending frequency   ? 1046

Frequency step size? 3

Duration each sound? .125
```

The sound generated by block 300 repeats until you press ESC. When you press ESC, the program starts over at line 110. To get a falling pitch, enter a

larger number for the beginning frequency, a smaller number for the ending
frequency, and a negative step size, as shown here:

```
Beginning frequency? 1046

Ending frequency  ? 523

Frequency step size? -3

Duration each sound? .125
```

Examine block 400 of the program. If the ESC key is not pressed, then
INKEY$ < > CHR$(27) is true, and the computer goes to line 310. If the
ESC key is pressed, the condition is false. The computer goes to line 420,
which sends it to line 110 to get data for a new sound. Here is another way
to write block 400:

```
400 REM ** Go repeat the sound, unless ESC was pressed **
405 ' If ESC was pressed, go get data for a new sound
410 IF INKEY$ = CHR$(27) THEN 110     'CHR$(27) is the ESC key
420 GOTO 310
```

You can use the keyword ELSE to combine lines 410 and 420 into a single
IF statement, as shown here:

```
410 IF INKEY$ = CHR$(27) THEN 110 ELSE 310 'CHR$(27) = ESC key
```

This IF…THEN…ELSE statement tells the computer to go to line 110 if the
condition (INKEY$ = CHR$(27)) is true, but (ELSE) go to line 310 if the
condition is false. Here is another way to write line 420:

```
410 IF INKEY$ <> CHR$(27) THEN 310 ELSE 110   'CHR$(27) = ESC
key
```

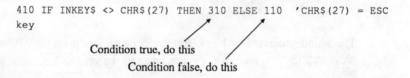

Condition true, do this
Condition false, do this

You can end the program by using CTRL+BREAK when the computer asks for the beginning frequency. Or, you could add a line between lines 210 and 220 to let you end the program by entering an invalid frequency as the beginning frequency. Since the smallest valid frequency is 37, use 0 as the signal to end the program. For example, add the following line.

```
215 IF BeginFreq = 0 THEN END
```

Make this change and run the modified program. End the program as indicated here:

```
Beginning frequency? 0
Ok
_
```

Now write another program to experiment with sound effects. Your program should make a sound that goes from a low frequency to a high frequency, then back down to the low frequency, then repeat the sequence if ESC has not been pressed. Begin by acquiring data as shown here:

```
Low frequency           ? 523

High frequency          ? 1046

Frequency step size     ? 3

Duration of each sound  ? .125
```

For variables, consider using *LoFreq, HiFreq, StepSize,* and *duration.* After entering the values of the variables, you should hear a rising pitch from 523 Hz to 1046 Hz in steps of 3 Hz, then a falling pitch from 1046 Hz to 523 Hz in steps of −3, and so on until you press ESC.

A MULTIPLE-CHOICE STATEMENT: ON...GOTO

At the beginning of this chapter, you saw Program GWME0601, Negative, Zero, or Positive #1. This program uses three IF statements to determine whether a number is negative, zero, or positive, and prints an appropriate

```
1 REM ** Negative, Zero, or Positive #2 **
2 ' GW-BASIC Made Easy, Chapter 6.  File: GWME0612.BAS

100 REM ** Assign messages to string variables **
110 n$ = "negative"
120 z$ = "zero"
130 p$ = "positive"

200 REM ** Tell what to do **
210 CLS : KEY OFF
220 PRINT "Enter a number and I will tell you whether"
230 PRINT "your number is negative, zero, or positive."

300 REM ** Ask for a number **
310 PRINT                                'Top of loop
320 INPUT "Number, please"; number

400 REM ** Tell about the number **
410 OneTwoThree = SGN(number) + 2
420 ON OneTwoThree GOTO 430, 440, 450
430 PRINT n$: GOTO 310                   'After executing one of
440 PRINT z$: GOTO 310                   'these lines, go to the
450 PRINT p$: GOTO 310                   'top of the loop
```

PROGRAM GWME0612   Negative, Zero, or Positive #2

message. Now Program GWME0612 (Negative, Zero, or Positive #2) uses an ON...GOTO statement to make a three-way decision.

Compare this new program with program GWME0601. Note that block 1 is slightly different; blocks 100, 200, and 300 are the same; block 400 is different. There is no block 500; its function is now included in block 400. A sample run is shown in Figure 6-8.

Block 400 is shown below. Lines 410 and 420 together decide whether to go to line 430, line 440, or line 450. The selected line prints a message, and then sends control to the top of the loop at line 310.

```
400 REM ** Tell about the number **
410 OneTwoThree = SGN(number) + 2
420 ON OneTwoThree GOTO 430, 440, 450
430 PRINT n$: GOTO 310                   'After executing one of
440 PRINT z$: GOTO 310                   'these lines, go to the
450 PRINT p$: GOTO 310                   'top of the loop
```

```
Enter a number and I will tell you whether
your number is negative, zero, or positive.

Number, please? 0
zero

Number, please? -1
negative

Number, please? 1
positive

Number, please? _
```

FIGURE 6-8   Sample output of Program GWME0612

In line 410, the statement

OneTwoThree = SGN(*number*) + 2

assigns to the variable *OneTwoThree* a value that depends on whether the value of *number* is negative, zero, or positive. SGN is a numeric function that can have three possible values, −1, 0, or 1, as follows:

If *number* is negative, then SGN(*number*) is −1.

If *number* is zero, then SGN(*number*) is 0.

If *number* is positive, then SGN(*number*) is 1.

Therefore, the value of SGN(*number*) + 2 is 1, 2, or 3, as follows:

If *number* is negative, then SGN(*number*) + 2 is 1.

If *number* is zero, then SGN(*number*) + 2 is 2.

If *number* is positive, then SGN(*number*) + 2 is 3.

The value of SGN(*number*) + 2 is assigned to the numeric variable *OneTwoThree*, whose name is chosen to indicate its possible values.
The statement

ON OneTwoThree GOTO 430, 440, 450

tells the computer to go to one of the three lines (430, 440, or 450), as determined by the value of *OneTwoThree*.

If *OneTwoThree* is 1, go to line 430.

If *OneTwoThree* is 2, go to line 440.

If *OneTwoThree* is 3, go to line 450.

Suppose the value of *number* is 3.14. Then SGN(*number*) + 2 is 3, and line 420 sends the computer to line 450. Line 450 prints the value of *p$*, which is "positive," then sends control to line 310.

Now try to trace the path through the program for a negative value of *number*, and for *number* equal to zero.

```
Response (1, 2, 3, 4, or 0 to quit)?   1

Response (1, 2, 3, 4, or 0 to quit)?   3

Response (1, 2, 3, 4, or 0 to quit)?   1

Response (1, 2, 3, 4, or 0 to quit)?   2

Response (1, 2, 3, 4, or 0 to quit)?   2.72
Oops!  Invalid response.  Try again.

Response (1, 2, 3, 4, or 0 to quit)?   5
Oops!  Invalid response.  Try again.

Response (1, 2, 3, 4, or 0 to quit)?   0

Total 'Yes' responses:          2
Total 'No' responses:           1
Total 'Sometimes' responses:    1
Total 'None of above' responses: 0

Press any key to continue
```

FIGURE 6-9   Output of Program GWME0613

```
1 REM ** The People's Poll #1 **
2 ' GW-BASIC Made Easy, Chapter 6.  File: GWME0613.BAS

100 REM ** Set up **
110 CLS : KEY OFF

200 REM ** Set tallies for the 4 possible responses to zero **
210 TallyOne = 0
220 TallyTwo = 0
230 TallyThree = 0
240 TallyFour = 0

300 REM ** Tell what to do **
310 PRINT "Does your computer understand you?"
320 PRINT
330 PRINT "1 = Yes, 2 = No, 3 = Sometimes, 4 = None above"
340 PRINT
350 PRINT "To quit, enter zero (0) as your response."

400 REM ** Get response **
410 PRINT
420 INPUT "Response (1, 2, 3, 4, or 0 to quit)"; response
430 IF response = 0 THEN 710

500 REM ** Tally the response **
510 IF response = 1 THEN TallyOne = TallyOne + 1: GOTO 410
520 IF response = 2 THEN TallyTwo = TallyTwo + 1: GOTO 410
530 IF response = 3 THEN TallyThree = TallyThree + 1: GOTO 410
540 IF response = 4 THEN TallyFour = TallyFour + 1: GOTO 410

600 REM ** You get here only if response not 1, 2, 3, or 4 **
610 PRINT "Oops!  Invalid response.  Try again.": GOTO 410

700 REM ** Print the final tallies **
710 PRINT
720 PRINT "Total 'Yes' responses:          "; TallyOne
730 PRINT "Total 'No' responses:           "; TallyTwo
740 PRINT "Total 'Sometimes' responses:    "; TallyThree
750 PRINT "Total 'None of above' responses:"; TallyFour
```

PROGRAM GWME0613   The People's Poll #1

THE PEOPLE'S POLL

Here's the questionnaire for a recent survey by the People's Poll.

```
        Does your computer understand you?
        Circle one answer.
        1. Yes
        2. No
        3. Sometimes
        4. None of the above
```

You can use Program GWME0613 (The People's Poll #1) to tally the responses. A test run is shown below. No actual responses are entered. This test run merely tests the entry of zero to end the program.

```
Does your computer understand you?

1 = Yes, 2 = No, 3 = Sometimes, 4 = None of above

To quit, enter zero (0) as your response.

Response (1, 2, 3, 4, or 0 to quit)? 0

Total 'Yes' responses:             0
Total 'No' responses:              0
Total 'Sometimes' responses:       0
Total 'None of above' responses:   0
```

The results of another run are shown in Figure 6-9 on page 184. Four valid and two invalid responses were entered.

Program GWME0614, The People's Poll #2, uses an ON...GOTO statement to replace the IF statements of Program GWME0613. A different method is used to reject an invalid response.

The ON...GOTO statement in line 510 works properly only if the value of *response* is an integer, either 1, 2, 3, or 4. Therefore, lines 440 and 450 are added to reject an invalid response. Line 440 rejects any response that is not an integer. The value of FIX(*response*) is the integer part of *response*.

```
1 REM ** The People's Poll #2 **
2 ' GW-BASIC Made Easy, Chapter 6.  File: GWME0614.BAS

100 REM ** Set up **
110 CLS : KEY OFF
115 ' Assign error message to string variable Oops$
120 Oops$ = "Oops!  Invalid response.  Try again."

200 REM ** Set tallies for the 4 possible responses to zero **
210 TallyOne = 0
220 TallyTwo = 0
230 TallyThree = 0
240 TallyFour = 0

300 REM ** Tell what to do **
310 PRINT "Does your computer understand you?"
320 PRINT
330 PRINT "1 = Yes, 2 = No, 3 = Sometimes, 4 = None above"
340 PRINT
350 PRINT "To quit, enter zero (0) as your response."

400 REM ** Get response **
410 PRINT
420 INPUT "Response (1, 2, 3, 4, or 0 to quit)"; response
430 IF response = 0 THEN 710
435 ' If response is not an integer, reject it
440 IF response < > FIX(response) THEN PRINT Oops$: GOTO 410
445 ' If response is less than 1 or more than 4, reject it
450 IF response < 1 OR response > 4 THEN PRINT Oops$: GOTO 410

500 REM ** Tally the response **
510 ON response GOTO 520, 530, 540, 550
520 TallyOne = TallyOne + 1: GOTO 410
530 TallyTwo = TallyTwo + 1: GOTO 410
540 TallyThree = TallyThree + 1: GOTO 410
550 TallyFour = TallyFour + 1: GOTO 410

700 REM ** Print the final tallies **
710 PRINT
720 PRINT "Total 'Yes' responses:          "; TallyOne
730 PRINT "Total 'No' responses:           "; TallyTwo
740 PRINT "Total 'Sometimes' responses:    "; TallyThree
750 PRINT "Total 'None of above' responses:"; TallyFour
```

PROGRAM GWME0614   The People's Poll #2

For example, FIX(3.14) is 3, FIX(7.99) is 7, FIX (1), and FIX(4) is 4.

- If *response* is not an integer, then response < > FIX(response) is true. The computer prints an error message (value of Oops$), and goes to line 410.

- If *response* is an integer, then *response* < > FIX(*response*) is false. The computer does not print an error message, nor does it go to line 410. Instead, it continues in line number order.

- If the value of *response* is an integer, the computer goes to line 450, which checks to see if the integer is in the range 1 to 4. If the response is less than 1 or more than 4, it is rejected. The computer prints the error message (value of Oops$), and goes back to line 410.

A value of *response* that successfully runs the gauntlet of lines 430 through 450 must be an integer from 1 to 4, and hence is a valid response. It is tallied in block 500.

REVIEW

This chapter introduced powerful control structures you can use to make your programs more automatic and more useful. You can use the IF statement to provide decision-making capabilities within a program while it is running. The ON...GOTO statement provides the means for multiple-choice decision making.

A WHILE...WEND loop repeats a set of instructions while a certain condition is true. It is very useful for constructing time delays. You can control loops that continue until you press any key, or a designated key.

The FOR...NEXT loop is especially designed for counting, or for executing a set of instructions for a sequence of values of a variable.

When you first enter GW-BASIC, the screen colors are white letters on a black background. You can use the COLOR statement to select any of 16 colors as the color for printing text.

You can use the SOUND statement to direct the computer to make a sound of a specified frequency (pitch) and duration (length of time). Use SOUND with FOR...NEXT loops to produce interesting sound effects.

CHR$ and INKEY$ are string functions. The value of CHR$ is a single character that corresponds to a number called an ASCII code. The INKEY$ function scans the keyboard and returns information about a key press, if any.

FIX and SGN are numeric functions. The FIX of a number is the integer part of the number. The SGN of a number is −1 if the number is negative, 0 if the number is zero, or 1 if the number is positive.

The first six chapters of this book have introduced the keywords shown below. Now is a good time to review these keywords, before you move on to the next chapter.

BEEP	CHR$	CLS	COLOR	DATE$	ELSE	END	FILES
FIX	FOR	GOTO	IF	INKEY$	INPUT	INPUT$	KEY
LIST	LLIST	LOAD	LOCATE	LPRINT	NEW	NEXT	OFF
ON	PRINT	REM	RUN	SAVE	SGN	SOUND	STEP
SYSTEM	TAB	THEN	TIME$	TO	USING	WEND	WHILE

7

FUNCTION JUNCTION

This chapter will teach you about some of the functions that are built into GW-BASIC. You will learn how to name and define your own user-defined functions. In particular, you will learn

- more about numeric functions used in previous chapters: FIX, TIMER

- more about some new numeric functions: ASC, INSTR, INT, LEN, RND

- more about string functions used in previous chapters: CHR$, DATE$, INKEY$, INPUT$, TIME$

- some new string functions: MID$, SPACE$

- how to name, define, and use your own user-defined functions

- several new statements: DATA, DEF FN, RANDOMIZE, READ, RESTORE

- how to print ASCII codes and characters

You will also discover how to use GW-BASIC in applications such as making random music, random colors, and random words; creating fantasy role-playing game characters; and finding dictionary words that have certain values (Wordsworth).

```
1 REM ** Demonstrate TIMER and INKEY$ Functions **
2 ' GW-BASIC Made Easy, Chapter 7.  File:GWME0701.BAS

10 CLS : KEY OFF

20 TIME$ = "23:59"     'One minute before midnight

30 WHILE INKEY$ = ""   'Loop while no key press
40   PRINT TIMER,
50 WEND
```

PROGRAM GWME0701   Demonstrate TIMER and INKEY$ Functions

BUILT-IN FUNCTIONS

GW-BASIC has a rich repertoire of built-in *functions*. A function is a keyword that, when used, returns a *value;* this value is the result computed by the function. GW-BASIC has *numeric functions* and *string functions*. The value of a numeric function is a number; the value of a string function is a string. In other words, a numeric function returns a numeric value, and a string function returns a string value. String function names, like string variable names, end with a dollar sign ($).

Some functions require *arguments;* others do not. An argument is a number or string on which the function operates to produce the value of the function.

Functions Without Arguments

The simplest type of function is one that does not require an argument. You have already used this type of function. For example, TIMER is a numeric function that does not require an argument. INKEY$ is a string function that does not require an argument.

TIMER NUMERIC FUNCTION   TIMER is a numeric function. This function returns the number of elapsed seconds since midnight, according to the computer's clock. At midnight, the value of TIMER is zero (0). At high noon, the value of TIMER is 43200. At one minute before midnight, the value of TIMER is 86340.

INKEY\$ STRING FUNCTION   INKEY\$ is a string function. INKEY\$ scans the keyboard for a key press. If a key or combination of keys has been pressed, the value of INKEY\$ is a 1- or 2-byte string that corresponds to the key or key combination. If no key has been pressed, the value of INKEY\$ is the null, or empty, string (""). INKEY\$ does not wait for a key press, as does the INPUT\$ function, described later in this section.

Program GWME0701 (Demonstrate TIMER and INKEY\$ Functions) uses both the TIMER numeric function and the INKEY\$ string function. This program sets the timer to one minute before midnight, then starts printing the value of TIMER. You can press any key (the space bar is a good choice) to stop the program. Use it to check your reaction time—how soon

```
86398.72      86398.72      86398.72      86398.72      86398.78
86398.78      86398.78      86398.78      86398.84      86398.84
86398.84      86398.89      86398.89      86398.89      86398.89
86398.94      86398.94      86398.94      86398.94      86399
86399         86399         86399         86399.06      86399.06
86399.06      86399.11      86399.11      86399.11      86399.11
86399.18      86399.18      86399.18      86399.18      86399.22
86399.22      86399.22      86399.28      86399.28      86399.28
86399.28      86399.33      86399.33      86399.33      86399.33
86399.39      86399.39      86399.39      86399.39      86399.44
86399.44      86399.44      86399.5       86399.5       86399.5
86399.5       86399.55      86399.55      86399.55      86399.55
86399.61      86399.61      86399.61      86399.61      86399.66
86399.66      86399.66      86399.72      86399.72      86399.72
86399.72      86399.77      86399.77      86399.77      86399.77
86399.83      86399.83      86399.83      86399.83      86399.88
86399.88      86399.88      86399.94      86399.94      86399.94
86399.94      0             0             0             0
.05           .05           .05           9.999999E-02
9.999999E-02                9.999999E-02                .16
.16           .16           .21           .21           .21
.21           .27           .27           .27
Ok

_
```

FIGURE 7-1   Values of TIMER before and after midnight

after midnight (TIMER = 0) can you stop the program? Figure 7-1 shows a sample run, where the program was stopped a fraction of a second after midnight, and the value of TIMER was reset to zero.

DATE$ AND TIME$ STRING FUNCTIONS   You can use DATE$ and TIME$ either as string functions, or as statements. Here are examples of both these keywords, used

- as statements: DATE$ = "1-1-90"
                    TIME$ = "7:30"

- as functions: PRINT DATE$
                    PRINT TIME$

When you use DATE$ and TIME$ as statements, you can assign values to them. These values are automatically updated as time passes. When you use DATE$ and TIME$ as functions, they return string values: either the current date, or the current time.

RND NUMERIC FUNCTION   RND is a numeric function. Its value is a *random number* between 0 and 1. The numbers generated by the RND function are not truly random, as are numbers obtained, for example, by rolling dice. Rather, RND generates *pseudorandom numbers*. To see the difference between truly random and pseudorandom numbers, run the following short program at least twice:

```
10 CLS
20 PRINT RND, RND, RND, RND, RND
```

Two runs are shown here. Note that both runs produced the same set of numbers. First run:

```
.1213501      .651861      .8688611      .7297625      .798853
```

Second run:

```
.1213501      .651861      .8688611      .7927625      .798853
```

RND generates the same sequence of numbers each time you run the program. These numbers are pseudorandom; if RND generated truly random numbers, the numbers produced would be unpredictable.

You can avoid this replication of so-called random numbers by using the RANDOMIZE statement with the TIMER function, as shown in the next program. RANDOMIZE TIMER is needed only once in each program. It starts the computer's random number generator at a place determined by the value of TIMER, which, as you know, is constantly changing. Thus you will see a different sequence of numbers when you run the program at different times.

```
10 RANDOMIZE TIMER
20 CLS
30 PRINT RND, RND, RND, RND, RND
```

Two runs of this program are shown next. Notice that these two runs produced different sets of random numbers. First run:

```
.6274775      .4732618      .3228105      .8009587      .7236309
```

Next run:

```
.3198908      .9272718      .3670305      .4495488      .4341107
```

The RND function generates a random number between 0 and 1, but never 0 or 1. That is, RND is a random number greater than 0 and less than 1. Thus:

$$0 < RND < 1$$

To obtain random numbers in another range of values, just multiply RND by an appropriate number. For example, 10 * RND is a random number between 0 and 10, but never 0 or 10. That is, 10 * RND is a random number greater than 0 and less than 10. So:

$$0 < 10 * RND < 10$$

Now use RND to make some strange "music." Program GWME0702 (Random Music) makes random sounds at frequencies between 37 Hz and 2037 Hz. Enter and run the program. You will hear short sounds at random frequencies between 37 Hz and 2037 Hz. Press the ESC key to stop the program.

```
1 REM ** Random Music **
2 ' GW-BASIC Made Easy, Chapter 7.  File: GWME0702.BAS

10 CLS : KEY OFF

20 RANDOMIZE TIMER                    'Scramble the RND function

30 PRINT "Random music.  Press ESC to stop."

40 WHILE INKEY$ <> CHR$(27)
50    frequency = 2000 * RND + 37     'Random between 37 & 2037
60    duration = 1                    '1 tick, about 1/18 second
70    SOUND frequency, duration
80 WEND
```

PROGRAM GWME0702   Random Music

Line 40 generates a random number between 37 and 2037, and assigns it as the value of *frequency*. The number 37 is the lowest valid frequency for the SOUND statement; 2037 was chosen arbitrarily. The result of 2000 * RND is a random number beween 0 and 2000. Add 37 to get a random number between 37 and 2037. Thus:

$$0 < 2000 * RND < 2000$$
$$37 < 2000 * RND + 37 < 2037$$

To hear even stranger-sounding music, change line 50 to the following:

```
50    duration = .125
```

Or make *duration* random. Try any of the following versions of line 50:

```
50    duration = RND              'Between 0 and 1 tick
```

```
50    duration = 2 * RND          'Between 0 and 2 ticks
```

```
50    duration = 2 * RND + 1      'Between 1 and 3 ticks
```

Try your own variations of lines 40 and 50.

THINGS TO REMEMBER GW-BASIC has two kinds of functions: numeric functions and string functions. The name of a string function ends in a dollar sign ($). The value of a numeric function is a number; the value of a string function is a string. Some names of functions are listed here:

Numeric functions: RND   TIMER

String functions: DATE$ INKEY$ TIME$

Functions That Require Arguments

Many GW-BASIC functions operate on arguments to compute the value of the function. The value of the function can depend on the value of the argument. The argument is enclosed in parentheses, and follows the name of the function. This section describes several useful functions that require arguments.

INT NUMERIC FUNCTION The INT function is a numeric function of a numeric argument. It returns the integer value of the argument enclosed in parentheses. More precisely, INT(*number*) is the greatest integer that is less than or equal to the value of number.

For example, INT(6 * RND) returns the integer value of the argument (6 * RND). Thus, if the value of RND is .3151505, then the value of 6 * RND is 1.890903, and the value of INT(6 * RND) is 1. Some examples of the INT function are shown here:

Non-negative numbers: INT(0) = 0   INT(3.142) = 3

Negative numbers: INT(−1) = −1   INT(−3.14) = − 4

In this book, most applications using INT involve numbers that are not negative. If you want to compute the integer part of a number, regardless of its sign, you can use another function, called FIX.

FIX NUMERIC FUNCTION FIX is a numeric function of a numeric argument. It returns the integer part of its numeric argument. More precisely, if a number is positive, FIX (*number*) returns the first integer that is less than or equal to the number; if a number is negative, FIX (*number*) returns the

```
1 REM ** Demonstrate FIX and INT Numeric Functions **
2 ' GW-BASIC Made Easy, Chapter 7.  File: GWME0703.BAS

10 CLS : KEY OFF

20 WHILE 1
30   INPUT "Argument, please"; argument
40   PRINT "FIX(argument) is "; FIX(argument)
50   PRINT "INT(argument) is "; INT(argument)
60   PRINT
70 WEND
```

PROGRAM GWME0703   Demonstrate FIX and INT Numeric Functions

first integer that is greater than or equal to the number. For example:

$$FIX(0) = 0 \quad FIX(3.14) = 3 \quad FIX(-3.14) = -3$$

Use Program GWME0703 (Demonstrate FIX and INT Numeric Functions) to learn more about FIX and INT. A sample run follows. You can use the program to verify that, for integer arguments, FIX and INT return the same results. The results are also the same for positive noninteger arguments. For negative noninteger arguments, however, the values differ by one.

```
Argument, please? 1
FIX(argument) is  1
INT(argument) is  1

Argument, please? -1
FIX(argument) is -1
INT(argument) is -1

Argument, please? .123
FIX(argument) is  0
INT(argument) is  0

Argument, please? -.123
FIX(argument) is  0
INT(argument) is -1

Argument, please? _
```

```
1 REM ** Print a Name in Random Colors **
2 ' GW-BASIC Made Easy, Chapter 7.  File: GWME0704.BAS

10 CLS : KEY OFF: WIDTH 40      'Use big letters

20 RANDOMIZE TIMER              'Scramble the RND function

30 WHILE INKEY$ <> CHR$(27)     'Loop while ESC not pressed
40    COLOR INT(15 * RND) + 1   'Random integer, 1 to 15
50    PRINT "Mariko  ";
60 WEND

70 COLOR 7: WIDTH 80            'Return screen to normal
```

PROGRAM GWME0704   Print a Name in Random Colors

The INT function is used in Program GWME0704 (Print a Name in Random Colors). This program prints Mariko's name repeatedly in big letters, using randomly selected colors.

When you run this program, you will see Mariko's name printed five times on every line. Each name is printed in one of 15 colors, randomly selected. Each name is printed in double-width letters, because WIDTH 40 is used in line 10. Line 20 *randomizes* the RND function, so that a different sequence of colors is selected when the program is run at different times.

The statement:

```
COLOR INT(15 * RND) + 1
```

selects one of 15 random colors. The result of $15 * RND$ is a random number between 0 and 15, but never 0 or 15. Therefore, $INT(15 * RND)$ is a random integer from 0 to 14, inclusive; and $INT(15 * RND) + 1$ is a random integer from 1 to 15. Table 7-1 shows how the integer color numbers are computed by line 40.

Since the value of RND is always a positive number, you can use either INT or FIX to obtain the integer part of $15 * RND$. Therefore, you can also write line 40 as shown here:

```
40    COLOR FIX(15 * RND) + 1   'Random integer, 1 to 15
```

Value of RND	15 * RND	INT(15 * RND)	INT(15 * RND) + 1
.7055475	10.58321	10	11
.301948	4.52922	4	5
1.401764E-02	.2102646	0	1
.81449	12.21735	12	13
4.535276E-02	.6802914	0	1
.2637929	3.956894	3	4
.9495566	14.24335	14	15

TABLE 7-1   How Color Numbers Are Computed by Program GWME0704

To see Mariko's name (or any name) in both blinking and nonblinking colors, including black (color number 0 or 16), change the COLOR statement to generate a random integer in the range 0 to 31, as follows:

```
40   COLOR INT(32 * RND)        'Random integer, 0 to 31
```

To see the name only in blinking colors, excluding black, change the COLOR statement so that it generates a random integer from 17 to 31, like this:

```
40   COLOR INT(15 * RND) + 17  'Random integer, 17 to 31
```

You can modify the program so that the color number is an integer from 1 to 31, except 16 (black). Also try changing the program so that names are alternately blinking and nonblinking. Invent your own combinations!

INPUT$ STRING FUNCTION   INPUT$(*n*) is a string function with a numeric argument. INPUT$(*n*) tells the computer to wait for a string of *n* characters to be entered from the keyboard. For example, INPUT$(1) tells the computer to wait for one character to be entered from the keyboard. You can press a letter key, a number key, or a punctuation key. SHIFT plus another key counts as one key. Use Program GWME0705 (Demonstrate INPUT$ String Function) to learn more about INPUT$. Press the ESC key to end the program.

```
1 REM ** Demonstrate INPUT$ String Function **
2 ' GW-BASIC Made Easy, Chapter  7.  File: GWME0705.BAS

10 CLS : KEY OFF

20 WHILE anykey$ <> CHR$(27)      'Loop while ESC not pressed
30   PRINT "Press a key"
40   anykey$ = INPUT$(1)
50   PRINT "You pressed "; anykey$
60   PRINT
70 WEND

80 PRINT "You pressed the ESC key, which ends the program."
```

PROGRAM GWME0705   Demonstrate INPUT$ String Function

Figure 7-2 shows an annotated run of Program GWME0705. Note that some keys, such as ENTER or the cursor control keys (arrow keys), are nonprinting keys. Try pressing these keys when you run the program, and see what happens.

ASCII CODES AND CHARACTERS   You can print many different characters on the screen. Some of these characters are visible on the keyboard, and you can use the keyboard to enter them. For example:

Uppercase letters   A B C D

Lowercase letters   a b c d

Digits   1 2 3 4

Punctuation   . , ; :

Special characters   @ # $ *

There are also characters you don't see on the keyboard. Some are shown after Figure 7-2.

```
Press a key
You pressed a

Press a key
You pressed A          SHIFT+A counts as one key

Press a key
You pressed 8

Press a key
You pressed *          SHIFT+8 counts as one key

Press a key
You pressed            Some keys are nonprinting

Press a key
You pressed ←          Press ESC to end the program

You pressed the ESC key, which ends the program.
Ok
_
```

FIGURE 7-2   An annotated run of Program GWME0705

Card characters: ♥ ♦ ♣ ♠

Greek letters: α β ε π Σ

Math symbols: √ ± ≤ ≡ ≈

Graphics characters: ▓ ╡ ╬ ╩ ╪

Every computer character has an *ASCII code*. An ASCII code is an integer in the range 0 to 255. ASCII stands for American Standard Code for Information Interchange. Here are some examples:

The ASCII code for A is 65

The ASCII code for B is 66

The ASCII code for a is 97

The ASCII code for b is 98

```
1 REM ** Demonstrate CHR$ String Function **
2 ' GW-BASIC Made Easy, Chapter 7.  File: GWME0706.BAS

10 CLS : KEY OFF: WIDTH 40                'Do it in big letters

20 WHILE 1
30   INPUT "ASCII code (0 to 255)"; ascii
40   IF ascii < 0 OR ascii > 255 THEN 80      'Go to end if invalid
50   PRINT "Thanks for calling my number! "; CHR$(ascii)
60   PRINT
70 WEND

80 WIDTH 80: END                          'Return to normal width
```

PROGRAM GWME0706   Demonstrate CHR$ String Function

The ASCII code for ∗ is 42

The ASCII code for ♥ is 3

You have probably guessed that the ASCII code for *C* is 67. For the uppercase letters *A* to *Z*, the ASCII codes are 65 to 90. For the lowercase letters *a* to *z*, the ASCII codes are 97 to 122. Digits also have ASCII codes; the codes for the digits 0 to 9 are 48 to 57. ASCII codes from 128 to 255 are codes for special characters, such as foreign alphabets, graphics characters, and math symbols.

CHR$ STRING FUNCTION   You can use the CHR$ string function to print ASCII characters on the screen. CHR$ is a string function of a numeric argument. The argument must be an ASCII code, an integer in the range 0 to 255. The value of CHR$ is the one-character string that corresponds to the ASCII code.

Use Program GWME0706 (Demonstrate CHR$ String Function) to see ASCII characters of your choice. To see a character printed on the screen, type its ASCII code (0 to 255) and press ENTER. To quit, enter an invalid code (a number less than zero or greater than 255); for example, −1 or 256. Figure 7-3 shows some typical results.

You can use Program GWME0707 (ASCII Codes and Characters) to print lots of ASCII codes and characters on the screen. You enter the first

```
ASCII code (0 to 255)? 1
Thanks for calling my number! ☻      CHR$(1) is a tiny face

ASCII code (0 to 255)? 3
Thanks for calling my number! ♥      CHR$(3) is a heart

ASCII code (0 to 255)? 65
Thanks for calling my number! A      CHR$(65) is uppercase A

ASCII code (0 to 255)? 42
Thanks for calling my number! *      CHR$(42) is an asterisk

ASCII code (0 to 255)? 219
Thanks for calling my number! ■      CHR$(219) is a graphics
                                                 character

ASCII code (0 to 255)? 227
Thanks for calling my number! π      CHR$(227) is a Greek letter

ASCII code (0 to 255)? _
```

FIGURE 7-3   An annotated run of Program GWME0706

```
1 REM ** ASCII Codes and Characters **
2 ' GW-BASIC Made Easy, Chapter 7.  File: GWME0707.BAS

10 CLS : KEY OFF

20 INPUT "First ASCII code"; FirstCode
30 INPUT "Last ASCII code "; LastCode

40 CLS

60 FOR ascii = FirstCode TO LastCode
70   PRINT ascii; CHR$(ascii); SPACE$(2);
80   IF (ascii - FirstCode + 1) MOD 10 = 0 THEN PRINT : PRINT
90 NEXT ascii
```

PROGRAM GWME0707   ASCII Codes and Characters

128 ç	129 ü	130 é	131 â	132 ä	133 à	134 å	135 ç	136 ê	137 ë
138 è	139 ï	140 î	141 ì	142 Ä	143 Å	144 É	145 æ	146 Æ	147 ô
148 ö	149 ò	150 û	151 ù	152 ÿ	153 Ö	154 Ü	155 ¢	156 £	157 ¥
158 ₧	159 ƒ	160 á	161 í	162 ó	163 ú	164 ñ	165 Ñ	166 ª	167 º
168 ¿	169 ⌐	170 ¬	171 ½	172 ¼	173 ¡	174 «	175 »	176 ░	177 ▒
178 ▓	179 │	180 ┤	181 ╡	182 ╢	183 ╖	184 ╕	185 ╣	186 ║	187 ╗
188 ╝	189 ╜	190 ╛	191 ┐	192 └	193 ┴	194 ┬	195 ├	196 ─	197 ┼
198 ╞	199 ╟	200 ╚	201 ╔	202 ╩	203 ╦	204 ╠	205 ═	206 ╬	207 ╧
208 ╨	209 ╤	210 ╥	211 ╙	212 ╘	213 ╒	214 ╓	215 ╫	216 ╪	217 ┘
218 ┌	219 █	220 ▄	221 ▌	222 ▐	223 ▀	224 α	225 ß	226 Γ	227 π

Press any key to continue

FIGURE 7-4   ASCII codes and characters printed by Program GWME0707

ASCII code and last ASCII code. The program then prints all ASCII codes and corresponding characters from your first code to your last code. Code and character pairs are printed ten to a line, and the lines are double spaced. Figure 7-4 is a sample run showing 100 codes and characters, from ASCII code 128 to ASCII code 227.

The statement:

```
PRINT ascii; CHR$(ascii); SPACE$(2);
```

prints the ASCII code (value of *ascii*), the ASCII character (value of CHR$(*ascii*)), and two spaces. The value of *ascii* is printed with a leading and a trailing space. SPACE$ is a string function of a numeric argument. SPACE$(2) creates two spaces, which are then printed.

The statement:

```
IF (ascii - FirstCode + 1) MOD 10 = 0 THEN PRINT: PRINT
```

causes two empty PRINT statements to occur after every ten pairs of codes and characters. This causes the lines to be double-spaced so you can read them more easily. MOD is an arithmetic operator. The value of *a* MOD *b* is the remainder after dividing *a* by *b*. For example, 37 MOD 10 is 7, and 40 MOD 10 is 0. You can experiment with MOD by running the following small program:

```
10 CLS
20 INPUT "a = "; a
30 INPUT "b = "; b
40 PRINT "a MOD b is"; a MOD b
50 PRINT : GOTO 20
```

ASC NUMERIC FUNCTION   The ASC function is just the opposite of the CHR$ function. ASC is a numeric function of a string argument. ASC returns the ASCII code of a character. For example, ASC("A") is 65, and ASC("*") is 42. If the argument consists of two or more characters, the ASC function returns the ASCII code of the first character. For example, ASC("ABC") is 65, and ASC("abc") is 97. Note that ASC(" ") is illegal and causes an error.

You can use Program GWME0708 (Demonstrate ASC Numeric Function) to print on the screen the ASCII codes of keyboard characters. Enter the letter **Q** to quit.

Figure 7-5 is an annotated run of Program GWME0708. Entering the first four characters (a, A, 2, and @) is easy. However, it is a little more difficult to enter the tiny face, the solid graphics character, and the Greek letter pi (π).

```
1 REM ** Demonstrate ASC Numeric Function **
2 ' GW-BASIC Made Easy, Chapter 7.  File: GWME0708.BAS

10 CLS : KEY OFF: WIDTH 40          'Do it in big letters

20 WHILE 1
30   INPUT "Keyboard character (press Q to quit)"; anykey$
35   ' Quit if value of anykey$ is Q or q
40   IF anykey$ = "Q" OR anykey$ = "q" THEN 80
50   PRINT "Here's my number:"; ASC(anykey$)
60   PRINT
70 WEND

80 WIDTH 80: END                    'End in normal width
```

PROGRAM GWME0708   Demonstrate ASC Numeric Function

```
Keyboard character (press Q to quit)? a
Here's my number: 97

Keyboard character (press Q to quit)? A        SHIFT A
Here's my number: 65

Keyboard character (press Q to quit)? 2
Here's my number: 50

Keyboard character (press Q to quit)? @        SHIFT 2
Here's my number: 64

Keyboard character (press Q to quit)? ☺        ALT 1
Here's my number: 1

Keyboard character (press Q to quit)? ■        ALT 219
Here's my number: 219

Keyboard character (press Q to quit)? π        ALT 227
Here's my number: 227

Keyboard character (press Q to quit)? _
```

FIGURE 7-5   An annotated run of Program GWME0708

To type these characters, you use the ALT key with the numeric key pad on the right side of the keyboard.

- To enter the tiny face (☺), hold down the ALT key, press the 1 key on the numeric key pad, release the 1 key, and then release the ALT key. You should see the tiny face on the screen. If not, use BACKSPACE to erase any incorrect character and try again. When you see the tiny face, press ENTER.

- To enter the solid graphics character (■), hold down the ALT key, type 219 on the numeric key pad, and then release the ALT key. Press ENTER.

- To enter the Greek letter pi (π), hold down the ALT key, type 227 on the numeric key pad, and then release the ALT key. Press ENTER.

In general, to type any ASCII character on the screen, hold down the ALT key, type the character's ASCII code on the numeric key pad, and then release the ALT key. Try this with ASCII codes in the range 128 to 255, or codes in the range 0 to 31. Some of the codes in the range 0 to 31 may cause an "Illegal function call" error message.

MID\$ STRING FUNCTION   MID\$ is a string function of three arguments—one string argument and two numeric arguments. When a function has more than one argument, the arguments are separated by commas. You use MID\$ to select a portion of a string (a *substring*) from within a string. For example, consider the word "proverb." It contains these shorter words:

pro   prove   prover   rove   rover   over   verb

You can use MID\$ to select these words within "proverb," or to select the entire word itself. Enter and run the following program:

```
10 CLS

20 word$ = "proverb"

30 PRINT MID$(word$, 1, 3)
40 PRINT MID$(word$, 1, 5)
50 PRINT MID$(word$, 1, 6)
60 PRINT MID$(word$, 1, 7)
70 PRINT MID$(word$, 2, 4)
80 PRINT MID$(word$, 2, 5)
90 PRINT MID$(word$, 3, 4)
100 PRINT MID$(word$, 4, 4)
```

A run of this program produces the following "words within words":

```
pro
prove
prover
proverb
rove
rover
over
verb
```

The value of the MID\$ function is a substring of the function's first argument. The second argument is numeric; it specifies the position within the string (the first argument) at which to begin. The third argument is also numeric; it specifies how many characters to select, counting from where the substring begins (the second argument). The following illustrates this:

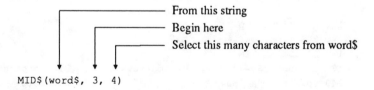

Since the value of *word$* is "proverb," the value of MID$(*word$, 3, 4*) is obtained by starting at the third character of "proverb" (o), and selecting four characters. Thus, MID$(*word$, 3, 4*) is "over."

WORD MAKER PROGRAM Suppose you want to name a new product, or even a new company. Perhaps you are writing a novel and want to create unusual names for characters or places. Why not use your computer to help you invent names? How would you write a program to print names that are pronounceable, but seem exotic, or even fantastic?

Program GWME0709 (Word Maker) generates five-letter words in this format: consonant, vowel, consonant, vowel, consonant (cvcvc). In this program, the letter *y* can appear as either a consonant or vowel. Here are some possible random words:

kobar   nigom   conan   zyydx   dufet

Program GWME0709 uses MID$ to select random consonants from the string *consonant$*, and random vowels from the string *vowel$*. The string variables *consonant$* and *vowel$* are assigned values during the setup block of the program, in lines 130 and 140. These variables are used later in the program to select random consonants or vowels.

The statement:

```
word$ = ""
```

tells the computer to assign the null string as the value of *word$*. Each time the GOTO loop is repeated, *word$* is reset to the null string, thus erasing any previous value it may contain.

The statement:

```
word$ = word$ + MID$(consonant$, INT(21 * RND) + 1, 1)
```

```
1 REM ** Word Maker **
2 ' GW-BASIC Made Easy, Chapter 7.  File: GWME0709.BAS

100 REM ** Set up **
110 CLS : KEY OFF
120 RANDOMIZE TIMER
130 consonant$ = "bcdfghjklmnpqrstvwxyz"    '21 consonants
140 vowel$ = "aeiouy"                       '6 vowels

200 REM ** GOTO loop to make words. Press ESC to quit **

210 BEEP: PRINT "Press a key for a word or ESC to quit"
220 anykey$ = INPUT$(1): IF anykey$ = CHR$(27) THEN END

225 ' To make a word, start with the empty string ("") and
226 ' add a consonant, vowel, consonant, vowel, consonant.
230 word$ = ""
240 word$ = word$ + MID$(consonant$, INT(21 * RND) + 1, 1)
250 word$ = word$ + MID$(vowel$, INT(6 * RND) + 1, 1)
260 word$ = word$ + MID$(consonant$, INT(21 * RND) + 1, 1)
270 word$ = word$ + MID$(vowel$, INT(6 * RND) + 1, 1)
280 word$ = word$ + MID$(consonant$, INT(21 * RND) + 1, 1)

300 REM ** Print the word and go to top of loop **
310 PRINT "Your random 'cvcvc' word is "; word$
320 PRINT
330 GOTO 210
```

PROGRAM GWME0709   Word Maker

in lines 240, 260, and 280 tells the computer to select one random letter from the string variable *consonant$,* and concatenate (join) it to the value of *word$.* When used with strings, the plus sign (+) means concatenate, or put together with, or attach to. The following MID$ function illustrates how this single letter is selected from *consonant$.*

The statement:

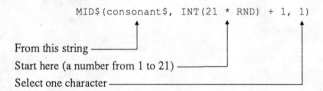

```
        MID$(consonant$, INT(21 * RND) + 1, 1)
```

From this string
Start here (a number from 1 to 21)
Select one character

The statement:

```
word$ = word$ +  MID$(vowel$, INT(6 * RND) + 1, 1)
```

in lines 250 and 270 tells the computer to select a random character from *vowel$* and concatenate it to the value of *word$*.

A sample run is shown below. When you run this program, the words generated will probably be different, since the letters in the words are randomly selected. Press ESC to end the program.

```
Press a key for a word or ESC to quit
Your random 'cvcvc' word is surig

Press a key for a word or ESC to quit
Your random 'cvcvc' word is kadeb

Press a key for a word or ESC to quit
Your random 'cvcvc' word is gusep

Press a key for a word or ESC to quit
Your random 'cvcvc' word is meyyy

Press a key for a word or ESC to quit
Your random 'cvcvc' word is bogox

Press a key for a word or ESC to quit
```

You can easily modify the program to generate words with a different consonant-vowel structure.

Remember: Modifying a program is a good way for you to make sure you understand how the program works. The best way to learn how to program is to write programs and make them work. In programming, you can usually do things in more than one way. Try writing your own versions of programs you see in this book.

MORE THINGS TO REMEMBER GW-BASIC has many built-in functions. A function returns one value, and may or may not require an argument. A function can be a numeric function or a string function. A numeric function returns a numeric value and string function returns a string value. Arguments can be numeric or string. Some examples of functions are shown in the following.

Numeric functions: TIMER
                      RND
                      FIX(numeric argument)
                      INT(numeric argument)
                      ASC(string argument)

String functions: DATE$
                      TIME$
                      INKEY$
                      INPUT$(numeric argument)
                      CHR$(numeric argument)
                      SPACE$(numeric argument)
                      MID$(string and numeric arguments)

USER-DEFINED FUNCTIONS

You can design your own functions and use them in the same ways you use built-in functions. Functions that you write are called *user-defined functions*. In this section, you will learn how to name, define, and use your own user-defined functions. You can define functions that do or do not require arguments. Function definitions must appear in the program before the user-defined function is activated, as described in the next section.

User-Defined Functions Without Arguments

To define and name your own function, use the DEF FN statement. Here is a user-defined function to "roll" one six-sided die. This function returns a random integer in the range 1 to 6.

```
DEF FNrollD6 = INT(6 * RND) + 1
```

The name of this function is FNrollD6. The name of a user-defined function always begins with FN. The part of the name following FN must conform to the rules for naming GW-BASIC variables. The function definition is to the right of the equal sign (=). This function FNrollD6 has no argument. In Program GWME0710 (Roll Two Six-Sided Dice (Roll 2D6)) FNrollD6 is used twice (in line 340).

```
1 REM ** Roll Two Six-Sided Dice (Roll 2D6) **
2 ' GW-BASIC Made Easy, Chapter 7.  File: GWME0710.BAS

100 REM ** Define FNrollD6, a function to 'roll' one die **
105 ' Returns an integer, 1 to 6
110 DEF FNrollD6 = INT(6 * RND) + 1

200 REM ** Set up **
210 CLS : KEY OFF
220 RANDOMIZE TIMER

300 REM ** WHILE...WEND loop to roll dice.  Hit ESC to quit **
310 WHILE 1
320   BEEP: PRINT "Press a key to roll, or ESC to quit"
330   anykey$ = INPUT$(1): IF anykey$ = CHR$(27) THEN END
340   PRINT "The roll is"; FNrollD6 + FNrollD6
350   PRINT
360 WEND
```

PROGRAM GWME0710   Roll Two Six-Sided Dice (Roll 2D6)

A sample run is shown next. In it, a key other than ESC was pressed three times to get three simulated rolls of two dice. The computer is waiting for another key press. Press ESC to end the program.

```
Press a key to roll, or ESC to quit
The roll is 6

Press a key to roll, or ESC to quit
The roll is 11

Press a key to roll, or ESC to quit
The roll is 9

Press a key to roll, or ESC to quit
```

You could also define a single function to simulate the rolling of two dice, then use it once in your program. Modify program GWME0710 to define and use the function FNroll2D6, shown next:

```
DEF FNroll2D6 = INT(6 * RND) + INT(6 * RND) + 2
```

```
1 REM ** Roll a Character Using the Trust-to-Luck Method **
2 ' GW-BASIC Made Easy, Chapter 7.  File: GWME0711.BAS

100 REM ** Define a function to 'roll' 3D6 **
110 DEF FNroll3D6 = INT(6 * RND) + INT(6 * RND) + INT(6 * RND) + 3

200 REM ** Set up **
210 CLS : KEY OFF
220 RANDOMIZE TIMER

300 REM ** Get ready to roll **
310 CLS
320 PRINT "Here is a character:"
330 PRINT

400 REM ** Roll 3D6 for each of 7 characteristics **
410 PRINT "Strength", FNroll3D6
420 PRINT "Constitution", FNroll3D6
430 PRINT "Size", FNroll3D6
440 PRINT "Intelligence", FNroll3D6
450 PRINT "Intuition", FNroll3D6
460 PRINT "Dexterity", FNroll3D6
470 PRINT "Appearance", FNroll3D6

500 REM ** Tell how to do again **
510 PRINT
520 PRINT "Press a key for another, or ESC to quit"
530 anykey$ = INPUT$(1)
540 IF anykey$ <> CHR$(27) THEN 310 ELSE END
```

PROGRAM GWME0711   Roll a Character Using Trust-to-Luck Method

ROLL A FANTASY GAME CHARACTER   Roll?! Relax...no mugging intended. Millions of game players know that rolling a character means creating a character in a fantasy role-playing game such as *Dungeons & Dragons, Land of Ninja,* or *RuneQuest.* A character is defined by a set of basic characteristics. For example, in one game system, a character has these seven characteristics: Strength, Constitution, Size, Intelligence, Intuition, Dexterity, and Appearance.

One way to create a character is by the Trust-to-Luck Method used in Program GWME0711. You roll 3D6 (three dice with six sides each) for each characteristic. Therefore, each characteristic is a value from 3 to 18, the higher the better.

The function FNroll3D6 defined in line 110 simulates rolling three six-sided dice. It is used seven times in block 400 to obtain values for the seven characteristics. A "roll" is a number from 3 to 18, with 10 or 11 being an average roll. Values below 10 are considered to be below average; values above 11 are considered to be above average.

```
Sample run #1:

Here is a character:

Strength       17        Barostan is big, strong, rugged, and
Constitution   16        agile, but not too bright. He is
Size           14        good to have on your side in a
Intelligence    8        fight, if someone will tell him who
Intuition       7        to attack.  He acts first, then
Dexterity      16        thinks later, if at all.
Appearance     10


Sample run #2:

Here is a character:

Strength       13        Joleen is a clown, mime, acrobat,
Constitution   11        dancer, or whatever else might
Size            7        entertain an audience. She wants to
Intelligence   13        travel with a troupe of wandering
Intuition      12        entertainers, and perform at fairs
Dexterity      18        and festivals.  She will charm you.
Appearance     13


Sample run #3:

Here is a character:

Strength       10        Rokana is quiet and introspective.
Constitution    9        She wants to study and become a
Size           11        sage, healer, and magic user.  Her
Intelligence   17        high intelligence and intuition make
Intuition      18        her well suited to achieve her goal.
Dexterity      10
Appearance     11
```

FIGURE 7-6   Fantasy role-playing game characters, Program GWME0711

```
1 REM ** Roll a Character Using the Trust-to-Luck Method #2 **
2 ' GW-BASIC Made Easy, Chapter 7.  File: GWME0712.BAS

100 REM ** Define a function to 'roll' 3D6 **
110 DEF FNroll3D6 = INT(6 * RND) + INT(6 * RND) + INT(6 * RND) + 3

200 REM ** Set up **
210 CLS : KEY OFF
220 RANDOMIZE TIMER

300 REM ** Get ready to roll **
310 CLS
320 PRINT "Here is a character:"
330 PRINT
340 Total = 0                    'Set total points to zero

400 REM ** Roll a character and compute total points **
410 Strength = FNroll3D6: Total = Total + Strength
420 Constitution = FNroll3D6: Total = Total + Constitution
430 Size = FNroll3D6: Total = Total + Size
440 Intelligence = FNroll3D6: Total = Total + Intelligence
450 Intuition = FNroll3D6: Total = Total + Intuition
460 Dexterity = FNroll3D6: Total = Total + Dexterity
470 Appearance = FNroll3D6: Total = Total + Appearance

500 REM ** Print characteristics and total points **
510 PRINT "Strength"; TAB(15);
515 PRINT USING "##"; Strength
520 PRINT "Constitution"; TAB(15);
525 PRINT USING "##"; Constitution
530 PRINT "Size"; TAB(15);
535 PRINT USING "##"; Size
540 PRINT "Intelligence"; TAB(15);
545 PRINT USING "##"; Intelligence
550 PRINT "Intuition"; TAB(15);
555 PRINT USING "##"; Intuition
560 PRINT "Dexterity"; TAB(15);
565 PRINT USING "##"; Dexterity
570 PRINT "Appearance"; TAB(15);
575 PRINT USING "##"; Appearance
580 PRINT
590 PRINT "Total points"; TAB(15);
595 PRINT USING "##"; Total
```

```
600 REM ** Tell how to do again **
610 PRINT
620 PRINT "Press a key for another, or ESC to quit"
630 anykey$ = INPUT$(1)
640 IF anykey$ <> CHR$(27) THEN 310 ELSE END
```

PROGRAM GWME0712   Roll a Character Using Trust-to-Luck Method #2
                        (*continued*)

Figure 7-6 shows annotated results from three sample runs of Program GWME0711. These were selected from several runs made in search of interesting characters to play in a role-playing game. Each character is named and given a rudimentary "personality." The personality will be refined during game play.

You can easily modify Program GWME0711 so that it rolls an *Advanced Dungeons and Dragons* (AD&D) character. An AD&D character has these six characteristics: Strength, Intelligence, Wisdom, Dexterity, Constitution, and Charisma. Then modify Program GWME0711 (or your own program) so that all information is printed to the printer, or to both the screen and the printer. While you are doing this, you can make improvements. For example, you can use TAB functions and PRINT USING statements to make the printed results neater, with the digits of the results right-aligned instead of left-aligned.

The next program is a modification of Program GWME0711. Program GWME0712 (Roll a Character Using Trust-to-Luck Method #2) prints the individual characteristics, and also the total number of points. That is, the program adds the values of the individual characteristics and prints this total. This is handy when the game master allows only characters whose total points lie in some range, say 81 to 84.

Figure 7-7 shows annotated results from two sample runs of Program GWME0712. Many runs were made to get these two, with the "right stuff" in a range of total points from 81 to 84, inclusive.

READ, DATA, AND RESTORE   Program GWME0713 (Roll a Character Using Trust-to-Luck Method #3) introduces three new statements: the READ statement, the DATA statement, and the RESTORE statement. Look for these statements in lines 410, 420, 430, and 450 of the program.

```
Sample run #1:

Here is a character:

Strength      12        Dernfara is a thief—quick, strong,
Constitution  13        and deft; smart enough to plan a
Size           8        decent caper.  He will enter your
Intelligence  13        house and steal you blind, even
Intuition     11        while you entertain the sheriff in
Dexterity     18        your dining room. Dernfara abhors
Appearance     9        violence—he would rather run than
                        fight. Few can catch him.


Total points  84

Sample run #2:

Here is a character:

Strength      13        Your turn.  Give this character a
Constitution  14        name and a personality.
Size           7
Intelligence  17
Intuition     12
Dexterity     13
Appearance     7

Total points  83
```

FIGURE 7-7   Fantasy role-playing game characters, Program GWME0712

The names of characteristics are stored as strings in DATA statements (lines 420 and 430). These names are read as values of the string variable *character$* by a READ statement (line 450). Since the READ statement is within a FOR…NEXT loop, all seven values are read, one at a time, and used in the PRINT statement in line 470. The RESTORE statement in line 410 tells the computer to start at the first value in the first DATA statement.

Lines 450, 460, and 470 are executed seven times. Each time, one characteristic name is read from a DATA statement (line 450). Line 460 rolls a numerical value and adds it to the total points. Line 470 prints the name of the characteristic and its numerical value. Note that line 470 has two statements, separated by a colon (:).

```
1 REM ** Roll a Character Using the Trust-to-Luck Method #3 **
2 ' GW-BASIC Made Easy, Chapter 7.  File: GWME0713.BAS

100 REM ** Define a function to 'roll' 3D6 **
110 DEF FNroll3D6 = INT(6 * RND) + INT(6 * RND) + INT(6 * RND) + 3

200 REM ** Set up **
210 CLS : KEY OFF
220 RANDOMIZE TIMER

300 REM ** Get ready to roll **
310 CLS
320 PRINT "Here is a character:"
330 PRINT
340 Total = 0                  'Set total points to zero

400 REM ** Roll character, print individual characteristics **
410 RESTORE
420 DATA Strength, Constitution, Size, Intelligence
430 DATA Intuition, Dexterity, Appearance
440 FOR k = 1 TO 7
450    READ character$
460    value = FNroll3D6: Total = Total + value
470    PRINT character$; TAB(15); : PRINT USING "##"; value
480 NEXT k

500 REM ** Print total points **
510 PRINT
520 PRINT "Total points"; TAB(15); : PRINT USING "##"; Total

600 REM ** Tell how to do again **
610 PRINT
620 PRINT "Press a key for another, or ESC to quit"
630 anykey$ = INPUT$(1)
640 IF anykey$ <> CHR$(27) THEN 310 ELSE END
```

PROGRAM GWME0713   Roll a Character Using Trust-to-Luck Method #3

User-Defined Functions with Arguments

The user-defined functions you have seen so far do not require arguments.
You can also define functions, however, that do have arguments. As with

```
1 REM **  Coin Flipper **
2 ' GW-BASIC Made Easy, Chapter 7.  File: GWME0714.BAS

100 REM ** Define FNran, a random integer function **
105 ' Returns random integer in the range, 1 to n
110 DEF FNran (n) = INT(n * RND) + 1

200 REM ** Set up **
210 CLS : KEY OFF
220 RANDOMIZE TIMER

300 REM ** WHILE...WEND loop to flip coins, ESC to quit **
310 WHILE 1
320    BEEP: PRINT "Press a key to flip a coin (ESC to quit)"
330    anykey$ = INPUT$(1)
340    IF anykey$ = CHR$(27) THEN END
350    OneOrTwo = FNran(2)
360    IF OneOrTwo = 1 THEN PRINT "HEADS"
370    IF OneOrTwo = 2 THEN PRINT "TAILS"
380    PRINT
390 WEND
```

PROGRAM GWME0714   Coin Flipper

built-in functions, the argument is enclosed in parentheses following the name of the function. The function FNran, shown next, is a function of one numeric argument, *n*. The value of FNran (*n*), is a random integer in the range 1 to *n*.

```
DEF FNran (n) = INT(n * RND) + 1
```

The argument *n* is a *local variable;* that is, the value of *n* has no meaning outside of the function definition. You may use *n* as a *variable* name elsewhere in the program, without affecting its use as an argument name. The argument *n* is chosen arbitrarily. You can replace *n* on both sides of the equal sign with any name. For example:

```
DEF FNran (range) = INT(range * RND) + 1
```

FNRAN NUMERIC FUNCTION   Program GWME0714, Coin Flipper, uses the function FNran to generate a random number, 1 or 2, which is then used to print HEADS or TAILS. Here is a short sample run of Program GWME0714:

```
Press a key to flip a coin (ESC to quit)
TAILS

Press a key to flip a coin (ESC to quit)
TAILS

Press a key to flip a coin (ESC to quit)
HEADS

Press a key to flip a coin (ESC to quit)
```

Remember: There are many ways to write a program. For example, since the value of *OneorTwo* must be 1 or 2, you can combine lines 360 and 370 into a single line, as in:

```
360    IF OneOrTwo = 1 THEN PRINT "HEADS" ELSE PRINT "TAILS"
```

If you do this, remember to delete line 370.

Here is a very different way to write block 300:

```
300 REM ** GOTO loop to flip coins, ESC to quit **
310 BEEP: PRINT "Press a key to flip a coin (ESC to quit)"
320 anykey$ = INPUT$(1)
330 IF anykey$ = CHR$(27) THEN END
340 ZeroOrOne = FNran(2) - 1
360 PRINT MID$("HEADSTAILS", 5 * ZeroOrOne + 1, 5)
370 PRINT : GOTO 310
```

In line 340, the value of FNran(2) is 1 or 2. Therefore, the value of *ZeroOrOne* is, well, 0 or 1. If *ZeroOrOne* is 0, then the MID$ function in line 360 selects HEADS; if *ZeroOrOne* is 1, then the MID$ function selects TAILS.

Now write another version of the coin flip program. Use the FNcoin function, defined below. The value of FNcoin is HEADS or TAILS, selected at random.

```
DEF FNcoin = MID$("HEADSTAILS", 5 * INT(2 * RND) + 1, 5)
```

```
1 REM ** Word Maker with Random Character Function **
2 ' GW-BASIC Made Easy, Chapter 7.  File: GWME0715.BAS

100 REM ** Define FNranchr$, a random character function **
105 ' Returns one random character from a string argument
110 DEF FNranchr$ (s$) = MID$(s$, INT(LEN(s$) * RND) + 1, 1)

200 REM ** Set up **
210 CLS : KEY OFF
220 RANDOMIZE TIMER
230 consonant$ = "bcdfghjklmnpqrstvwxyz"    '21 consonants
240 vowel$ = "aeiouy"                       '6 vowels, including y

300 REM ** GOTO loop to make words. Press ESC to quit **
310 BEEP: PRINT "Press a key to make a word (ESC to quit)"
320 anykey$ = INPUT$(1): IF anykey$ = CHR$(27) THEN END

325 ' To make a word, start with the empty string ("") and
326 ' add a consonant, vowel, consonant, vowel, consonant.
330 word$ = ""
340 word$ = word$ + FNranchr$(consonant$)   'Add a consonant
350 word$ = word$ + FNranchr$(vowel$)       'Add a vowel
360 word$ = word$ + FNranchr$(consonant$)   'Add a consonant
370 word$ = word$ + FNranchr$(vowel$)       'Add a vowel
380 word$ = word$ + FNranchr$(consonant$)   'Add a consonant

400 REM ** Print the word and go to top of loop **
410 PRINT "Your random 'cvcvc' word is "; word$
420 PRINT : GOTO 310
```

PROGRAM GWME0715   Word Maker with Random Character Function

FNRANCHAR$ STRING FUNCTION In programming, you can always do things in more than one way. Program GWME0715 (Word Maker with Random Character Function) uses a defined function, called FNranchr$, to generate random words. The value of FNranchar$ is a single character selected at random from a string argument. A run of this program will produce results similar to results produced by Program GWME0709.

This new Word Maker program introduces a new function called LEN. LEN is a numeric function of a string argument. Its value is the number of characters, including spaces (if any), in the string argument. For example, LEN("abc") is 3, and LEN("a b c") is 5.

WORDSWORTH

This has been a long chapter, containing many new ideas and many programs. Now take some time for a recreational activity called Wordsworth.

Assign a letter score to each letter of the alphabet, A through Z, as follows:

A=1	B=2	C=3	D=4	E=5	F=6	G=7
H=8	I=9	J=10	K=11	L=12	M=13	N=14
O=15	P=16	Q=17	R=18	S=19	T=20	U=21
V=22	W=23	X=24	Y=25	Z=26		

For any dictionary word you choose, compute two numbers, called *Wordsworth +* and *Wordsworth *,* as follows:

- *Wordsworth +* is the numerical value of a word, obtained by adding the letter scores of all the letters in the word. For example:

  hobbit is worth 8 + 15 + 2 + 2 + 9 + 20 = 56 points
  dragon is worth 4 + 18 + 1 + 7 + 15 + 14 = 59 points

- *Wordsworth *** is the numerical value of a word, obtained by multiplying the letter scores of all the letters in the word. For example:

  hobbit is worth 8 * 15 * 2 * 2 * 9 * 20 = 86,400 points
  dragon is worth 4 * 18 * 1 * 7 * 15 * 14 = 105,840 points

In other words, *Wordsworth +* is the sum of the letter scores of all the letters in a word; *Wordsworth *** is the product of the letter scores of all the letters in a word. You can use Program GWME0716 (Wordsworth) to compute and print *Wordsworth +* and *Wordsworth *** for a word entered from the keyboard.

The program uses the LEN and MID$ functions introduced previously, and a new function called INSTR. INSTR is a numeric function of two string arguments. INSTR returns a numeric value that depends on whether the second argument is a substring of the first argument. If not, the value of INSTR is zero (0); if there is a match, the value of INSTR is the position in the first argument where the second argument matches. Table 7-2 shows values of INSTR for several pairs of arguments.

```
1 REM ** Wordsworth **
2 ' GW-BASIC Made Easy, Chapter 7.  File: GWME0716.BAS

100 REM ** Set up **
110 CLS : KEY OFF
120 Upper$ = "ABCDEFGHIJKLMNOPQRSTUVWXYZ"
130 Lower$ = "abcdefghijklmnopqrstuvwxyz"

200 REM ** Get a word **
210 INPUT "Your word"; word$
220 PRINT

300 REM ** Set Words Worth sum and product to zero **
305 ' Product# is a double precision variable
310 Sum = 0
320 Product# = 1

400 REM ** Compute Wordsworth + and Wordsworth * **
410 FOR k = 1 TO LEN(word$)
420    Letter$ = MID$(word$, k, 1)
430    Lscore = INSTR(Upper$, Letter$) + INSTR(Lower$, Letter$)
440    IF Lscore = 0 THEN 470
450    Sum = Sum + Lscore
460    Product# = Product# * Lscore
470 NEXT k

500 REM ** Print Wordsworth + and *, go to top of loop **
510 PRINT "Wordsworth + is"; Sum
520 PRINT "Wordsworth * is"; Product#
530 PRINT : GOTO 210
```

PROGRAM GWME0716   Wordsworth

Figure 7-8 is an annotated run of Program GWME0716. Note that words can be entered in all uppercase letters, all lowercase letters, or a mixture of both. The program ignores characters that are not letters.

Now use the program to help you answer one or more of the following questions. An answer must be a real dictionary word.

1. What three-letter word has the smallest *Wordsworth +?* Or *Wordsworth *?*

INSTR("abc", "a") is 1	Match at position 1 of first argument
INSTR("abc", "b") is 2	Match at position 2 of first argument
INSTR("abc", "c") is 3	Match at position 3 of first argument
INSTR("abc", "*") is 0	No match; no asterisk in first argument
INSTR("abc", "A") is 0	No match; no A in first argument
INSTR("abc", "ab") is 1	Match at position 1 of first argument
INSTR("abc", "bc") is 2	Match at position 2 of first argument
INSTR("abc", "abc") is 1	Match at first position of first argument
INSTR("ab", "abc") is 0	No match; abc is not in first argument

TABLE 7-2   Values of INSTR for Several Pairs of Arguments

2. What three-letter word has the largest *Wordsworth +?* Or *Wordsworth *?*

3. What four-letter word has the smallest *Wordsworth +?* Or *Wordsworth *?*

4. What four-letter word has the largest *Wordsworth +? Wordsworth *?*

5. What is the first word (alphabetically) to have a *Wordsworth +* of exactly 100? *Wordsworth ** of exactly 100?

6. What is the last word (alphabetically) to have a *Wordsworth +* of exactly 100? *Wordsworth ** of exactly 100?

7. In the entire dictionary, what word has the largest *Wordsworth +?* Or *Wordsworth *?*

8. What is the longest word (most letters) that has a *Wordsworth +* equal to the number of weeks in a year?

9. What word has a *Wordsworth ** closest to one million? The value can be less than one million or greater than one million.

```
Your word? dragon                Word entered in all lowercase
                                 letters
Wordsworth + is 59
Wordsworth * is 105840

Your word? DRAGON                Word entered in all uppercase
                                 letters
Wordsworth + is 59
Wordsworth * is 105840

Your word? Dragon                Word entered in mixture of upper-
                                 and lowercase
Wordsworth + is 59
Wordsworth * is 105840

Your word? R2D2                  Characters other than letters are
                                 ignored
Wordsworth + is 22
Wordsworth * is 72
```

FIGURE 7-8   An annotated run of Program GWME0716

Most of the work and play in answering these questions is people play: browsing through a dictionary, thinking about what to do, creating strategies—most enjoyable! People do this well. Some of the work, such as looking up letter scores and calculating, is grungy stuff. Let the computer do those things.

REVIEW

GW-BASIC has many built-in functions. When you use a function, it returns one value. A function can be a numeric function, returning a numeric value, or a string function, returning a string value. The name of a string function ends with a dollar sign ($).

Some functions require arguments; others do not. An argument is a number or a string upon which the function operates to produce the value of the function. Here are some examples of functions, as used in this chapter:

- Numeric functions with no argument: RND, TIMER

- String functions with no argument: DATE$, INKEY$, TIME$

- Numeric functions of a numeric argument: FIX(3.14), INT(3.14)

- Numeric functions of a string argument: ASC(anykey$), LEN(word$)

- Numeric functions of two string arguments: INSTR(Lower$,Letter$)

- String functions of a numeric argument: CHR$(ascii), SPACE$(2)

- String function, mixed arguments: MID$(word$, k, 1)

You can use the DEF FN statement to define your own functions. Some user-defined functions are:

- Numeric function with no argument: FNroll3D6

- Numeric function of a numeric argument: FNran(2)

- String function of a string argument: FNranchr$(vowel$)

User-defined functions are tools that you can design to make your programming tasks easier and more enjoyable.

8

SUBROUTINES

In this chapter, you will learn how to use *subroutines*. A subroutine is a self-contained set of statements that can be used from anywhere in a program. The subroutine performs its task, then returns control to the part of the program that called the subroutine. You can divide a large program into smaller, more manageable blocks, write a subroutine for each block, and then write a main program to call upon the subroutines as needed. In particular, you will learn how to

- Use the GOSUB and ON...GOSUB statements to call, or use, subroutines.

- Use the RETURN statement in a subroutine to return control to the proper place in the program.

- Use the MERGE statement to merge a subroutine from a disk with a program in memory.

- Use the RENUM statement to renumber lines in a program.

- Trace a program. A trace shows the order in which lines are executed when you run a program.

- Use the F7 function key to turn on the trace mode. You can also use the TRON statement for this purpose.

- Use the F8 function key to turn off the trace mode. You can also use the TROFF statement to do this.

- Use the VIEW PRINT statement to divide the screen into two areas. In one area, you can print and scroll through information. The other area is "locked in" and cannot be used for printing new information.

As you read this chapter, think about starting your personal collection of subroutines that you can use in writing programs.

GOSUB AND RETURN

A subroutine is a piece of a program designed to be called (used) from anywhere in the program, except from the subroutine itself. Think of the entire program divided into a main program and one or more subroutines. You use a GOSUB statement in the main program to call a subroutine. When the subroutine completes its task, it executes a RETURN statement, which returns control to the part of the program that called the subroutine.

```
1 REM ** Beep with Time Delay Subroutine **
2 ' GW-BASIC Made Easy, Chapter 8.  File: GWME0801.BAS

10 CLS

20 PRINT "You will hear a beep every second"

30 BEEP                    'Loop top

40 GOSUB 80                'Use time delay subroutine

50 GOTO 30                 'Loop bottom

70 END                     'End of main program

80 start = TIMER: WHILE TIMER < start + 1: WEND: RETURN
```

PROGRAM GWME0801   Beep with Time Delay Subroutine

A Time Delay Subroutine

Program GWME0801 (Beep with Time Delay Subroutine) has a main program in lines 10 through 70, and a time delay subroutine in line 80.

The program executes lines 10 and 20, then enters the GOTO loop in lines 30 through 50. Each time through the loop, the computer beeps (line 30), goes to the subroutine (from line 40), executes the subroutine (line 80), returns to line 50 (via RETURN in line 80), and goes to the top of the loop (from line 50). Line 70 is never executed. It is there to mark the end of the main program and separate it from the subroutine that follows the main program.

When you run the program, you will see the message "You will hear a beep every second" near the top of the screen and hear a beep once every second. Use CTRL+BREAK to interrupt the program.

TRACING A PROGRAM A program executes its lines in line number order, except when the order is changed by statements such as GOTO and GOSUB. For example, Program GWME0801 executes lines in the following order:

1. 10, 20   (executed once)
2. 30, 40, 80, 50
3. 30, 40, 80, 50
4. 30, 40, 80, 50
5. And so on...

This sequence of line numbers is called a *trace* of the program. GW-BASIC has the ability to trace a program for you, by printing the line number of each line as it is executed. You use the F7 function key to turn the trace on, and the F8 function key to turn the trace off. When you turn the trace on and run the program, the computer will print the line number of each line it executes. Let's try this.

First, turn on the trace.

Press:

F7

```
[20]You will hear a beep every second
[30] [40] [80] [50] [30] [40] [80] [50] [30] [40] [80] [50] [30] [40] [80] [50] [30] [40] [80] [50]
[30] [40] [80] [50] [30] [40] [80] [50] [30] [40] [80] [50] [30] [40] [80] [50] [30] [40] [80] [50]
[30] [40] [80] [50] [30] [40] [80] [50] [30] [40] [80] [50] [30] [40] [80]
Break in 80
Ok
_
```

FIGURE 8-1   Trace of Program GWME0801

Now, run the program.

Press:

F2

Figure 8-1 shows a trace of the program. The trace was interrupted by using CTRL+BREAK.

Important: While the program is running, you cannot turn off the trace by pressing the F8 function key. After interrupting a trace with CTRL+BREAK, press the F8 key to turn off the trace, unless you want to trace again.

```
1 REM ** Information About Trace **
2 ' GW-BASIC Made Easy, Chapter 8.  File: GWME0802.BAS

10 CLS

20 PRINT "Use F7 to turn on the trace and F8 to turn it off."
30 PRINT "Labels for F7 and F8 are on the key line (7TRON and"
40 PRINT "8TROFF).  When the trace is on, the computer prints"
50 PRINT "the line number of each line it executes."
60 PRINT
70 GOSUB 100                    'Use time delay subroutine
80 GOTO 20                      'Go to top of loop
90 END                          'End of main program

100 start = TIMER: WHILE TIMER < start + 1: WEND: RETURN
```

PROGRAM GWME0802   Information About Trace

```
Use F7 to turn on the trace and F8 to turn it off.
Labels for F7 and F8 are on the key line (7TRON and
8TROFF).  When the trace is on, the computer prints
the line number of each line it executes.

Use F7 to turn on the trace and F8 to turn it off.
Labels for F7 and F8 are on the key line (7TRON and
8TROFF).  When the trace is on, the computer prints
the line number of each line it executes.


Break in 100
Ok

_
```

FIGURE 8-2   Sample run of Program GWME0802 with trace off

Note that line 10 does not appear in the trace shown in Figure 8-1. Actually, it appeared briefly, then disappeared as the computer executed line 10, which is a CLS statement. You do see line 20 in the trace, along with the information printed by line 20. The rest of the trace shows lines 30, 40, 80, and 50 being repeated until the program is interrupted with CTRL+BREAK.

Program GWME0802 (Information About Trace) prints information about trace on (TRON) and trace off (TROFF) on the screen. This program has a main program in lines 10 through 90. Line 70 calls a time delay subroutine in line 100. The subroutine then returns to line 80. Figure 8-2 shows a run of Program GWME0802 with the trace off. Figure 8-3 shows a run of the program with the trace on.

You can turn the trace on by using the keyword TRON as a direct statement. You can turn off the trace by using TROFF as a direct statement. Let's try this.

To turn on the trace,

Type:

TRON

and press ENTER.

```
[20]Use F7 to turn on the trace and F8 to turn it off.
[30]Labels for F7 and F8 are on the key line (7TRON and
[40]8TROFF).  When the trace is on, the computer prints
[50]the line number of each line it executes.
[60]
[70][100][80][20]Use F7 to turn on the trace and F8 to turn
it off.
[30]Labels for F7 and F8 are on the key line (7TRON and
[40]8TROFF).  When the trace is on, the computer prints
[50]the line number of each line it executes.
[60]
[70][100]
Break in 100
Ok
—
```

FIGURE 8-3   Sample run of Program GWME0802 with trace on

To turn off the trace,

Type:

TROFF

and press ENTER.

Of course, it is much faster to press F7 or F8 than to type TRON or TROFF, and you are less likely to make a mistake.

The time delay used in Program GWME0801 and Program GWME0802 causes a one-second delay. If you want a two-second delay, call the subroutine twice. To do this in Program GWME0801, change lines 20 and 40 to the following:

```
20 PRINT "You will hear a beep every two seconds"
40 GOSUB 80: GOSUB 80      'Use time delay subroutine twice
```

After making this change, trace the program. Figure 8-4 shows a trace of the program. Note that line number 80 appears twice in each execution of the GOTO loop in lines 30 through 50. Remember, line 40 has two GOSUB

```
[20]You will hear a beep every two seconds
[30][40][80][80][50][30][40][80][80][50][30][40][80][80][50][30][40][80][80][50]
[30][40][80][80][50][30][40][80][80][50][30][40][80][80][50][30][40][80][80][50]
[30][40][80][80][50][30][40][80][80][50][30][40][80][80]
Break in 80
Ok
_
```

FIGURE 8-4   Trace of Program GWME0801 with modified lines 20 and 40

statements. The first GOSUB sends control to the subroutine in line 80, which then sends control back to the second GOSUB in line 40. The second GOSUB sends control to the subroutine, which then sends control back to line 50.

A Variable Time Delay

The time delay subroutine used in Programs GWME0801 and GWME0802 provides a fixed time delay of one second. A variable time delay subroutine is shown next:

```
80 start = TIMER: WHILE TIMER < start + delay: WEND: RETURN
```

To use this subroutine, first assign the amount of delay (in seconds) as the value of *delay*, then call the subroutine. For example, for a one-second delay, do this:

```
delay = 1: GOSUB 80
```

If you want a two-second delay, do this:

```
delay = 2: GOSUB 80
```

```
1 REM ** Beep with Variable Time Delay Subroutine **
2 ' GW-BASIC Made Easy, Chapter 8.  File: GWME0803.BAS

10 CLS

20 PRINT "You'll hear a beep every second (Press ESC to quit)"

30 WHILE INKEY$ <> CHR$(27)      'Loop while ESC not pressed
40    BEEP
50    delay = 1: GOSUB 80         'Set delay & use subroutine
60 WEND

70 END                           'End of main program

80 start = TIMER: WHILE TIMER < start + delay: WEND: RETURN
```

PROGRAM GWME0803   Beep with Variable Time Delay Subroutine

Program GWME0803 (Beep with Variable Time Delay Subroutine) demonstrates the use of the time delay subroutine. Enter and run this program. Press the ESC key to exit from the WHILE...END loop. The program then executes the END statement in line 70 and the program ends.

If line 70 were not there, the computer would try to execute the time delay subroutine without entering it by means of a GOSUB statement. In this situation, you would see the error message "RETURN without GOSUB in 80." To verify this, delete line 70, run the program, then press ESC. It is good programming practice to put an END statement just before a block of subroutines, to prevent this sort of problem from occurring.

COUNT DOWN...BLAST OFF!   Here is another version of the Count Down...Blast Off! program previously shown in Chapter 6 (GWME0606). This new Program GWME0804 (Count Down...Blast Off! with Variable Time Delay Subroutine) uses a variable time delay subroutine. The subroutine is in line 910. Lines 900 and 905 are REM statements that provide information about the subroutine. The subroutine is called from lines 230, 260, 380, 430, and 470.

```
1 REM ** Countdown...Blastoff! with Time Delay Subroutine **
2 ' GW-BASIC Made Easy, Chapter 8.  File: GWME0804.BAS

100 REM ** Clear screen & turn off key line **
110 CLS : KEY OFF

200 REM ** Countdown **
210 FOR count = 10 TO 0 STEP -1
220   BEEP: PRINT count
230   delay = 1: GOSUB 910              'Use time delay subroutine
240 NEXT count
250 PRINT "Blastoff!!!"
260 delay = 1: GOSUB 910               'Use time delay subroutine

300 REM ** Show bird on the launch pad **
310 CLS
320 LOCATE 18, 36: PRINT "    *";
330 LOCATE 19, 36: PRINT "   *U*";
340 LOCATE 20, 36: PRINT "   *S*";
350 LOCATE 21, 36: PRINT "   *A*";
360 LOCATE 22, 36: PRINT " *****";
370 LOCATE 23, 36: PRINT "*******";
380 delay = 1: GOSUB 910                'Use time delay subroutine

400 REM ** Launch the bird **
410 FOR k = 1 TO 3
420   LOCATE 24, 36: PRINT "  !!!"
430   delay = 1 / k: GOSUB 910          'Use time delay subroutine
440 NEXT k
450 FOR k = 4 TO 26
460   PRINT
470   delay = 1 / k: GOSUB 910          'Use time delay subroutine
480 NEXT k

500 REM ** Announce a successful launch **
510 LOCATE 12, 20
520 PRINT "All systems are go.  Everything is AOK."
530 END

900 REM ** SUBROUTINE: Variable time delay **
905 ' Assign a value to delay before calling this subroutine
910 start = TIMER: WHILE TIMER < start + delay: WEND: RETURN
```

PROGRAM GWME0804   Count Down...Blast Off! with Variable Time Delay
Subroutine

Lines 230, 260, and 380 set the delay to one second and then call the subroutine, as follows:

```
delay = 1: GOSUB 910
```

Lines 430 and 470 are inside FOR...NEXT loops. They set the delay to a value determined by the variable in the FOR statement, and then call the subroutine, like this:

```
delay = 1 / k: GOSUB 910
```

Since the value of k increases each time through the loop, the value of $1 / k$ decreases. Therefore, each time the subroutine is called, the delay is shorter than the previous time. This is intended to show the bird (spaceship) accelerating as it zooms up the screen and out of sight.

The FOR...NEXT loop in lines 410 through 440 is shown here:

```
410 FOR k = 1 TO 3
420    LOCATE 24, 36: PRINT "  !!!"
430    delay = 1 / k: GOSUB 910     'Use time delay subroutine
440 NEXT k
```

Note that line 430 is executed three times, for $k = 1$, $k = 2$, and $k = 3$. Therefore, the time delays are 1 second, $\frac{1}{2}$ second, and $\frac{1}{3}$ second. The time delays continue decreasing in the FOR...NEXT loop in lines 450 through 480, as follows:

```
450 FOR k = 4 TO 26
460    PRINT
470    delay = 1 / k: GOSUB 910     'Use time delay subroutine
480 NEXT k
```

As this FOR...NEXT is carried out, the time delays are $\frac{1}{4}$ second, $\frac{1}{5}$ second, $\frac{1}{6}$ second, and so on, down to $\frac{1}{26}$ second.

```
1 REM ** Word Maker with Subroutines **
2 ' GW-BASIC Made Easy, Chapter 8.  File: GWME0805.BAS

100 REM ** Define FNran, a random integer function **
105 ' Returns random integer in the range, 1 to n
110 DEF FNran (n) = INT(n * RND) + 1

200 REM ** Set up **
210 CLS : KEY OFF
220 RANDOMIZE TIMER

300 REM ** Find out how many words to make **
310 CLS : INPUT "How many words shall I make"; NumberOfWords
320 PRINT

400 REM ** Make and print the words **
410 FOR k = 1 TO NumberOfWords
420    GOSUB 710                     'Use make a word subroutine
430    PRINT word$,                  'Print the word
440    IF k MOD 5 = 0 THEN PRINT     'Double spaces lines
450 NEXT k

500 REM ** Tell how to do again or quit **
510 PRINT : PRINT
520 PRINT "Press a key for more words (ESC to quit)";
530 BEEP: anykey$ = INPUT$(1)
540 IF anykey$ <> CHR$(27) THEN 310 ELSE END

700 REM ** SUBROUTINE: Make a 'cvcvc' word **
710 word$ = ""
720 GOSUB 810                     'Add a consonant
730 GOSUB 910                     'Add a vowel
740 GOSUB 810                     'Add a consonant
750 GOSUB 910                     'Add a vowel
760 GOSUB 810                     'Add a consonant
770 RETURN

800 REM ** SUBROUTINE: Add a consonant **
810 consonant$ = "bcdfghjklmnpqrstvwxyz"
820 letter$ = MID$(consonant$, FNran(21), 1)  'Random consonant
830 word$ = word$ + letter$                   'Attach it to word
840 RETURN
```

PROGRAM GWME0805   Word Maker with Subroutines

```
900 REM ** SUBROUTINE: Add a vowel **
910 vowel$ = "aeiou"
920 letter$ = MID$(vowel$, FNran(5), 1)        'Random vowel
930 word$ = word$ + letter$                    'Attach it to word
940 RETURN
```

PROGRAM GWME0805   Word Maker with Subroutines (*continued*)

Word Maker with Subroutines

The next program has a main program, a user-defined function, and three subroutines. The main program calls one subroutine, which then calls the other two subroutines, as needed. Two of the subroutines use the user-defined function. Here is an annotated REM outline of Program GWME0805 (Word Maker with Subroutines).

```
1 REM ** Word Maker with Subroutines **
2 ' GW-BASIC Made Easy, Chapter 8.  File: GWME0805.BAS

100 REM ** Define FNran, a random integer function **   Defined function

200 REM ** Set up **

300 REM ** Find out how many words to make **

400 REM ** Make and print the words **                  Main program

500 REM ** Tell how to do again or quit **

700 REM ** SUBROUTINE: Make a 'cvcvc' word **

800 REM ** SUBROUTINE: Add a consonant **               Subroutines

900 REM ** SUBROUTINE: Add a vowel **
```

Figure 8-5 shows a sample run of Program GWME0805. This run was selected from many runs because it generated an easily recognized word, "sixes." If you run the program many times, you will probably see few actual English words. Since there are 21 consonants and 5 vowels in our language, the number of possible consonant-vowel combinations can be calculated as

```
How many words shall I make? 23

vipim        sixes        jotuk        pahol        qawob

qenor        dumom        vupet        fusip        kiloz

sixik        nojik        waroy        tuwed        debec

sitay        qukuw        jekih        gilor        fehan

zisuy        vobab        gezic

Press a key for more words (ESC to quit)
```

FIGURE 8-5   Sample run of Program GWME0805

follows: 21 * 5 * 21 * 5 * 21 = 231,525. About how many of these do you
think are English words of the form consonant, vowel, consonant, vowel,
consonant (cvcvc)?

Program GWME0805 makes words of the form *cvcvc*. To make words
with a different consonant-vowel structure, rewrite only the Make-a-word
subroutine in block 700. For example, here is a subroutine to make a word
of the form *cvc* (consonant, vowel, consonant):

```
700 REM ** SUBROUTINE: Make a 'cvc' word **
710 word$ = ""
720 GOSUB 810                          'Add a consonant
730 GOSUB 910                          'Add a vowel
740 GOSUB 810                          'Add a consonant
750 RETURN
```

Make this change and run the modified program. You will probably see more
recognizable words. Then change the subroutine again, so that it makes a
word of the form *vccvcv*, as shown here:

```
700 REM ** SUBROUTINE: Make a 'vccvc' word **
710 word$ = ""
720 GOSUB 910                          'Add a vowel
730 GOSUB 810                          'Add a consonant
740 GOSUB 810                          'Add a consonant
750 GOSUB 910                          'Add a vowel
```

```
760 GOSUB 810                    'Add a consonant
770 GOSUB 910                    'Add a vowel
780 RETURN
```

What word structure would you like? Write the subroutine so that it makes the words you want.

A Multiple-Choice Subroutine Caller

In Chapter 6, you learned how to use the ON...GOTO statement to go to one line number in a list of line numbers. GW-BASIC also has a multiple-choice statement for use with subroutines, called ON...GOSUB. Program GWME0806 (Negative, Zero, or Positive #3) demonstrates the use of the ON...GOSUB statement. Look for it in line 420.

```
1 REM ** Negative, Zero, or Positive #3 **
2 ' GW-BASIC Made Easy, Chapter 8.  File: GWME0806.BAS

100 REM ** Assign messages to string variables **
110 n$ = "negative"
120 z$ = "zero"
130 p$ = "positive"

200 REM ** Tell what to do **
210 CLS : KEY OFF
220 PRINT "Enter a number and I will tell you whether"
230 PRINT "your number is negative, zero, or positive."

300 REM ** Ask for a number **
310 PRINT                        'Top of loop
320 INPUT "Number, please"; number

400 REM ** Tell about the number **
410 OneTwoThree = SGN(number) + 2
420 ON OneTwoThree GOSUB 440, 450, 460
430 GOTO 310                     'Bottom of loop

440 PRINT n$: RETURN             'Subroutine (number < 0)
450 PRINT z$: RETURN             'Subroutine (number = 0)
460 PRINT p$: RETURN             'Subroutine (number > 0)
```

PROGRAM GWME0806   Negative, Zero, or Positive #3

Block 400, in which the ON…GOSUB statement appears, is shown here:

```
400 REM ** Tell about the number **
410 OneTwoThree = SGN(number) + 2
420 ON OneTwoThree GOSUB 440, 450, 460
430 GOTO 310                           'Bottom of loop

440 PRINT n$: RETURN                   'Subroutine (number < 0)
450 PRINT z$: RETURN                   'Subroutine (number = 0)
460 PRINT p$: RETURN                   'Subroutine (number > 0)
```

Remember, the value of SGN(*number*) is −1 for negative numbers, 0 for zero, and 1 for positive numbers. Therefore, the value of SGN(*number*) + 2 is 1, 2, or 3.

- If the value is 1, line 420 calls the subroutine in line 440.

- If the value is 2, line 420 calls the subroutine in line 450.

- If the value is 3, line 420 calls the subroutine in line 460.

No matter which subroutine is called, it returns control to line 430.

Think of lines 440 through 460 as a set of three subroutines. You can also think of lines 440 through 460 as one subroutine with three entry points.

DIVIDE AND CONQUER

You can save yourself lots of time and trouble by dividing long programs into a main program and several subroutines. The main program consists of GOSUB statements, and control statements such as IF…THEN. The main program and accompanying remarks clearly show the overall structure of the program. The main program controls the flow of the program and calls subroutines as needed to get the work done.

The People's Poll

Program GWME0807 (The People's Poll #3) is the latest in the series of People's Poll programs that began in Chapter 6. A listing of the main program follows.

```
1 REM ** The People's Poll #3 **
2 ' GW-BASIC Made Easy, Chapter 8.  File: GWME0807.BAS
3 ' Tallies responses (1, 2, 3, 4) entered from keyboard

100 REM ** Main program **
110 GOSUB 1010                          'Set up
120 GOSUB 2010                          'Clear tallies to zero
130 GOSUB 3010                          'Tell what to do
140 GOSUB 4010                          'Get response.  Loop top
150 IF response$ = CHR$(27) THEN 170    'If ESC pressed, GOTO 170
160 GOSUB 5010: GOTO 140                'Tally & go to loop top
170 GOSUB 6010                          'Print final tallies
180 END                                 'End of main program
```

You can build Program GWME0807 a few blocks at a time, and check out each block to make sure it works. Begin by entering the title block (block 1), part of the main program, and the first two subroutines, as shown here:

```
1 REM ** The People's Poll #3 **
2 ' GW-BASIC Made Easy, Chapter 8.  File: GWME0807.BAS
3 ' Tallies responses (1, 2, 3, 4) entered from keyboard

100 REM ** Main program **
110 GOSUB 1010                          'Set up
120 GOSUB 2010                          'Clear tallies to zero
180 END                                 'End of main program

1000 REM ** SUBROUTINE: Set up **
1010 CLS : KEY OFF
1020 RETURN

2000 REM ** SUBROUTINE: Clear tallies to zero **
2010 TallyOne = 0
2020 TallyTwo = 0
2030 TallyThree = 0
2040 TallyFour = 0
2050 RETURN
```

Run this part of the program. It clears the screen, turns off the key line, and sets the four tally variables to zero. You will see a clear screen, except for Ok and the blinking cursor. Use a direct PRINT statement to check the values of the variables.

Type:

PRINT TallyOne, TallyTwo, TallyThree, TallyFour

and press ENTER.

It prints:

```
 0              0            0             0
Ok
_
```

Save the program under the filename GWME0807.V01. The extension .V01 means "version 1." You will create version 2, version 3, and so on, until the program is complete. These partial versions give you an "audit trail" that you can use if something goes amiss.

Now add line 130 and the subroutine it calls, as follows:

```
130 GOSUB 3010                          'Tell what to do

3000 REM ** SUBROUTINE: Tell what to do **
3010 LOCATE 20, 1: PRINT STRING$(78, 205);
3020 LOCATE 21, 1: PRINT "Does your computer understand you?;

3030 LOCATE 23, 1
3040 PRINT "1 = Yes, 2 = No, 3 = Sometimes, 4 = None above
3050 LOCATE 25, 1
3060 PRINT "To quit, press the ESC key.";
3070 VIEW PRINT 1 TO 19
3080 RETURN
```

After adding these lines, list the program. It should look like this:

```
1 REM ** The People's Poll #3 **
2 ' GW-BASIC Made Easy, Chapter 8.  File: GWME0807.BAS
3 ' Tallies responses (1, 2, 3, 4) entered from keyboard

100 REM ** Main program **
110 GOSUB 1010                   'Set up
120 GOSUB 2010                   'Clear tallies to zero
130 GOSUB 3010                   'Tell what to do
180 END                          'End of Main program

1000 REM ** SUBROUTINE: Set up **
1010 CLS : KEY OFF
1020 RETURN
```

```
2000 REM ** SUBROUTINE: Clear tallies to zero **
2010 TALLYONE = 0
2020 TALLYTWO = 0
2030 TALLYTHREE = 0
2040 TALLYFOUR = 0
2050 RETURN

3000 REM ** SUBROUTINE: Tell what to do **
3010 LOCATE 20, 1: PRINT STRING$(78, 205);
3020 LOCATE 21, 1: PRINT "Does your computer understand you?";
3030 LOCATE 23, 1
3040 PRINT "1 = Yes, 2 = No, 3 = Sometimes, 4 = None above";
3050 LOCATE 25, 1
3060 PRINT "To quit, press the ESC key as your response";
3070 VIEW PRINT 1 TO 19
3080 RETURN
```

Save this program as version 2, with the filename GWME0807.V02; then run it. Figure 8-6 shows how a run should look. Correct any mistakes, and

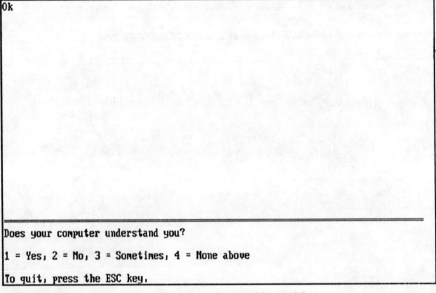

FIGURE 8-6   Sample run of Program GWME0807.V02

save the program again in its correct form.

The "Tell what to do" subroutine in block 3000 introduces a new statement—the VIEW PRINT statement. This statement defines a text view port, which restricts the screen area in which information can be printed.

The statement VIEW PRINT 1 TO 19 establishes lines 1-19 of the screen as a view port, in which information is displayed. Any information previously written in lines 20-25 remains on the screen. Since the instructions to the user are printed in screen lines 20-25 before the VIEW PRINT 1 TO 19 statement is executed, the instructions remain on the screen and do not scroll off. The screen is thus divided into two areas, as shown in Figure 8-7.

The statement

```
3010 LOCATE 20, 1: PRINT STRING$(78,205);
```

draws a double line across the screen by printing 78 copies of ASCII character 205 (=). This line is drawn in row 20. It separates the instructions in lines 21-25 from the view port in lines 1-19. The VIEW PRINT instruction

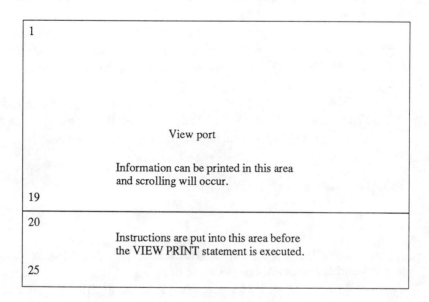

FIGURE 8-7   VIEW PRINT divides the screen into two areas

then "locks in" the instructions. Changing information is restricted to lines 1-19.

Now add the next piece of the program, as shown in the following.

```
140 GOSUB 4110                          'Get response.  Loop top
150 IF response$ = CHR$(27) THEN 170 'If ESC pressed, GOTO 170
160 GOTO 140
170 PRINT "ESC was pressed"
180 END


4000 REM ** SUBROUTINE: Get a response **
4010 ' Valid responses are 1, 2, 3, 4, or ESC key
4020 PRINT : PRINT "Response (1, 2, 3, 4, or ESC to quit)? ";
4030 response$ = CHR$(32)
4040 WHILE INSTR("1234" + CHR$(27), response$) = 0
4050    BEEP: response$ = INPUT$(1)
4060 WEND
4070 PRINT response$                    'Echo the response
4080 response = VAL(response$)    'Numeric equivalent to string
4090 RETURN
```

Lines 160 and 170 are temporary—they will be replaced as you add more pieces to the program. They are used here as a means for checking out the subroutine in block 4000.

After you add lines 140, 150, 160, 170, and the subroutine, list the program to make sure it is all there, then save it under the filename GWME0807.V03. Figure 8-8 shows a run of this latest version of The People's Poll #3.

The "Get a response" subroutine in block 4000 contains a WHILE...WEND loop to acquire the response. This loop accepts only 1, 2, 3, 4, or the ESC key as valid responses. The loop is shown here:

```
4020 response$ = CHR$(32)
4030 WHILE INSTR("1234" + CHR$(27), response$) = 0
4040    BEEP: response$ = INPUT$(1)
4050 WEND
```

Line 4020 assigns a space (ASCII code 32) as the value of the string variable *response$*. For this value of *response$*, the value of the function INSTR("1234" + CHR$(27), response$) is zero (0). Therefore, line 4040 is executed; the computer beeps and waits for you to enter one character. If you press a key other than 1, 2, 3, 4, or ESC, your entry is ignored. Try it when

```
Response (1, 2, 3, 4, or ESC to quit)? 1

Response (1, 2, 3, 4, or ESC to quit)? 2

Response (1, 2, 3, 4, or ESC to quit)? 3

Response (1, 2, 3, 4, or ESC to quit)? 4

Response (1, 2, 3, 4, or ESC to quit)? ←
ESC was pressed
Ok




_____

Does your computer understand you?

1 = Yes, 2 = No, 3 = Sometimes, 4 = None above

To quit, press the ESC key.
```

FIGURE 8-8   Sample run of Program GWME0807.V03

you run the program; press **5** or **6** or **A**. The computer will keep beeping and waiting for 1, 2, 3, 4, or ESC. When you press one of these keys, the value of the INSTR function becomes non-zero, the WHILE…WEND loop ends, and the computer continues with the rest of the program.

Any response you enter is a string value. It is assigned to the string variable *response$*. Line 4080 uses the VAL function to obtain the numerical equivalent of the string value of *response$* and assigns it as the value of the numeric variable *response*. For example, if the value of *response$* is 3, then the value of *response* will be 3. If you press the ESC key, the value of *response* will be zero (0), since ESC is not a number.

Now add the subroutine that tallies the response. Also add line 160, which calls the subroutine and then goes to the top of the loop.

```
160 GOSUB 5010: GOTO 140          'Tally & go to loop top

5000 REM ** SUBROUTINE: Tally the response **
5010 ON response GOTO 5020, 5030, 5040, 5050
```

```
5020 TallyOne = TallyOne + 1: RETURN
5030 TallyTwo = TallyTwo + 1: RETURN
5040 TallyThree = TallyThree + 1: RETURN
5050 TallyFour = TallyFour + 1: RETURN
```

You have now expanded the program to version 4; save it as GWME0807.V04. Next, run it and enter several responses. For example, enter one 1, two 2s, three 3s, and four 4s. Then press ESC to end the program. Finally, use a direct PRINT statement to find out if your responses are properly tallied.

Type:

PRINT TallyOne, TallyTwo, TallyThree, TallyFour

and press ENTER.

You should see the correct tallies for the responses you entered prior to pressing the ESC key.

The program is almost complete. To complete it, add the following subroutine and line 170, which calls the subroutine.

```
170 GOSUB 6010                          'Print final tallies

6000 REM ** SUBROUTINE: Print the final tallies **
6010 VIEW PRINT: CLS
6020 PRINT "Total 'Yes' responses:"; TAB(35); TallyOne
6030 PRINT "Total 'No' responses:'; TAB(35); TallyTwo
6040 PRINT "Total 'Sometimes' responses:"; TAB(35); TallyThree
6050 PRINT "Total 'None above' responses:"; TAB(35); TallyFour
6060 RETURN
```

The results of a sample run are shown here:

```
Total 'Yes' responses            1
Total 'No' responses:            2
```

```
Total 'Sometimes' responses:        3
Total 'None above' responses:       4
Ok

_
```

Save the complete program as GWME0807.BAS.

```
1 REM ** The People's Poll #3 **
2 ' GW-BASIC Made Easy, Chapter 8.  File: GWME0807.BAS
3 ' Tallies responses (1, 2, 3, 4) entered from keyboard

100 REM ** Main program **
110 GOSUB 1010                      'Set up
120 GOSUB 2010                      'Clear tallies to zero
130 GOSUB 3010                      'Tell what to do
140 GOSUB 4010                      'Get response.  Loop top
150 IF response$ = CHR$(27) THEN 170 'If ESC pressed, GOTO 170
160 GOSUB 5010: GOTO 140            'Tally & go to loop top
170 GOSUB 6010                      'Print final tallies
180 END                            'End of main program

1000 REM ** SUBROUTINE: Set up **
1010 CLS : KEY OFF
1020 RETURN

2000 REM ** SUBROUTINE: Clear tallies to zero **
2010 TallyOne = 0
2020 TallyTwo = 0
2030 TallyThree = 0
2040 TallyFour = 0
2050 RETURN

3000 REM ** SUBROUTINE: Tell what to do **
3010 LOCATE 20, 1: PRINT STRING$(78, 205);
3020 LOCATE 21, 1: PRINT "Does your computer understand you?";
```

PROGRAM GWME0807   The People's Poll #3

```
3030 LOCATE 23, 1
3040 PRINT "1 = Yes, 2 = No, 3 = Sometimes, 4 = None above";
3050 LOCATE 25, 1
3060 PRINT "To quit, press the ESC key.";
3070 VIEW PRINT 1 TO 19
3080 RETURN

4000 REM ** SUBROUTINE: Get a response **
4005 ' Valid responses are 1, 2, 3, 4, or ESC key
4010 PRINT : PRINT "Response (1, 2, 3, 4, or ESC to quit)? ";
4020 response$ = CHR$(32)
4030 WHILE INSTR("1234" + CHR$(27), response$) = 0
4040    BEEP: response$ = INPUT$(1)
4050 WEND
4060 PRINT response$                'Echo the response
4070 response = VAL(response$)      'Numeric equivalent to string
4080 RETURN

5000 REM ** SUBROUTINE: Tally the response **
5010 ON response GOTO 5020, 5030, 5040, 5050
5020 TallyOne = TallyOne + 1: RETURN
5030 TallyTwo = TallyTwo + 1: RETURN
5040 TallyThree = TallyThree + 1: RETURN
5050 TallyFour = TallyFour + 1: RETURN

6000 REM ** SUBROUTINE: Print the final tallies **
6010 VIEW PRINT: CLS
6020 PRINT "Total 'Yes' responses:"; TAB(35); TallyOne
6030 PRINT "Total 'No' responses:"; TAB(35); TallyTwo
6040 PRINT "Total 'Sometimes' responses:"; TAB(35); TallyThree
6050 PRINT "Total 'None above' responses:"; TAB(35); TallyFour
6060 RETURN
```

PROGRAM GWME0807   The People's Poll #3 (*continued*)

If you wish, you can now delete the earlier versions of the program from the disk. Use the KILL statement. For example, delete Program GWME0807.V01 like this:

Type:

KILL "GWME0807.V01"

and press ENTER.

A good way to learn more about programming is to modify an existing program. Some modifications to Program GWME0807 are suggested here:

- Tally responses to three questions, instead of four questions. The possible responses are 1, 2, 3, or ESC.

- Tally responses to five questions. The possible responses are 1, 2, 3, 4, 5, or ESC.

- Instead of numbers, use letters as responses. For example, let the possible responses be *a, b, c, d,* or ESC.

- In the subroutine to print the final tallies, also compute and print the total number of responses. That is, print the sum of the values of *TallyOne, TallyTwo, TallyThree,* and *TallyFour.*

- In the subroutine that prints the final tallies, use PRINT USING statements, so that the printed numbers line up properly for values greater than 9.

- Compute and print the percent of the total for each response, as well as the number of responses. For example, a run might end like this:

```
Total 'Yes' responses:           5    10%
Total 'No' responses:           18    36%
Total 'Sometimes' responses:    15    30%
Total 'None above' responses:   12    24%

Total of all responses          50   100%
```

PREFABRICATED PROGRAMS

One way to reduce the work in programming is to save useful subroutines as ASCII files on your work disk. Then, when you need one of these subroutines in a program, use the MERGE statement to merge the subroutine with the program you are writing. Think of your collection of subroutines as prefabricated building blocks that you can use to make programming easier.

To save a subroutine, you must choose line numbers for the lines in the subroutine. A line number must be an integer in the range 1 to 65529. One way to save subroutines is to begin numbering at, say, 60000. Then, when you merge a subroutine, you use the RENUM command to renumber the subroutine to fit your program. If you use this convention, use line numbers less than 60000 in all your programs, so you can merge subroutines without replacing any lines in your program.

The Variable Time Delay Subroutine

Begin building your personal subroutine library by saving the variable time delay subroutine to your work disk.

Type:

NEW

and press ENTER.

Next, enter the variable time delay subroutine, as shown here:

```
60000 REM ** SUBROUTINE: Variable time delay **
60010 ' Assign a value to delay before calling this subroutine
60020 start = TIMER: WHILE TIMER < start + delay: WEND: RETURN
```

Save this subroutine in ASCII format (see Chapter 3) to your work disk under the filename DELAY.SUB. The extension .SUB will tell you that this is a subroutine when you look at a list of filenames on the disk. After saving the subroutine, erase it from memory.

Now check out the subroutine. To do so, you will write a main program, merge the subroutine with the main program, renumber the subroutine to fit the main program, and then run it to make sure everything is in good working order.

Type:

NEW

and press ENTER.

Enter the following main program:

```
10 CLS
20 INPUT "Delay"; delay
30 BEEP: GOSUB 60020
40 GOTO 30
50 END
```

Now merge the subroutine with the main program. If you saved the subroutine to the default disk drive, merge it from that drive as follows:

Type:

MERGE "DELAY.SUB", A

and press ENTER.

To merge the subroutine from a disk drive other than the default drive, include the drive designation as part of the filename. For example, to merge the subroutine from disk drive B, do this:

Type:

MERGE "B:DELAY.SUB", A

and press ENTER.

After merging the subroutine with the main program, list the resulting program. A listing is shown here:

```
10 CLS
20 INPUT "Delay"; delay
30 BEEP: GOSUB 60020
40 GOTO 30
50 END
60000 REM ** SUBROUTINE: Variable time delay **
60010 ' Assign a value to delay before calling this subroutine
60020 START = TIMER: WHILE TIMER < START + DELAY: WEND: RETURN
```

Finally, run the program. Enter the delay of your choice, and listen to the computer go beep...beep...beep. Use CTRL+BREAK to stop. Try several values of *delay* to make sure the subroutine is working properly.

Renumbering a Program

You can use the RENUM command to renumber all or part of a program. Use it now to renumber the preceding program.

Type:

RENUM

and press ENTER.

The RENUM command renumbers all lines in a program. The renumbered lines will be numbered 10, 20, 30, and so on. Line number references following GOTO, GOSUB, and so on, are changed so they still refer to the correct lines.

List the program. It should now look like this:

```
10 CLS
20 INPUT "Delay"; DELAY
30 BEEP: GOSUB 80
40 GOTO 30
50 END
60 REM ** SUBROUTINE: Variable time delay **
70 ' Assign a value to delay before calling this subroutine
80 START = TIMER: WHILE TIMER < START + DELAY: WEND: RETURN
```

Note that the subroutine is now numbered 60, 70, and 80. Also note that the GOSUB statement in line 30 has been renumbered so that it still sends control to the proper line in the time delay subroutine.

Now renumber lines 60, 70, and 80 so that they become lines 100, 105, and 110.

Type:

RENUM 100, 60, 5

and press ENTER.

List the program. It should appear as shown here:

```
10 CLS
20 INPUT "Delay"; DELAY
30 BEEP: GOSUB 110
40 GOTO 30
50 END
100 REM ** SUBROUTINE: Variable time delay **
105 ' Assign a value to delay before calling this subroutine
110 START = TIMER: WHILE TIMER < START + DELAY: WEND: RETURN
```

The command:

```
RENUM 100, 60, 5
```

tells the computer to renumber old line 60 as new line 100, and continue renumbering in increments of 5 from the new line 100.

The LOCASE Subroutine

Suppose you are writing a trivia program. One of the questions is, "What are the colors of a rainbow?" If red is one of the colors, people might enter it as red or RED or Red, or perhaps even as ReD. This could make it a bit difficult to determine if the answer is correct.

The LOCASE subroutine changes all letters in a string to lowercase. Subroutine LOCASE is shown here:

```
60000 REM ** SUBROUTINE: LOCASE **
60010 ' Changes letters in strng$ to lower case
60020 FOR kk% = 1 TO LEN(strng$)
60030    character$ = MID$(strng$, kk%, 1)
60040    code% = ASC(character$)
60050    IF code% > 64 AND code% < 91 THEN code% = code% + 32
60060    character$ = CHR$(code%)
60070    MID$(strng$, kk%, 1) = character$
60080 NEXT kk%
60090 RETURN
```

Save the subroutine under the filename LOCASE.SUB. Does it work? To test it, enter the following main program, merge the subroutine, and run the resulting program.

```
10 CLS
20 INPUT "String, please"; strng$
```

```
30 GOSUB 60020
40 PRINT "LOCASE string is "; strng$
50 PRINT : GOTO 20
60 END
```

A sample run is shown here. For the string R2D2, note that the subroutine leaves characters that are not letters unchanged. Uppercase letters are changed to lowercase. Lowercase letters are not changed.

```
String, please? RED
LOCASE string is red

String, please? Red
LOCASE string is red

String, please? red
LOCASE string is red

String, please? R2D2
LOCASE string is r2d2

String, please? _
```

The subroutine uses two integer variables, *kk%* and *code%*, and two string variables, *strng$* and *character$*. Only one of these variables (strng$) appears in the main program. Its original value can be changed by the main program. The following variation of the main program preserves the value of the string you enter:

```
10 CLS
20 INPUT "String, please"; ThinRope$
30 strng$ = ThinRope$: GOSUB 60020
40 PRINT "You entered: "; ThinRope$
50 PRINT "I changed it to: "; strng$
60 PRINT : GOTO 20
70 END
```

Line 30 assigns the value of *ThinRope$* as the value of *strng$* and calls the subroutine. Since the variable *ThinRope$* is not used in the subroutine, its value remains unchanged by the execution of the subroutine. Enter this version of the main program, merge the subroutine, and run the resulting program to see how it works.

HOW SUBROUTINE LOCASE WORKS The LOCASE subroutine consists of a FOR...NEXT loop that extracts each character of *strng$* and checks to see if it is an uppercase letter. An uppercase letter is changed to lowercase and inserted back into the string.

In line 60030, the value of *character$* is one character from the value of *strng$*. Line 60040 assigns the ASCII code of this character to *code%*. Uppercase letters have ASCII codes 65-90 for *A* through *Z*. Lowercase letters have ASCII codes 97-122 for *a* through *z*. Therefore, the ASCII code for a lowercase letter is exactly 32 more than the code for the corresponding uppercase letter.

If the value of *code%* is in the range 65-90, inclusive, line 60050 adds 32 to it, thus changing it to the value for a lowercase letter. Otherwise, *code%* is not changed. Line 60060 converts the value of *code%* to a one-character string, and assigns it to *character$*.

In line 60070, MID$ is used as a statement, not as a function. The statement:

```
MID$(strng$, kk%, 1) = character$
```

replaces the character at position *kk%* in *strng$* with the value of *character$*. For example, suppose *strng$* is "RED", *kk%* is 1, and *character$* is *r*. The MID$ statement replaces *R* with *r* in position 1.

Your turn. Write a subroutine, called UPCASE, that replaces all lowercase letters in *strng$* with uppercase letters.

REVIEW

A subroutine is a self-contained piece of a program. You can break a long program into short subroutines, and then write a main program to call, or use, the subroutines as needed. You use GOSUB or ON...GOSUB statements to call subroutines. A subroutine must contain one or more RETURN statements that return control to the part of the program called the subroutine.

A subroutine can be used in more than one program. Therefore, if you think a subroutine will be useful in the future, save it in ASCII format on your work disk. When you need the subroutine, use the MERGE statement to merge it with a program you are writing. You can use the RENUM statement to renumber the lines in the subroutine so that they fit your program.

A program executes its lines in line number order, except when the order is changed by statements such as GOTO and GOSUB. You can tell the computer to trace a program, displaying line numbers as lines are executed. In this way, you can follow the flow of the program and see how it works. This is especially useful if the program is *not* working; a trace will help you "debug" the program. Use the F7 function key or a TRON statement to turn on a trace. Use the F8 function key or a TROFF statement to turn off a trace.

You can use a VIEW PRINT statement to divide the screen into two areas. After doing so, you can print in one area, but not in the other area. One application of VIEW PRINT is to print instructions to the user in part of the screen, then "lock them in" by means of a VIEW PRINT. You can print new information to the other part of the screen without disturbing the instructions.

9

ARRAYS

In this chapter you will learn about a new kind of variable—the array variable—and about arrays of array variables. In particular, you will learn about

- subscripts and array variables

- arrays, lists, or sets of array variables

- array dimensions and how to use the DIM statement to reserve memory space for arrays

- using the DEFINT keyword to define some or all numeric variables as integers, unless designated otherwise

- using two or three related arrays to calculate and print line items and dot products

- using the SWAP keyword to exchange values in an array

- scrambling arrays into random order

- sorting both numeric and string arrays

ARRAYS

In previous chapters you have used simple numeric and string variables. For example:

Numeric variables: *number   delay!   k   Value#*

String variables: *anykey$ vowel$ word$*

Now you will learn about *arrays* and *array variables*. An array is a set, or collection, of array variables. Each individual array variable in an array is called an *element* of the array. An array has a name. An array variable consists of the name of the array followed by a *subscript*.

Array Variables

An array variable consists of a variable name followed by a subscript enclosed in parentheses. All array variables in an array have the same variable name, which is also the name of the entire array. An array variable can be numeric or string.

For example:

Numeric array variables: *Price(5)   temperature!(3)*

String array variables: *StateName$(50)   word$(23)*

Note that a string array variable name ends in a dollar sign. A numeric array variable name may end in a numeric type designator (%, !, or #), which designates the array as an integer array, single precision array, or double precision array. These numeric type designators were introduced and explained in Chapter 4.

The *subscript* of an array variable is the number enclosed in parentheses following the variable name, as shown on the next page.

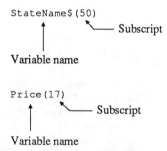

A subscript can be a number, a numeric variable, or a numeric expression consisting of any legal combination of numbers, numeric variables, and numeric functions, as in the following:

- as a number: *temperature!(7)*.

- as a numeric variable: *word$(WordNumber%)*.

- as a numeric expression: *number*(INT(49 * RND) + 1).

Subscripts must be integers. If you use a subscript that is not an integer, GW-BASIC will round it to the nearest integer.

Remember: An array variable consists of these parts, in this order:

	Numeric	*String*
1. a variable name:	*number*	*word$*
2. left parenthesis:	*number(*	*word$(*
3. a numeric subscript:	*number(3*	*word$(3*
4. right parenthesis:	*number(3)*	*word$(3)*

Array Dimensions

An array is a list of array variables. A numeric array with four array variables follows. Note that the subscripts begin with 0, followed by 1, 2, and 3.

```
                                   DaysInMonth%(0)
                                   DaysInMonth%(1)
                                   DaysInMonth%(2)
                                   DaysInMonth%(3)
                                   DaysInMonth%(4)
                                   DaysInMonth%(5)
                                   DaysInMonth%(6)
              DaysInMonth%()       DaysInMonth%(7)
                                   DaysInMonth%(8)
                                   DaysInMonth%(9)
                                   DaysInMonth%(10)
                                   DaysInMonth%(11)
                                   DaysInMonth%(12)
```

FIGURE 9-1   The array *DaysInMonth%( )*

```
Price(0)      Price(1)      Price(2)      Price(3)
```

A string array with five array variables is shown next. The subscripts are 0, 1, 2, 3, and 4.

```
word$(0)      word$(1)      word$(2)      word$(3)      word$(4)
```

Unless you tell it otherwise, GW-BASIC assumes that an array has 11 elements, with subscripts 0 through 10. These are GW-BASIC's default values for the smallest (0) up to the largest (10) subscripts.

THE DIM STATEMENT   You can use the DIM statement to specify a maximum subscript different from 10. The keyword DIM is a shortened form of the word "dimension." In this book, all programs that use arrays will contain a DIM statement. Some examples of DIM statements are

```
DIM temperature!(7)
DIM DaysInMonth%(12)
DIM AcctBalance#(1000)
DIM StateName$(50)
```

The statement DIM *temperature!(7)* defines a single precision numeric array of eight elements, *temperature!(0)* through *temperature!(7)*. Zero (0) is the smallest subscript; 7 is the largest subscript.

The statement DIM *DaysInMonth%(12)* defines an integer array of 13 elements, *DaysInMonth%(0)* through *DaysInMonth%(12)*. Elements 1 through 12 might be the number of days in the 12 months, January through December.

The statement DIM *AcctBalance#(1000)* defines a double precision numeric array of 1001 elements; that is, *AcctBalance#(0)* through *AcctBalance#(1000)*.

In this book, an array name followed by an empty set of parentheses is used to refer to an entire array. This convention is used so you can easily distinguish an array from a simple, nonsubscripted variable or a single array variable, as demonstrated here.

Simple variables:	*Price*	*word$*
Single array variables:	*Price(6)*	*word$(3)*
Entire array:	*Price( )*	*word$( )*

For example, *DaysInMonth%()* is an integer array defined by the following DIM statement:

```
DIM DaysInMonth%(12)
```

DaysInMonth%(), then, refers to the entire array consisting of 13 elements, as shown in Figure 9-1. The array *temperature!()* is a single precision array defined by this DIM statement:

```
DIM temperature!(7)
```

Figure 9-2 shows the array *temperature!()*, defined by this DIM statement.

The DIM statement reserves memory space for the specified number of array elements, and clears this space to zeros for numeric arrays, or to null strings for string arrays. For example:

• The statement

  DIM *temperature!(7)*

allocates memory space for 8 single precision array variables, *temperature!(0)* through *temperature!(7)*. A single precision number requires 4 bytes of memory. Therefore, 32 bytes are reserved.

- The statement

DIM *DaysInMonth%(12)*

allocates memory space for 13 integer array variables, from *DaysInMonth%(0)* through *DaysInMonth%(12)*. An integer requires 2 bytes of memory. Therefore, 26 bytes are reserved.

- The statement

DIM *AcctBalance#(1000)*

allocates memory space for 1001 double precision array variables, *AcctBalance#(0)* through *AcctBalance#(1000)*. A double precison number requires 8 bytes of memory. Therefore, 8008 bytes are reserved.

Strings are variable in length, from no bytes (the null string) to a maximum of 255 bytes. The DIM statement allocates a 3-byte string *pointer* for each array variable. Additional memory space is allocated later when string array variables are assigned values.

```
                              temperature!(0)
                              temperature!(1)
                              temperature!(2)
temperature!()                temperature!(3)
                              temperature!(4)
                              temperature!(5)
                              temperature!(6)
                              temperature!(7)
```

FIGURE 9-2   The array *temperature!( )*

```
1 REM ** High, Low, and Average Temperature for One Week **
2 ' GW-BASIC Made Easy, Chapter 9.  File: GWME0901.BAS

100 REM ** Define all variables as integer variables **
110 ' Use !, #, and $ to designate other variable types
120 DEFINT A-Z

200 REM ** Dimension single precision array, temperature!() **
210 DIM temperature!(7)

300 REM ** Setup **
310 SCREEN 0: CLS : KEY OFF

400 REM ** Main program **
410 CLS : GOSUB 1010        'Get temperature data
420 GOSUB 2010              'Find high temperature
430 GOSUB 3010              'Find low temperature
440 GOSUB 4010              'Compute average temperature
450 PRINT : GOSUB 5010      'Print the results
460 PRINT : END             'End of main program

1000 REM ** SUBROUTINE: Get temperature data for one week **
1010 PRINT "Enter temperature data for each day of the week."
1020 PRINT
1030 INPUT "Sunday    "; temperature!(1)
1040 INPUT "Monday    "; temperature!(2)
1050 INPUT "Tuesday   "; temperature!(3)
1060 INPUT "Wednesday"; temperature!(4)
1070 INPUT "Thursday "; temperature!(5)
1080 INPUT "Friday    "; temperature!(6)
1090 INPUT "Saturday "; temperature!(7)
1100 RETURN

2000 REM ** SUBROUTINE: Find high temperature **
2010 High! = temperature!(1)
2020 FOR k = 2 TO 7
2030   IF temperature!(k) > High! THEN High! = temperature!(k)
2040 NEXT k
2050 RETURN
```

PROGRAM GWME0901   High, Low, and Average Temperature for One Week

```
3000 REM ** SUBROUTINE: Find low temperature **
3010 Low! = temperature!(1)
3020 FOR k = 2 TO 7
3030    IF temperature!(k) < Low! THEN Low! = temperature!(k)
3040 NEXT k
3050 RETURN

4000 REM ** SUBROUTINE: Compute average temperature **
4010 Total! = 0
4020 FOR k = 1 TO 7
4030    Total! = Total! + temperature!(k)
4040 NEXT k
4050 Average! = Total! / 7
4060 RETURN

5000 REM ** SUBROUTINE: Print high, low, average temperature **
5010 PRINT "High:    "; High!
5020 PRINT "Low:     "; Low!
5030 PRINT "Average:"; Average!
5040 RETURN
```

PROGRAM GWME0901   High, Low, and Average Temperature for One Week
                         (*continued*)

PROGRAMMING WITH ARRAYS

Arrays add a new dimension to your ability to make the computer do what you want it to do, the way you want it done. You can use arrays to write programs that would be impractical, or even impossible, to write without arrays.

High, Low, and Average Temperature for One Week

Program GWME0901 (High, Low, and Average Temperature for One Week) uses the array *temperature!( )* to store the temperatures for each of the seven days of the week, Sunday through Saturday. The values of *temperature!(1)* through *temperature!(7)* are entered from the keyboard;

```
Enter the temperature for each day of the week.

Sunday    ? 1
Monday    ? 2
Tuesday   ? 3
Wednesday? 4
Thursday  ? 5
Friday    ? 6
Saturday  ? 7

High:     7
Low:      1
Average:  4
```

FIGURE 9-3   Test run of High, Low, and Average Temperature Program

then the program computes and prints the high temperature, low temperature, and average temperature for the week. Array element *temperature!(0)* is not used.

A test run of Program GWME0901 is shown in Figure 9-3. The temperatures entered in this run are very low, so that the program can be verified easily. As you will see if you check the printed results yourself, the

```
Enter the temperature for each day of the week.

Sunday    ? 3
Monday    ? 6
Tuesday   ? 1
Wednesday? 5
Thursday  ? 7
Friday    ? 2
Saturday  ? 4

High:     7
Low:      1
Average:  4
```

FIGURE 9-4   Second test run of High, Low, and Average Temperature Program

```
Enter the temperature for each day of the week.

Sunday    ? 68
Monday    ? 67
Tuesday   ? 70
Wednesday? 72
Thursday  ? 75
Friday    ? 80
Saturday  ? 77


High:      80
Low:       67
Average: 72.71429
```

FIGURE 9-5   Practical run of High, Low, and Average Temperature Program

answers are correct. A second test of the program in Figure 9-4 shows another run of the program with the same numbers, but in scrambled order; again the results were correct. A more realistic application of this program is shown in the sample run in Figure 9-5; the temperatures entered in this run were taken at the same time each day.

Program GWME0901 introduces a new keyword, DEFINT. It appears in block 100 of the program, shown here:

```
100 REM ** Define all variables as integer variables **
110 ' Use !, #, and $ to designate other variable types
120 DEFINT A-Z
```

The statement DEFINT A-Z tells the computer to regard all variables beginning with the letters *A* to *Z* as integer variables. Since uppercase and lowercase letters are considered by the program to be the same (in variable names), and since all variables must begin with a letter, this statement defines all numeric variables as integers. Many programmers use this convention, because integers take the least amount of memory and operate the fastest. You can use the variable type designators ! and # to specify individual numeric variable names as other than integer (! for single precision and # for double precision variables).

The next block in the program (block 200) defines the array *temperature!()* as a single precision array with seven elements, or array variables.

```
200 REM ** Dimension single precision array, temperature!() **
210 DIM temperature!(7)
```

The rest of the program consists of a setup block, a main program, and five subroutines. The main program is shown here:

```
400 REM ** Main program **
410 CLS : GOSUB 1010          'Get temperature data
420 GOSUB 2010               'Find high temperature
430 GOSUB 3010               'Find low temperature
440 GOSUB 4010               'Compute average temperature
450 PRINT : GOSUB 5010       'Print the results
460 PRINT : END              'End of main program
```

Line 410 clears the screen and calls the subroutine that acquires the values of the array variables, *temperature!(1)* through *temperature!(7)*. The subroutine is shown next:

```
1000 REM ** SUBROUTINE: Get temperature data for one week **
1010 PRINT "Enter temperature data for each day of the week."
1020 PRINT
1030 INPUT "Sunday    "; temperature!(1)
1040 INPUT "Monday    "; temperature!(2)
1050 INPUT "Tuesday   "; temperature!(3)
1060 INPUT "Wednesday"; temperature!(4)
1070 INPUT "Thursday "; temperature!(5)
1080 INPUT "Friday    "; temperature!(6)
1090 INPUT "Saturday "; temperature!(7)
1100 RETURN
```

The values of *temperature!(1)* through *temperature!(7)* entered in the third sample run of GWME0901 (Figure 9-5) are shown in Table 9-1. After acquiring the values of *temperature!(1)* through *temperature!(7)*, the subroutine executes line 1100, which returns control to the main program.

Next, line 420 calls the subroutine to find the highest temperature. It is shown here:

```
2000 REM ** SUBROUTINE: Find high temperature **
2010 High! = temperature!(1)
2020 FOR k = 2 TO 7
2030    IF temperature!(k) > High! THEN High! = temperature!(k)
2040 NEXT k
2050 RETURN
```

Array variable	Value
temperature!(1)	68
temperature!(2)	67
temperature!(3)	70
temperature!(4)	72
temperature!(5)	75
temperature!(6)	80
temperature!(7)	77

TABLE 9-1   Values of Array Variables, Third Sample Run

The value of *High!* is set equal to the first number in the array, the value of *temperature!(1)*. The FOR...NEXT loop then searches the rest of the array (subscripts 2 through 7). If any value in the array is higher than the value of *High!*, it is assigned as the new value of *High!*.

A similar method is used in the subroutine to find the lowest temperature and assign it as the value of *Low!*, as follows:

```
3000 REM ** SUBROUTINE: Find low temperature **
3010 Low! = temperature!(1)
3020 FOR k = 2 TO 7
3030   IF temperature!(k) < Low! THEN Low! = temperature!(k)
3040 NEXT k
3050 RETURN
```

In the next subroutine, called in line 4010, a FOR...NEXT loop uses the variable *Total!* to add up the week's temperatures. *Total!* is first set to zero. Each value in *temperature!()* is then added to *Total!*, one at a time, as the value of *k* goes from 1 to 7. *Total!* is then divided by seven (the number of elements) to obtain the average (*Average!*) temperature.

```
4000 REM ** SUBROUTINE: Compute average temperature **
4010 Total! = 0
4020 FOR k = 1 TO 7
4030   Total! = Total! + temperature!(k)
4040 NEXT k
4050 Average! = Total! / 7
4060 RETURN
```

Remember: The variable *k,* used in each of the FOR...NEXT loops in this program, is an integer variable. The DEFINT statement in block 100 of the program defines all variables as integers, unless designated otherwise.

The computational part of the program is now complete. All that is left to do is to print the results. This is done by the following subroutine, which is called by line 450 of the main program.

```
5000 REM ** SUBROUTINE: Print high, low, average temperature **
5010 PRINT "High:    "; High!
5020 PRINT "Low:     "; Low!
5030 PRINT "Average:"; Average!
5040 RETURN
```

In the third sample run (Figure 9-5), the value of *Average!* is 72.71429. You can use a PRINT USING statement to round this value to the nearest degree or nearest tenth of a degree. To round *Average!* to the nearest degree, use a statement like this:

```
PRINT "Average:"; : PRINT USING "###"; Average!
```

To round *Average!* to the nearest tenth of a degree, use this PRINT USING statement:

```
PRINT "Average"; : PRINT USING "###.#"; Average!
```

A More General High, Low, and Average Temperature Program

Program GWME0901 is fine if you have exactly one week's worth of temperatures to process. But what if you want to use temperatures for ten days, or a month, or even a year? Program GWME0902 (High, Low, and Average Temperature) allows you to enter up to 1000 temperatures, or even more if you change the DIM statement in line 210. When you run the program, you first enter the number of temperatures you want to process, and then enter the temperatures. Two sample runs of Program GWME0902 are shown in Figure 9-6 and Figure 9-7.

You can edit GWME0901 to obtain GWME0902. Change the name of the program in line 1, and change the filename in line 2. Block 100 remains

```
1 REM ** High, Low, and Average Temperature **
2 ' GW-BASIC Made Easy, Chapter 9.  File: GWME0902.BAS

100 REM ** Define all variables as integer variables **
110 ' Use !, #, and $ to designate other variable types
120 DEFINT A-Z

200 REM ** Dimension single precision array, temperature!() **
210 DIM temperature!(1000)

300 REM ** Setup **
310 SCREEN 0: CLS : KEY OFF

400 REM ** Get number of temperatures to process **
410 CLS
420 PRINT "High, Low, and Average Temperature Program"
430 PRINT
440 INPUT "How many temperatures"; NmbrOfElements
450 PRINT

500 REM ** Main program **
510 CLS : GOSUB 1010          'Get temperature data
520 GOSUB 2010                'Find high temperature
530 GOSUB 3010                'Find low temperature
540 GOSUB 4010                'Compute average temperature
550 PRINT : GOSUB 5010        'Print the results
560 PRINT : END               'End of main program

1000 REM ** SUBROUTINE: Get temperature data **
1010 PRINT "Enter the temperatures:"
1020 PRINT
1030 FOR k = 1 TO NmbrOfElements
1040   PRINT "Temperature #"; k; : INPUT temperature!(k)
1050 NEXT k
1060 RETURN

2000 REM ** SUBROUTINE: Find high temperature **
2010 High! = temperature!(1)
2020 FOR k = 2 TO NmbrOfElements
2030   IF temperature!(k) > High! THEN High! = temperature!(k)
2040 NEXT k
2050 RETURN
```

PROGRAM GWME0902   High, Low, and Average Temperature

```
3000 REM ** SUBROUTINE: Find low temperature **
3010 Low! = temperature!(1)
3020 FOR k = 2 TO NmbrOfElements
3030   IF temperature!(k) < Low! THEN Low! = temperature!(k)
3040 NEXT k
3050 RETURN

4000 REM ** SUBROUTINE: Compute average temperature **
4010 Total! = 0
4020 FOR k = 1 TO NmbrOfElements
4030   Total! = Total! + temperature!(k)
4040 NEXT k
4050 Average! = Total! / NmbrOfElements
4060 RETURN

5000 REM ** SUBROUTINE: Print high, low, average temperature **
5010 PRINT "High:   "; High!
5020 PRINT "Low:    "; Low!
5030 PRINT "Average:"; Average!
5040 RETURN
```

PROGRAM GWME0902   High, Low, and Average Temperature (*continued*)

unchanged. Change line 210 so that the program can process up to 1000 temperatures, as shown here:

```
200 REM ** Dimension single precision array, temperature!() **
210 DIM temperature!(1000)
```

The setup block (block 300) remains unchanged. The main program is then renumbered as lines 500 through 560 to make room for block 400, shown here:

```
400 REM ** Get number of temperatures to process **
410 CLS
420 PRINT "High, Low, and Average Temperature Program"
430 PRINT
440 INPUT "How many temperatures"; NmbrOfElements
450 PRINT
```

```
High, Low, and Average Temperature Program

How many temperatures? 7

Enter the temperatures:

Temperature # 1 ? 68
Temperature # 2 ? 67
Temperature # 3 ? 70
Temperature # 4 ? 72
Temperature # 5 ? 75
Temperature # 6 ? 80
Temperature # 7 ? 77

High:    80
Low:     67
Average: 72.71429
```

FIGURE 9-6   Sample run of High, Low, and Average Temperature Program

When you run the program, you will enter the value of *NmbrOfElements*, which, because of the DEFINT A-Z statement in line 120, is an integer variable. The variable *NmbrOfElements* appears in four of the remodeled subroutines.

Except for being renumbered, the main program is the same as it appeared in Program GWME0901. The subroutines that begin in lines 1000, 2000, 3000, and 4000 are changed only slightly. For example, here is the subroutine that begins in line 1000. Note that only line 1030 is different from the subroutine in Program GWME0901. Instead of 7, the variable *NmbrOfElements* is used in the FOR statement.

```
1000 REM ** SUBROUTINE:  Get temperature data **
1010 PRINT "Enter the temperatures:"
1020 PRINT
1030 FOR k = 1 TO NmbrOfElements
1040   PRINT "Temperature #"; k; : INPUT temperature!(k)
1050 NEXT k
1060 RETURN
```

```
High, Low, and Average Temperature Program

How many temperatures? 12

Enter the temperatures:

Temperature # 1 ? 36
Temperature # 2 ? 38
Temperature # 3 ? 43
Temperature # 4 ? 43
Temperature # 5 ? 39
Temperature # 6 ? 37
Temperature # 7 ? 34
Temperature # 8 ? 27
Temperature # 9 ? 25
Temperature # 10 ? 22
Temperature # 11 ? 23
Temperature # 12 ? 19


High:    43
Low:     19
Average: 32.16667
```

FIGURE 9-7   Second sample of High, Low, and Average Temperature Program

A similar change is made in line 2020 of the subroutine to find the high temperature, and in line 3030 of the subroutine to find the low temperature.

In the subroutine to compute the average temperature, two lines (4020 and 4050) are changed, as shown here:

```
4000 REM ** SUBROUTINE: Compute average temperature **
4010 Total! = 0
4020 FOR k = 1 TO NmbrOfElements
4030    Total! = Total! + temperature!(k)
4040 NEXT k
4050 Average! = Total! / NmbrOfElements
4060 RETURN
```

The subroutine to print the final results (block 5000) is the same as in Program GWME0901. As you can see, you can save lots of time by editing GWME0901 to obtain GWME0902.

Item	Quantity	Price Each	Line Total
Sleeping bag	1	89.95	89.95
Stuff bags	3	4.50	13.50
Stove	1	21.99	21.99
Fuel cartridges	6	1.75	10.50
Waterproof matches, boxes	4	.35	1.40
Total Amount (dot product)			137.34

TABLE 9-2   An Order for Camping Equipment

In Program GWME0901, the array *temperature!()* has eight elements, *temperature!(0)* through *temperature!(7)*. The program actually uses seven elements, the ones with subscripts 1 through 7. In Program GWME0902, the array *temperature!()* has 1001 elements, *temperature!(0)* through *temperature!(1000)*. During a run, the number of elements actually used is the value of *NmbrOfElements* that you enter at the beginning of the run. You can see this value used in the FOR...NEXT loops, and in the computation of the value of *Average!*. Compare these lines in both programs.

Program GWME0901:
```
1030 FOR k = 1 TO 7
2020 FOR k = 1 TO 7
3020 FOR k = 1 TO 7
4020 FOR k = 1 TO 7
4050 Average! = Total! / 7
```

Program GWME0902:
```
1030 FOR k = 1 TO NmbrOfElements
2020 FOR k = 1 TO NmbrOfElements
3020 FOR k = 1 TO NmbrOfElements
4020 FOR k = 1 TO NmbrOfElements
4050 Average! = Total! / NmbrOfElements
```

Dot Product of Two Arrays

The *dot product* of two arrays is the sum of the product of corresponding elements of the two arrays. For example, suppose the arrays *a( )* and *b( )* each consist of three elements, as follows.

array *a( )*:   *a(1)*   *a(2)*   *a(3)*

array *b( )*:   *b(1)*   *b(2)*   *b(3)*

The dot product of *a( )* and *b( )* is shown here:

```
DotProduct = a(1) * b(1) + a(2) * b(2) + a(3) * b(3)
```

The term *dot product* is borrowed from mathematics. A familiar application of the dot product is filling out an order form or an invoice. For example, an order for some camping equipment is shown in Table 9-2. The order has five line items. For each line, multiply the Quantity times the Price Each to obtain the Line Total. Add the five Line Totals to get the Total Amount of the order. The Total Amount of the order is the dot product.

Program GWME0903 (Dot Product of Two Arrays) computes and prints the dot product of two arrays called *Qty!()* and *Price#()*. The program does not print the individual line totals. In block 100, a DEFINT A-Z statement defines all variables to be integers, unless designated otherwise. Designated variables appear in the program, as follows:

Qty!( )	is a single precision array
Price#( )	is a double precision array
DotProduct#	is a double precision variable

In the subroutine to get data for the two arrays (block 1000), the values of array variables are acquired by means of the following FOR...NEXT loop.

```
1030 FOR k = 1 TO NumbrOfElements
1040    PRINT "Quantity   #"; k; : INPUT Qty!(k)
1050    PRINT "Price each #"; k; : INPUT Price#(k)
1060    PRINT
1070 NEXT k
```

The array values are entered in the order *Qty!(1)* and *Price#(1)*, *Qty!(2)* and *Price#(2)*, *Qty!(3)* and *Price#(3)*, and so on, as *k* increases from 1 to the value of *NmbrOfElements*.

The dot product is computed by another subroutine (block 2000). *DotProduct#* is first set to 0. Then, within a FOR...NEXT loop, the corresponding elements of *Qty!()* and *Price#()* are multiplied and added to *DotProduct#*.

```
1 REM ** Dot Product of Two Arrays **
2 ' GW-BASIC Made Easy, Chapter 9.  File: GWME0903.BAS

100 REM ** Define all variables as integer variables **
110 ' Use !, #, and $ to designate other variable types
120 DEFINT A-Z

200 REM ** Dimension arrays, Qty!() and Price#() **
210 DIM Qty!(100), Price#(100)

300 REM ** Setup **
310 SCREEN 0: CLS : KEY OFF

400 REM ** Get number of array elements **
410 CLS : PRINT "Dot product of arrays, Qty!() and Price#()"
420 PRINT : INPUT "How many line items"; NmbrOfElements

500 REM ** Main program **
510 PRINT : GOSUB 1010          'Get data for Qty!() & Price#()
520 GOSUB 2010                  'Compute dot product
530 GOSUB 3010                  'Print dot product
540 PRINT : END                 'End of main program

1000 REM ** SUBROUTINE: Get data for Qty!() & Price#()
1010 PRINT "Please enter data as requested."
1020 PRINT
1030 FOR k = 1 TO NmbrOfElements
1040   PRINT "Quantity  #"; k; : INPUT Qty!(k)
1050   PRINT "Price each #"; k; : INPUT Price#(k)
1060   PRINT
1070 NEXT k
1080 RETURN

2000 REM ** SUBROUTINE: Compute dot product, Qty!() & Price#() **
2010 DotProduct# = 0
2020 FOR k = 1 TO NmbrOfElements
2030   DotProduct# = DotProduct# + Qty!(k) * Price#(k)
2040 NEXT k
2050 RETURN

3000 REM ** SUBROUTINE: Print dot product Qty!() & Price#() **
3010 PRINT "The dot product is"; DotProduct#
3020 RETURN
```

PROGRAM GWME0903   Dot Product of Two Arrays

```
2000 REM ** SUBROUTINE: Compute dot product, Qty!() & Price#() **
2010 DotProduct# = 0
2020 FOR k = 1 TO NmbrOfElements
2030   DotProduct# = DotProduct# + Qty!(k) * Price#(k)
2040 NEXT k
2050 RETURN
```

Two test runs are shown in Figure 9-8. Notice that the Line Item totals are not printed by this program, although they are computed. Small quantities

---

```
Dot product of arrays, Qty!() and Price#()

How many line items? 3

Please enter data as requested.

Quantity   # 1 ? 1
Price each # 1 ? 1

Quantity   # 2 ? 1
Price each # 2 ? 2

Quantity   # 3 ? 1
Price each # 3 ? 3

The dot product is 6

Dot product of arrays, Qty!() and Price#()

How many line items? 3

Please enter data as requested.

Quantity   # 1 ? 1
Price each # 1 ? 1

Quantity   # 2 ? 2
Price each # 2 ? 1

Quantity   # 3 ? 3
Price each # 3 ? 1

The dot product is 6
```

FIGURE 9-8 Sample runs of Dot Product Program

and prices were chosen for these examples to let you verify easily that the program is running correctly. Run the program yourself using the values in Table 9-2.

The subroutine to print the dot product (block 3000) is very short. Try your hand at modifying it so that the results are printed rounded to dollars and cents (use PRINT USING). You might also want to compute and add the sales tax, and perhaps shipping charges. Tailor the program to your requirements.

Dot Product with Line Item Printout

Program GWME0904 (Dot Product with Line Item Printout) is an expanded version of Program GWME0903. It allows you to enter the name of each item, as well as the quantity and price. The item names are stored in the string array *ItemName$()*. After all information has been entered, the computer prints "Press a key," and then waits. After you press a key, each line item and line total is printed, followed by the grand total, or dot product.

```
1 REM ** Dot Product with Line Item Printout **
2 ' GW-BASIC Made Easy, Chapter 9.  File: GWME0904.BAS

100 REM ** Define all variables as integer variables **
110 ' Use !, #, and $ to designate other variable types
120 DEFINT A-Z

200 REM ** Dimension arrays ItemName$(), Qty!(), and Price#() **
210 DIM ItemName$(100), Qty!(100), Price#(100)

300 REM ** Setup **
310 SCREEN 0: CLS : KEY OFF

400 REM ** Get number of array elements **
410 CLS : PRINT "Dot product of arrays, Qty!() and Price#()"
420 PRINT : INPUT "How many line items?"; NmbrOfElements
```

PROGRAM GWME0904   Dot Product with Line Item Printout

```
500 REM ** Main program **
510 PRINT : GOSUB 1010          'Get data for Qty!() & Price#()
520 PRINT "Press a key"
530 akey$ = INPUT$(1)           'Wait for a key press
540 CLS : GOSUB 2010            'Print headings
550 PRINT : GOSUB 3010          'Print lines, compute dot product
560 PRINT : GOSUB 4010          'Print dot product
570 PRINT :END                  'End of main program

1000 REM ** SUBROUTINE: Get data for Qty!() & Price#()
1010 PRINT "Please enter data as requested."
1020 PRINT
1030 FOR k = 1 TO NmbrOfElements
1040    PRINT "Item name  #"; k; : LINE INPUT "? "; ItemName$(k)
1050    PRINT "Quantity   #"; k; : INPUT Qty!(k)
1060    PRINT "Price each #"; k; : INPUT Price#(k)
1070    PRINT
1080 NEXT k
1090 RETURN

2000 REM ** SUBROUTINE: Print headings **
2010 PRINT "Item name"; TAB(30); "Quantity";
2020 PRINT TAB(44); "Price each"; TAB(64); "Line total"
2030 PRINT
2040 RETURN

3000 REM ** SUBROUTINE: Print line data & compute dot product **
3010 DotProduct# = 0
3020 FOR k = 1 TO NmbrOfElements
3030    LineTotal# = Qty!(k) * Price#(k)
3040    DotProduct# = DotProduct# + LineTotal#
3050    PRINT LEFT$(ItemName$(k), 20);
3060    PRINT TAB(30); : PRINT USING "#######,"; Qty!(k);
3070    PRINT TAB(40); : PRINT USING "##########,.##"; Price#(k);
3080    PRINT TAB(60); : PRINT USING "##########,.##"; LineTotal#
3090 NEXT k
3100 RETURN

4000 REM ** SUBROUTINE: Print dot product (total amount) **
4010 PRINT TAB(27); "Total amount (dot product):"; TAB(60);
4020 PRINT USING "##########,.##"; DotProduct#
4030 RETURN
```

PROGRAM GWME0904 *Dot Product with Line Item Printout (continued)*

```
Please enter data as requested.

Item name   # 1 ? sleeping bag
Quantity    # 1 ? 1
Price each  # 1 ? 89.95

Item name   # 2 ? stuff bags
Quantity    # 2 ? 3
Price each  # 2 ? 4.50

Item name   # 3 ? stove
Quantity    # 3 ? 1
Price each  # 3 ? 21.99

Item name   # 4 ? fuel cartridges
Quantity    # 4 ? 6
Price each  # 4 ? 1.75

Item name   # 5 ? waterproof matches, boxes
Quantity    # 5 ? 4
Price each  # 5 ? .35

Press a key
```

FIGURE 9-9   Data entry of Dot Product with Line Items Program

Figure 9-9 shows the appearance of the screen during the data entry portion of a run. In this example, five items are entered, and some information has scrolled off the top of the screen. This scrolling does not affect the data stored in each array—all data entered for *ItemName$(), Qty!(),* and *Price#()* are retained, regardless of any screen scrolling. Figure 9-10 shows the results printed following a key press.

Note that part of the name of the fifth item name was not printed. The string function LEFT$ was used in line 3050 to print only the first 20 characters of *ItemName$(k),* thus truncating any element in *ItemName$()* longer than 20 characters. This is done so that long names like the one entered for *ItemName$(5)* do not encroach on the space reserved for the value of *Qty!(k),* which is printed under the heading "Quantity."

Item name	Quantity	Price Each	Line Total
sleeping bag	1	89.95	89.95
stuff bags	3	4.50	13.50
stove	1	21.99	21.99
fuel cartridges	6	1.75	10.50
waterproof matches	4	0.35	1.40
	Total Amount (dot product):		137.34

FIGURE 9-10 Printout of Dot Product with Line Items Program

If you enter more than 16 sets of data, part of the final printout will scroll off the screen. Therefore, rewrite the printout subroutines (blocks 3000 and 4000) so that the results are printed to the printer instead of to the screen.

REARRANGING AN ARRAY

You can use arrays to store lists of information and perform calculations, as in the preceding programs. You can also use arrays to rearrange information. For example, you can use arrays to sort lists of numbers or names into some desired sequence, such as least-to-greatest, or greatest-to-least. You can even use arrays to scramble information into random patterns.

Scramble an Array of Numbers

Sometimes, especially when creating computer simulations or games, you may want to scramble a list, or array, of numbers. For example, you can use an array of numbers 1 to 52 to represent the 52 cards in a deck of cards, and then "shuffle the deck" by scrambling the array. You can use Program GWME0905 (Scramble an Array of Numbers) to scramble a list of integers from 1 to *NmbrOfElements*, where you enter the value of *NmbrOfElements*.

```
1 REM ** Scramble an Array of Numbers **
2 ' GW-BASIC Made Easy, Chapter 9.  File: GWME0905.BAS

100 REM ** Setup **
110 SCREEN 0: CLS : KEY OFF  'Set up the screen
120 DEFINT A-Z              'Nondesignated variables = integer
130 DIM array(100)          'Dimension array
140 RANDOMIZE TIMER         'Start random numbers with TIMER

200 REM ** Get number of numbers to scramble **
210 CLS : PRINT "Scramble an array of numbers"
220 PRINT
230 INPUT "How many numbers shall I scramble?"; NmbrOfElements
240 PRINT

300 REM ** Main program **
310 GOSUB 1010                            'Generate numbers
320 PRINT "Here are the numbers:"
330 GOSUB 2010                            'Print numbers
340 GOSUB 3010                            'Scramble numbers
350 PRINT "Here are the scrambled numbers:"
360 GOSUB 2010                            'Print numbers
370 PRINT : END                           'End main program

1000 REM ** SUBROUTINE: Generate the unscrambled array **
1010 FOR k = 1 TO NmbrOfElements
1020    array(k) = k
1030 NEXT k
1040 RETURN

2000 REM ** SUBROUTINE: Print the array **
2010 PRINT
2020 FOR k = 1 TO NmbrOfElements
2030    PRINT array(k),          'Comma gives 5 numbers per line
2040 NEXT k
2050 PRINT : PRINT
2060 RETURN

3000 REM ** SUBROUTINE: Scramble the array **
3010 FOR k = 1 TO NmbrOfElements
3020    RandomSubscript = INT(NmbrOfElements * RND) + 1
3030    SWAP array(k), array(RandomSubscript)
3040 NEXT k
3050 RETURN
```

PROGRAM GWME0905   Scramble an Array of Numbers

```
Scramble an array of numbers

How many numbers shall I scramble? 7

Here are the numbers:

1                2                3                4                5
6                7

Here are the scrambled numbers:

5                4                1                6                2
7                3
```

FIGURE 9-11   Screen appearance of Scramble an Array Program

Figure 9-11 shows a sample run for a list of seven numbers, 1 through 7. Since there are 5040 different ways to arrange the integers 1 through 7, you are likely to see a different arrangement when you run the program and ask for seven numbers.

The original, unscrambled array is generated by assigning 1 to *array(1)*, 2 to *array(2)*, 3 to *array(3)*, and so on. If *NmbrOfElements* is 7, the unscrambled array will contain the values shown in Table 9-3. Since the variable name *array* does not have a numeric type designation, it is automatically an integer variable name because of the DEFINT A-Z statement in line 120. Therefore, *array( )* is an integer array.

Array Element	Value
array(1)	1
array(2)	2
array(3)	3
array(4)	4
array(5)	5
array(6)	6
array(7)	7

TABLE 9-3   Values of Elements in Unscrambled Array

The array is scrambled by the subroutine which follows. Within the FOR...NEXT loop, the value of each array element is exchanged, or swapped, for the value of a randomly selected array element.

```
3000 REM ** SUBROUTINE: Scramble the array **
3010 FOR k = 1 TO NmbrOfElements
3020   RandomSubscript = INT(NmbrOfElements * RND) + 1
3030   SWAP array(k), array(RandomSubscript)
3040 NEXT k
3050 RETURN
```

A value is assigned to *RandomSubscript*, and then the value of *array(1)* is exchanged for the value of *array(RandomSubscript)*. A new value is then assigned to *RandomSubscript*, and the value of *array(2)* is exchanged for the value of *array(RandomSubscript)*. This sequence continues until the value of *array(NmbrOfElements)* has been exchanged for the value of *array(RandomSubscript)*.

The statement

RandomSubscript = INT(NmbrOfElements * RND) + 1

tells the computer to generate a random integer in the range 1 to *NmbrOfElements*, and assign it as the value of *RandomSubscript*. A SWAP statement will then exchange the value of *array(k)* and the value of *array(RandomSubscript)*.

The statement

SWAP array(k), array(RandomSubscript)

tells the computer to exchange the values of *array(k)* and *array(RandomSubscript)*.

```
SWAP array(k),  array(RandomSubscript)
```

Exchange the values of these variables

```
1 REM ** Scramble and Sort an Array of Numbers **
2 ' GW-BASIC Made Easy, Chapter 9.  File: GWME0906.BAS

100 REM ** Setup **
110 SCREEN 0: CLS : KEY OFF   'Set up the screen
120 DEFINT A-Z                'Nondesignated variables = integer
130 DIM array(100)            'Dimension array
140 RANDOMIZE TIMER           'Start random numbers with TIMER

200 REM ** Get number of numbers to scramble **
210 CLS : PRINT "Scramble and Sort an array of numbers"
220 PRINT
230 INPUT "How many numbers shall I scramble?"; NmbrOfElements
240 PRINT

300 REM ** Main program **
310 GOSUB 1010                           'Generate numbers
320 GOSUB 3010                           'Scramble numbers
330 PRINT "Here are the scrambled numbers:"
340 GOSUB 2010                           'Print numbers
350 GOSUB 4010                           'Sort the numbers
360 PRINT "Here are the sorted numbers:"
370 GOSUB 2010                           'Print numbers
380 PRINT : END                          'End main program

1000 REM ** SUBROUTINE: Generate the unscrambled array **
1010 FOR k = 1 TO NmbrOfElements
1020    array(k) = k
1030 NEXT k
1040 RETURN

2000 REM ** SUBROUTINE: Print the array **
2010 PRINT
2020 FOR k = 1 TO NmbrOfElements
2030    PRINT array(k),              'Comma gives 5 numbers per line
2040 NEXT k
2050 PRINT : PRINT
2060 RETURN
```

PROGRAM GWME0906   Scramble and Sort an Array of Numbers

```
3000 REM ** SUBROUTINE: Scramble the array **
3010 FOR k = 1 TO NmbrOfElements
3020   RandomSubscript = INT(NmbrOfElements * RND) + 1
3030   SWAP array(k), array(RandomSubscript)
3040 NEXT k
3050 RETURN


4000 REM ** SUBROUTINE: Sort the array of numbers **
4010 FOR j = 1 TO NmbrOfElements - 1
4020   FOR k = j + 1 TO NmbrOfElements
4030     IF array(k) < array(j) THEN SWAP array(k), array(j)
4040   NEXT k
4050 NEXT j
4060 RETURN
```

PROGRAM GWME0906   Scramble and Sort an Array of Numbers (*continued*)

Scramble and Sort an Array of Numbers

The converse of scrambling an array is sorting an array. Program
GWME0906 (Scramble and Sort an Array) contains a subroutine to sort an
array of numbers into ascending order, with the smallest number in *array(1)*,
and the largest number in *array(NmbrOfElements)*. This program generates
an array of consecutive numbers (1, 2, 3, and so on), scrambles and prints the
array, sorts the array, and prints the sorted array. A sample run is shown in
Figure 9-12.

Much of Program GWME0906 is the same as Program GWME0905.
Therefore, you can save time by editing GWME0905 to obtain GWME0906.
In this way, you can quickly get all of the program except the subroutine that
does the sorting, shown here:

```
4000 REM ** SUBROUTINE: Sort the array of numbers **
4010 FOR j = 1 TO NmbrOfElements - 1
4020   FOR k = j + 1 TO NmbrOfElements
4030     IF array(k) < array(j) THEN SWAP array(k), array(j)
4040   NEXT k
4050 NEXT j
4060 RETURN
```

```
Scramble and Sort an array of numbers

How many numbers shall I scramble? 7

Here are the scrambled numbers:

  5            7            2            3            6
  1            4

Here are the sorted numbers:

  1            2            3            4            5
  6            7
```

FIGURE 9-12   Sample run of Scramble and Sort an Array of Numbers Program

This subroutine features a FOR...NEXT loop inside a FOR...NEXT loop. The inside loop (lines 4020 through 4040) runs through all its values of k for each value of j in the outside loop (lines 4010 through 4050).

Suppose that the value of *NmbrOfElements* is 4, and the values of the scrambled array are as shown in Table 9-4. The value of j (in the outside loop) will run from 1 to 3 and for each value of j, the value of k (in the inside loop) will run from $j+1$ to 4. Together, j and k will take on the values shown next.

Array Element	Value
array(1)	2
array(2)	4
array(3)	1
array(4)	3

TABLE 9-4   Scrambled *array( )* Values

```
j  k
1  2

   3

   4

2  3

   4

3  4
```

For each pair of values of *j* and *k*, the values of *array(k)* and *array(j)* are compared. If the value of *array(k)* is less than the value of *array(j)*, the two values are exchanged, thus putting the smaller value in *array(j)*. The following diagram shows what happens the first time through both FOR...NEXT loops, when *j* is 1, and *k* is 2, 3, and 4. Arrows indicate any exchanges that are made.

```
Array        Starting      j = 1     j = 1      j = 1
variable     order         k = 2     k = 3      k = 4

array(1)        2            2         2    1      1
array(2)        4            4         4    4      4
array(3)        1            1         1    2      2
array(4)        3            3         3    3      3
```

After the two FOR...NEXT loops have been executed once, *array(1)* contains the smallest number. The value of *k* has gone through all its values: 2, 3, and 4. The value of *j* then becomes 2, and *k* will now go through the values 3 and 4. The next diagram shows what happens the second time through; arrows indicate any exchanges that are made.

```
                           j = 2      j = 2
                           k = 3      k = 4

array(1)        1            1          1
array(2)        4            2          2
array(3)        2            4          4
array(4)        3            3          3
```

After the second pass ($j = 2$), the second smallest number is in *array(2)*. The third pass (and last, for an array of four elements) completes the sort. The next diagram shows the results of the third pass; again, the arrows indicate any exchanges made this time.

```
                       j = 3
                       k = 4

array(1)      1              1
array(2)      2              2
array(3)      4     ⟍    ⟋→ 3
array(4)      3    ⟋  ⟍  → 4
```

After the third pass, the array is in sorted order. The entire sorting process for this example is shown in Figure 9-13.

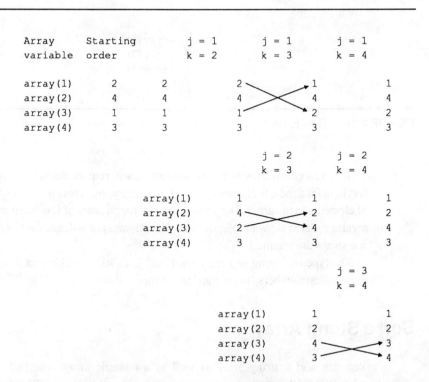

Array variable	Starting order	j = 1 k = 2	j = 1 k = 3	j = 1 k = 4
array(1)	2	2	2	1	1
array(2)	4	4	4	4	4
array(3)	1	1	1	2	2
array(4)	3	3	3	3	3

			j = 2 k = 3	j = 2 k = 4
array(1)		1	1	1
array(2)		4	2	2
array(3)		2	4	4
array(4)		3	3	3

				j = 3 k = 4
array(1)			1	1
array(2)			2	2
array(3)			4	3
array(4)			3	4

FIGURE 9-13   A complete sort of four elements, Program GWME0906

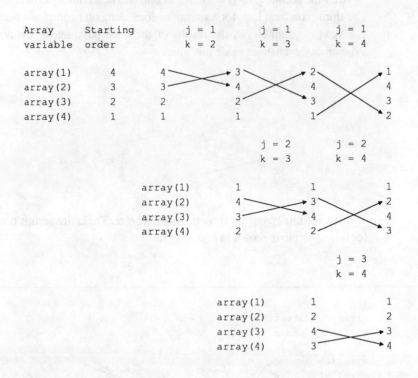

```
Array       Starting        j = 1        j = 1        j = 1
variable    order           k = 2        k = 3        k = 4

array(1)       4          4         3         2         1
array(2)       3          3         4         4         4
array(3)       2          2         2         3         3
array(4)       1          1         1         1         2

                                         j = 2        j = 2
                                         k = 3        k = 4

                       array(1)       1         1         1
                       array(2)       4         3         2
                       array(3)       3         4         4
                       array(4)       2         2         3

                                                    j = 3
                                                    k = 4

                       array(1)       1         1
                       array(2)       2         2
                       array(3)       4         3
                       array(4)       3         4
```

FIGURE 9-14   Reverse order sorting process

When an entire array is in reverse order, it will require the most swaps to sort it. In fact, there will be exactly *(n-1) * (n-2)* swaps, where *n* is the number of elements in the array. The sorting process for an array of four elements in reverse order is shown in Figure 9-14. For this array, *n = 4*, and *(4-1) * (4-2) = 6* swaps are required.

The type of sorting process shown here is called a bubble sort, because the smallest numbers "bubble up" to the top.

Sort a String Array

You can sort a string array as well as a numeric array. The following subroutine will sort strings into an order determined by the ASCII values of the characters in the string. A character is "less than" another character if its

```
1 REM ** Sort a String Array **
2 ' GW-BASIC Made Easy, Chapter 9.  File: GWME0907.BAS

100 REM ** Setup **
110 SCREEN 0: CLS : KEY OFF   'Setup the screen
120 DEFINT A-Z                'Nondesignated variables = integer
130 DIM array$(100)           'Dimension string array

200 REM ** Get number of strings to sort **
210 CLS : PRINT "Sort a string array"
220 PRINT
230 INPUT "How many strings shall I sort?"; NmbrOfElements
240 PRINT

300 REM ** Main program **
310 GOSUB 1010                         'Enter strings
350 GOSUB 4010                         'Sort the strings
360 PRINT "Here are the sorted strings:"
370 GOSUB 2010                         'Print strings
380 PRINT : END                        'End main program

1000 REM ** SUBROUTINE: Acquire strings via keyboard entry **
1010 FOR k = 1 TO NmbrOfElements
1020    LINE INPUT "String? "; array$(k)
1030 NEXT k
1040 RETURN

2000 REM ** SUBROUTINE: Print the array **
2010 PRINT
2020 FOR k = 1 TO NmbrOfElements
2030    PRINT array$(k)
2040 NEXT k
2050 PRINT
2060 RETURN

4000 REM ** SUBROUTINE: Sort the array of strings **
4010 FOR j = 1 TO NmbrOfElements - 1
4020    FOR k = j + 1 TO NmbrOfElements
4030       IF array$(k) < array$(j) THEN SWAP array$(k), array$(j)
4040    NEXT k
4050 NEXT j
4060 RETURN
```

PROGRAM GWME0907   Sort a String Array

ASCII value is less than the ASCII value of the other character. For example, the ASCII value of the letter *A* is 65, and the ASCII value of the letter *B* is 66. Therefore, *A* is less than *B*, and *A < B* is a true condition.

```
4000 REM ** SUBROUTINE: Sort the array of strings **
4010 FOR j = 1 TO NmbrOfElements - 1
4020   FOR k = j + 1 TO NmbrOfElements
4030     IF array$(k) < array$(j) THEN SWAP array$(k), array$(j)
4040   NEXT k
4050 NEXT j
4060 RETURN
```

Except for line 4030, this subroutine is the same as the subroutine used in Program GWME0906 to sort a numeric array. Line 4030 swaps the values of *array$(k)* and *array$(j)* if the value of *array$(k)* is "less than" the value of *array$(j)*, according to the ASCII values of the characters in the string values of these array variables.

Sample runs of Program GWME0907 (Sort a String Array) are shown in Figures 9-15, 9-16, and 9-17. Figure 9-15 shows a sort of three strings, each consisting of all lowercase letters. The program sorts these correctly. Figure 9-16 shows a sort of three strings, each consisting of all uppercase letters. The program sorts these correctly, also. Figure 9-17 shows a sort of three strings containing both lower- and uppercase letters. These strings are not sorted properly.

```
Sort a string array

How many strings shall I sort? 3

String? beta
String? alpha
String? gamma

Here are the sorted strings:

alpha
beta
gamma
```

FIGURE 9-15   Sorting strings consisting of all lowercase letters

```
Sort a string array

How many strings shall I sort? 3

String? BETA
String? ALPHA
String? GAMMA

Here are the sorted strings:

ALPHA
BETA
GAMMA
```

FIGURE 9-16   Sorting strings consisting of all uppercase letters

The subroutine in block 4000 will not properly sort strings that contain both lower- and uppercase letters. This happens because the ASCII codes for uppercase letters A through Z are 65 to 90, whereas the ASCII codes for the lowercase letters a through z are 97 to 122. Therefore, all uppercase letters will sort as "less than" any lowercase letters.

```
Sort a string array

How many strings shall I sort? 3

String? beta
String? alpha
String? Gamma

Here are the sorted strings:

Gamma
alpha
beta
```

FIGURE 9-17   Sorting strings consisting of mixed lower- and uppercase letters

You can fix this problem by using the LOCASE subroutine shown in Chapter 8, and modify the sort subroutine as shown here:

```
3000 REM ** SUBROUTINE: LOCASE **
3005 ' Changes letters in strng$ to lowercase
3010 FOR kk = 1 TO LEN(strng$)
3020    character$ = MID$(strng$, kk, 1)
3030    code = ASC(character$)
3040    IF code  > 64 AND code < 91 THEN code = code + 32
3050    character$ = CHR$(code)
3060    MID$(strng$, kk, 1) = character$
3070 NEXT kk
3080 RETURN

4000 REM ** SUBROUTINE: Sort the array of strings **
4010 FOR j = 1 TO NmbrOfElements - 1
4020    strng$ = array$(j): GOSUB 3010: jstrng$ = strng$
4030    FOR k = j + 1 TO NmbrOfElements
4040       strng$ = array$(k): GOSUB 3010: kstrng$ = strng$
4050       IF kstrng$ < jstrng$ THEN SWAP array$(k), array$(j)
4060    NEXT k
4070 NEXT j
4080 RETURN
```

Add the LOCASE subroutine to Program GWME0907, and modify the sort subroutine as just shown. Give the modified program the filename GWME0908 (Sort a String Array with LOCASE Subroutine).

```
1 REM ** Sort a String Array with LOCASE Subroutine **
2 ' GW-BASIC Made Easy, Chapter 9.  File: GWME0908.BAS

100 REM ** Setup **
110 SCREEN 0: CLS : KEY OFF   'Set up the screen
120 DEFINT A-Z                'Nondesignated variables = integer
130 DIM array$(100)           'Dimension string array

200 REM ** Get number of strings to sort **
210 CLS : PRINT "Sort a string array"
220 PRINT
230 INPUT "How many strings shall I sort?"; NmbrOfElements
240 PRINT
```

PROGRAM GWME0908   Sort a String Array with LOCASE Subroutine

```
300 REM ** Main program **
310 GOSUB 1010                                  'Enter strings
350 GOSUB 4010                                  'Sort the strings
360 PRINT "Here are the sorted strings:"
370 GOSUB 2010                                  'Print strings
380 PRINT : END                                 'End main program

1000 REM ** SUBROUTINE: Acquire strings via keyboard entry **
1010 FOR k = 1 TO NmbrOfElements
1020    LINE INPUT "String? "; array$(k)
1030 NEXT k
1040 PRINT : RETURN

2000 REM ** SUBROUTINE: Print the array **
2010 PRINT
2020 FOR k = 1 TO NmbrOfElements
2030    PRINT array$(k)
2040 NEXT k
2050 PRINT
2060 RETURN

3000 REM ** SUBROUTINE: LOCASE **
3005 ' Changes letters in strng$ to lowercase
3010 FOR kk = 1 TO LEN(strng$)
3020    character$ = MID$(strng$, kk, 1)
3030    code = ASC(character$)
3040    IF code >  64 AND code  < 91 THEN code = code + 32
3050    character$ = CHR$(code)
3060    MID$(strng$, kk, 1) = character$
3070 NEXT kk
3080 RETURN

4000 REM ** SUBROUTINE: Sort the array of strings **
4010 FOR j = 1 TO NmbrOfElements - 1
4020    strng$ = array$(j): GOSUB 3010: jstrng$ = strng$
4030    FOR k = j + 1 TO NmbrOfElements
4040       strng$ = array$(k): GOSUB 3010: kstrng$ = strng$
4050       IF kstrng$ < jstrng$ THEN SWAP array$(k), array$(j)
4060    NEXT k
4070 NEXT j
4080 RETURN
```

PROGRAM GWME0908   Sort a String Array with LOCASE Subroutine
(*continued*)

```
Sort a string array

How many strings shall I sort? 3

String? beta
String? alpha
String? Gamma

Here are the sorted strings:

alpha
beta
Gamma
```

FIGURE 9-18   Sorting strings consisting of mixed lower- and uppercase letters

The LOCASE subroutine changes all letters in the value of *strng$* to lowercase. In the modified sort subroutine, the LOCASE subroutine is used twice, in lines 4020 and 4040, to obtain strings called *jstrng$* and *kstrng$*. The value of *jstrng$* is the value of *array$(j)* with all letters changed to lowercase. The value of *kstrng$* is the value of *array$(k)* with all letters changed to lowercase. These strings are used in line 4050, to decide whether to swap the values of *array$(j)* and *array$(k)*.

In the LOCASE subroutine, note the use of *kk* as the FOR...NEXT loop variable. You cannot use *k* because it is used in the sort subroutine that calls the LOCASE subroutine. The value of *k* in the sort subroutine remains unchanged while the LOCASE subroutine (and *kk*) does its work.

Figure 9-18 shows a sample run of the modified Sort a String Array program. The strings are sorted correctly, even though one string has both lower- and uppercase letters.

REVIEW

An array is a set of variables referenced by the same name and a subscript. Arrays, like simple variables, can be numeric or string. Numeric arrays can be integer, single precision, or double precision arrays. The size of an array defaults to 11 elements, with subscripts 0 through 10. You can use a DIM statement to set the upper limit to a number other than 10. An array subscript can be a number, a numeric variable, or a numeric expression.

You can use arrays in many ways. Some are shown in this chapter. You can write short programs to manipulate large arrays of information. You can scramble an array into random order, or use a bubble sort to put an array into the order you want.

10

SEQUENTIAL FILES

In this chapter you will read about the different types of data files: sequential and random-access. You will learn about unstructured sequential files and structured sequential files and how to create and access records from each. In particular, you will learn how to

- create and scan structured and unstructured sequential files

- use the file statements OPEN, WRITE #, LINE INPUT #, INPUT #, and CLOSE #

- create and scan the NotePad.Txt file, an unstructured sequential file of free-form records

- create and scan the Japanese.Txt file, a structured sequential file of Japanese and English words and phrases

- use the Japanese.Txt file, or a similar file, as an aid to learning

- use the file functions EOF and LOF

- change the name of a file by using the NAME statement

TYPES OF DATA FILES

A file is a collection of information; the information contained in a file can be on any topic and organized in any way you choose. Think of a computer file as a file in a file cabinet: it contains information and notes that you want to save, about one or several topics.

There are several different kinds of computer files, including program files and data files. You have already used and created many different program files in previous chapters; each program you saved is a program file. In this chapter and in the next chapter, you will learn to create and use data files, which are used to store information. GW-BASIC has two types of data files: sequential files and random-access files.

Sequential Files

A data file is organized into records. A record in a bank statement file, for example, may contain the account number, the date, and the amount of a deposit or check. A *sequential file* is a file in which the records must be accessed sequentially; that is, to read the fifth record in a sequential file, records one through four must be accessed first. You might think of a cassette tape as a kind of sequential file. To hear the third song on the tape, you have to play or fast-forward past the first and second songs on the tape. This sequential file structure is depicted in Figure 10-1.

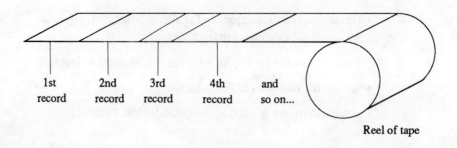

| 1st | 2nd | 3rd | 4th | and |
| record | record | record | record | so on... |

Reel of tape

FIGURE 10-1   Diagram of sequential file structure

Since each record in a sequential file must be accessed in order, using such files can be cumbersome—but they do have some advantages. A record in a sequential file can be any length, very short to very long, and uses only as much space as the data being stored. This means that sequential files store data efficiently, without wasting space. If a record is only 15 characters long, only 15 bytes (plus any special characters that identify the end of the record) are used to store it.

Sequential files also have some disadvantages. Although the data stored in a sequential file is stored in a minimum of space, the process of searching for a given record, especially in a large file, can be slow. Modifying, inserting, and deleting records in a sequential file can also be time consuming, usually requiring that the file be rewritten. In addition, sorting a large sequential file can be awkward, often considerably more difficult than sorting a random-access file.

For example, imagine how difficult it would be to delete a song from a cassette tape, or add one, or change the length of one—without leaving gaps or deleting parts of other songs. You would need to make an entirely new tape. Imagine trying to create a tape in which the songs appear in an entirely different order. This is the dilemma with sequential files.

A *random-access file* is one in which the records can be accessed in any order. You can access record 17, then record 4, then record 235, then record 2, and so on. A record can be accessed whether or not the previous records have already been accessed. This is similar to the way songs can be accessed on a compact disc. All records in a random-access file are the same length, which means that random-access files can be somewhat wasteful of storage space. Modifying a record in a random-access file, however, is much easier than modifying a record in a sequential file. Only the record being changed needs to be rewritten, rather than the entire file.

In this book, two types of sequential files are used: unstructured sequential files and structured sequential files. This chapter shows you how to create and use both types of sequential files. In Chapter 11, Random-Access Files, you will learn how to use random-access files.

UNSTRUCTURED SEQUENTIAL FILES

An *unstructured* sequential file is a sequential file in which one record is one string. A record can be any length up to 255 characters—the maximum length allowed for a GW-BASIC string. A record can even be a null (or empty) string. For example, a file that contains a letter to a friend can be an unstructured sequential file. Each line in the letter, including blank lines, is a record in the file. A GW-BASIC program saved in ASCII format is an unstructured sequential file. Each line of the program is one record in the file.

In contrast, a *structured* sequential file consists of records that have two or more *fields*. Each record has the same fields. A record in a bank statement file that contains an account number, date, and amount of check or deposit is an example of a structured record with three fields. A field in a structured file can be either string or numeric. A string field can be any length that a string variable can be, up to a maximum of 255 characters. Numeric fields are stored 1 byte per digit, and are limited in length by the numeric variables used to write the fields to the file.

Sequential files, whether unstructured or structured, are stored as ASCII text files. This means they can be used by word processors and other application programs that accept ASCII text. You could use a word processor to create, view, or modify a sequential file.

An Example of an Unstructured Sequential File

You will now create and use an unstructured sequential file called NotePad.Txt. This file consists of free-form records that are notes. A record in this file can be anything you wish, as long as it is typed as a single string. It might contain, for example, notes on how to use GW-BASIC. Or, as in Figure 10-2, it might hold notes on GW-BASIC, your appointments for April, and your favorite quotes from a book you're reading.

Remember: In an unstructured sequential file, each record is one string. One record can be the empty string (""), a string with 255 characters, or anything in between.

NAMING A FILE   Data files must be named. As with the programs you named in previous chapters, filenames for data files must conform to MS-DOS file-naming conventions. Filenames are limited to eight characters, plus a three-letter extension. The following example of a filename, used in a program later in this chapter, contains seven characters plus a three-letter extension:

NotePad.Txt

The three-letter extension (.Txt) was chosen to indicate that this is a text file. As you know, GW-BASIC does not distinguish between uppercase and

```
Record 1:   This is the NotePad.Txt file.

Record 2:   NotePad.Txt is an unstructured sequential file.

Record 3:   Each record is one string, up to 255 characters.

Record 4:   Use NotePad.Txt for notes of any kind.

Record 5:   Meet with Jester at noon on 4/1.

Record 6:   Library books due 4/15 -- also mail tax return.

Record 7:   Reality expands to fulfill the available fantasies.
```

FIGURE 10-2   A NotePad.Txt file with seven records

lowercase letters in filenames. Therefore, NotePad.Txt, notepad.txt, and NOTEPAD.TXT are considered the same name. When naming files, it is wise to choose names that reflect the contents of the file.

In this book, filenames will usually consist of only letters, or letters and numbers. If you wish, you can use any of the following ASCII characters in filenames and extensions:

A-Z a-z 0-9 $ – { } ~ ! # ( ) &

Creating the NotePad.Txt File

The NotePad.Txt file, shown in Figure 10-2, is a good example of an unstructured sequential file. To create this file, you will

1. open the file so that information can be entered into it

2. enter records from the keyboard and write them to the file

3. close the file after all records have been entered

To do this, you will use statements containing the following GW-BASIC keywords.

OPEN   : Open a file

LINE INPUT   : Obtain a string from the keyboard

WRITE #   : Write a record (string) to a file

CLOSE   : Close a file

A description of each of these statements follows, and each is used later in the program that creates NotePad.Txt.

THE OPEN STATEMENT   An OPEN statement is *required* before a file can be written to or read from. When a file is opened, it is assigned a file number. This file number is then used whenever the file is accessed or written to.

When you open a sequential file, you must declare the kind of access for which the file is to be opened: output, append, or input. A file opened for output can only be written to; if the file already exists, its contents will be emptied automatically before any records are written to it. If you attempt to read from a file opened for output, you will see an error message.

The statement

OPEN "NotePad.Txt" FOR OUTPUT AS #1

assigns the file NotePad.Txt as file #1, and allows you to write records to file #1. If this file already exists, it is emptied immediately. Therefore, before you use an OPEN...FOR OUTPUT statement, check the directory of the disk you are using to be sure that you will not be erasing the contents of a file that you wish to save.

A file opened for appending, like a file opened for output, can only be written to. However, its contents are not erased before any records are written to it. Also, as the term "append" implies, any records written to a file opened for appending are added to the end of the file.

The statement

OPEN "NotePad.Txt" FOR APPEND AS #1

assigns the file NotePad.Txt as file #1, and allows you to write records beginning at the end of file #1. Unlike a file opened for output, if this file already exists, its contents remain untouched.

If a file is opened for input, it can only be read from. If you attempt to write to a file opened for input, you will see an error messsage.

The statement

OPEN "NotePad.Txt" FOR INPUT AS #1

assigns the file NotePad.Txt as file #1, and allows you to read records from file #1. If a file opened for input does not already exist, you will see an error message.

Unless specified otherwise, a file is opened on the default disk drive, assumed to be drive A. In the following example, the file NotePad.Txt is opened for output on the default disk drive.

```
OPEN "NotePad.Txt" FOR OUTPUT AS #1
```

        ↑   ↑

    File name   File number

If you want the file to be opened on another disk drive, such as drive B, write the OPEN statement as follows:

```
OPEN "B:NotePad.Txt" FOR OUTPUT AS #1
```

      ↑

   Disk drive

If you wish, you can use NOTEPAD.TXT or notepad.txt as the filename, since GW-BASIC does not distinguish between lowercase and uppercase letters in a filename.

Remember: If there is already a file named NotePad.Txt on the disk, the OPEN...FOR OUTPUT statement will erase its contents before writing any new data to it.

THE CLOSE STATEMENT   When a file is no longer needed in a program, it should be closed. Any files still open at the end of a program should also be closed. In order to reassign a file number to a different file, the file previously assigned to that number must be closed.

The statement CLOSE #1 closes the file assigned as #1. Once a file has been closed, you can no longer read from or write to that file, unless you open it again. You may reuse the file number. If more than one file must be processed at once, use different numbers for the two files.

You may open a sequential file for output (or appending), or for input, but not both at the same time. If you need to write to and read from a sequential file in a program, you must close the file and then reopen it with a new access mode. You can open and close a file as many times as you wish within a program.

THE LINE INPUT STATEMENT   The LINE INPUT statement is well suited for entering records from the keyboard to be written to an unstructured sequential data file. Since each record in an unstructured file is a single string, each string entered when the LINE INPUT statement is executed is then written to the file as a single record.

The statement

LINE INPUT ">"; *record$*

assigns the characters entered to the variable *record$*. This string can then be written to the NotePad.Txt file as a single record.

THE WRITE # STATEMENT   You use the WRITE # statement to write information to a previously opened file.

The statement

WRITE #1, *record$*

writes the value of the string variable *record$* to the file previously opened as file #1. The numeral following the number sign (#) specifies which file is to be written to. If you were writing to a file opened as file #2, then the statement would look like this:

```
WRITE #2, record$
```

The WRITE # statement encloses the string written to the file in quotation marks. You can use another statement, the PRINT # statement, to write a string to a file without enclosing it in quotation marks. The PRINT # statement is not discussed in this book.

```
1 REM ** Create the NotePad.Txt File **
2 ' GW-BASIC Made Easy, Chapter 10.  File:GWME1001.BAS
3 ' NotePad.Txt is an unstructured sequential file

100 REM ** Setup **
110 SCREEN 0: CLS : KEY OFF
120 DEFINT A-Z                  'Undesignated variables are integer

200 REM ** Wait for a key press to begin **
210 PRINT "Press a key to begin"
220 akey$ = INPUT$(1)
230 PRINT

300 REM ** Open a new NotePad.Txt file for output as file #1 **
310 ' File is opened on the default disk drive
320 OPEN "NotePad.Txt" FOR OUTPUT AS #1

400 REM ** Enter records from keyboard and write to file **
410 LINE INPUT ">"; record$      'Top of GOTO loop
420 IF record$ = "" THEN 510     '  Exit loop if empty string
430 WRITE #1, record$            '  Write record to file #1
440 GOTO 410                     'Bottom of loop

500 REM ** Close the file and end the program **
510 CLOSE #1
520 END
```

PROGRAM GWME1001   Create the NotePad.Txt File

A Program to Create the NotePad.Txt File

Program GWME1001 (Create the NotePad.Txt File) creates an unstructured sequential file of records you enter from the keyboard. Each record can have up to 255 characters, which is the number of characters allowed by the LINE INPUT statement.

Program GWME1001 Explained

Program GWME1001 begins with a familiar setup block, then prints the message "Press a key to begin," and waits for a key press. Make sure that the disk on which you wish to create the NotePad.Txt file is in the default disk drive; then press a key. The program moves on to block 300, shown here:

```
300 REM ** Open a new NotePad.Txt file for output as file #1 **
310 ' File is opened on the default disk drive
320 OPEN "NotePad.Txt" FOR OUTPUT AS #1
```

The NotePad.Txt file is now open for output, and is empty. If the NotePad.Txt file already exists on the disk, opening it for output erases all records. If it is not already on the disk, opening it for output creates it as an empty file, ready to receive records.

After opening the file, the program moves on to block 400, shown next:

```
400 REM ** Enter records from keyboard and write to file **
410 LINE INPUT ">"; record$      'Top of GOTO loop
420 IF record$ = "" THEN 510     ' Exit loop if empty string
430 WRITE #1, record$            ' Write record to file #1
440 GOTO 410                     'Bottom of loop
```

Line 410 prints a prompt (>) and waits for a string. The screen appears as shown here:

```
Press a key to begin

>_
```

You can type any string and press ENTER. Your string is accepted as the value of the string variable *record$*. If you just press ENTER without first typing something, the value of *record$* will be the empty string (""). In this case, line 420 sends control to line 510. No record is written to the NotePad.Txt file. This ends the process of entering records and writing them to the file.

If you type anything, even one space, and press ENTER, your entry becomes the value of *record$* and is written to the file by line 430. Figure 10-3 shows the screen after entry of the seven records shown in Figure 10-2.

```
Press a key to begin

>This is the NotePad.Txt file.
>NotePad.Txt is an unstructured sequential file.
>Each record is one string, up to 255 characters.
>Use NotePad.Txt for notes of any kind.
>Meet Jester at noon on 4/1.
>Library books due 4/15 -- also mail tax return.
>Reality expands to fulfill the available fantasies.
>_
```

FIGURE 10-3   Entering records into the NotePad.Txt file

After entering the records shown in Figure 10-3, or other records of your choice, press ENTER to exit the GOTO loop in block 400 and go to block 500 (line 510), shown next:

```
500 REM ** Close the file and end the program **
510 CLOSE #1
520 END
```

Block 500 is very simple. It closes the file and ends the program. You will see the familiar "Ok" and cursor on the screen.

Use the FILES statement to verify that the NotePad.Txt file is on the default drive disk. You will see it listed as NOTEPAD.TXT.

Now use the SYSTEM statement to exit GW-BASIC and return to MS-DOS. Then use the MS-DOS DIR command to list all files on the disk that contain the NotePad.Txt file. You will see the filename and other information, including the size of the file in bytes. The directory entry for the NotePad.Txt file should be similar to the one shown here:

```
          .
          .
          .
NOTEPAD   TXT      316   3-23-90  10:58a
          .
          .
          .
```

```
1 REM ** Create an Unstructured Sequential File **
2 ' GW-BASIC Made Easy, Chapter 10.  File:GWME1002.BAS
3 ' Each record is one string--You supply disk drive & filename

100 REM ** Setup **
110 SCREEN 0: CLS : KEY OFF
120 DEFINT A-Z                    'Undesignated variables are integer

200 REM ** Get name of the file & disk drive **
210 LOCATE 1, 1: PRINT "Create an unstructured sequential file"
220 LOCATE 3, 1: INPUT "File name"; naym$
230 LOCATE 5, 1: INPUT "Disk drive"; drive$
240 filename$ = drive$ + ":" + naym$
250 CLS : PRINT "Create the "; naym$; " file on drive "; drive$
270 PRINT

300 REM ** Open a file for output as file #1 **
310 OPEN filename$ FOR OUTPUT AS #1

400 REM ** Enter records from keyboard and write to file **
410 LINE INPUT ">"; record$     'Top of GOTO loop
420 IF record$ = "" THEN 510     '  Exit loop if empty string
430 WRITE #1, record$            '  Write record to file #1
440 GOTO 410                     'Bottom of loop

500 REM ** Print size, close the file and end the program **
510 PRINT : PRINT filename$; " has"; LOF(1); "bytes"
520 CLOSE #1
530 END
```

PROGRAM GWME1002   Create an Unstructured Sequential File

Since NotePad.Txt is an ASCII file, you can use the MS-DOS TYPE command to print it on the screen, as shown here:

```
A>TYPE NotePad.Txt
"This is the NotePad.Txt file."
"NotePad.Txt is an unstructured sequential file."
"Each record is one string, up to 255 characters."
"Use NotePad.Txt for notes of any kind."
"Meet Jester at noon on 4/1."
```

```
"Library books due 4/15 -- also mail tax return."
"Reality expands to fulfill the available fantasies."

A>
```

Note that each record (string) is enclosed in quotation marks. These quotation marks were supplied by the WRITE # statement when it wrote the records to the file.

A More General File Creation Program

Program GWME1002 (Create an Unstructured Sequential File) creates a file using a filename and disk drive designation entered from the keyboard. You can edit Program GWME1001 to obtain Program GWME1002.

Run the program. It begins like this:

```
Create an unstructured sequential file

File name? _
```

Type the name of the file you want to create, and press ENTER. For example, here is what happens if you type **NotePad.Txt** and press ENTER:

```
Create an unstructured sequential file

File name? NotePad.Txt

Disk drive? _
```

Now type the disk drive letter (**a** or **A**, **b** or **B**, or another drive you want to use), but don't yet press ENTER. If you see something wrong, you can use CTRL+BREAK to interrrupt. When everything is as you want it, press ENTER. You will see a screen similar to the following:

```
Create the NotePad.Txt file on drive A

>_
```

The NotePad.Txt file has now been opened on disk drive A and is empty. Do not type anything; instead, just press ENTER. The computer prints the number of bytes in the file, as shown next, closes the file, and ends the program.

```
A:NotePad.Txt has 0 bytes
```

The file exists on the disk as an empty file—it has no records. You can use the FILES statement to verify that it is on the disk, although empty. In MS-DOS, you can use the DIR command to see the filename and number of bytes (0) in the file.

Run the program again, enter one short record as follows, and then press ENTER to end the run.

```
Create the NotePad.Txt file on drive A

>abc
>

A:NotePad.Txt has 7 bytes
```

The file now has one record, consisting of abc enclosed in quotation marks ("abc"); that accounts for five bytes. The other two bytes (for a total of seven bytes) consist of two characters that mark the end of the record. These are the CR (Carriage Return) and LF (Line Feed) characters. Every record ends with these two characters. The ASCII code for LF is 10, and the ASCII code for CR is 13.

Block 200 of the program acquires the name of the file and the disk drive letter. These are concatenated, along with a colon (:), and assigned as the value of *filename$*, as shown here:

```
240 filename$ = drive$ + ":" + naym$
```

The variable *filename$* is used in line 310 to open the file, like this:

```
310 OPEN filename$ FOR OUTPUT AS #1
```

If you want to append records to an existing file, change line 310 to the following:

```
310 OPEN filename$ FOR APPEND AS #1
```

You can make a few changes to Program GWME1002 to obtain Program GWME1003 (Append to an Unstructured Sequential File). Use Program GWME1003 when you want to append records to the end of an existing file,

```
1 REM ** Append to an Unstructured Sequential File **
2 ' GW-BASIC Made Easy, Chapter 10.  File:GWME1003.BAS
3 ' Append records to the end of an existing file

100 REM ** Setup **
110 SCREEN 0: CLS : KEY OFF
120 DEFINT A-Z                  'Undesignated variables are integer

200 REM ** Get name of the file & disk drive **
210 LOCATE 1, 1: PRINT "Append to unstructured sequential file"
220 LOCATE 3, 1: INPUT "File name"; naym$
230 LOCATE 5, 1: INPUT "Disk drive"; drive$
240 filename$ = drive$ + ":" + naym$
250 CLS : PRINT "Append to "; naym$; " file on drive "; drive$
260 PRINT

300 REM ** Open a file for append as file #1 **
310 OPEN filename$ FOR APPEND AS #1

400 REM ** Enter records from keyboard and write to file **
410 LINE INPUT ">"; record$    'Top of GOTO loop
420 IF record$ = "" THEN 510    '  Exit loop if empty string
430 WRITE #1, record$           '  Write record to file #1
440 GOTO 410                    'Bottom of loop

500 REM ** Print size, close the file and end the program **
510 PRINT : PRINT filename$; " has"; LOF(1); "bytes"
520 CLOSE #1
530 END
```

PROGRAM GWME1003   Append to an Unstructured Sequential File

thus increasing the size of the file. Program GWME1003 does not erase an existing file.

Scanning an Unstructured Sequential File

Program GWME1004 (Scan an Unstructured Sequential File) reads each record in an unstructured file and prints it on the screen, one record at a time.

```
1 REM ** Scan an Unstructured Sequential File **
2 ' GW-BASIC Made Easy, Chapter 10.  File:GWME1004.BAS
3 ' You enter disk drive letter & name of file

100 REM ** Setup **
110 SCREEN 0: CLS : KEY OFF
120 DEFINT A-Z               'Undesignated variables are integer

200 REM ** Get name of the file & disk drive **
210 LOCATE 1, 1: PRINT "Scan an unstructured sequential file"
220 LOCATE 3, 1: INPUT "File name"; naym$
230 LOCATE 5, 1: INPUT "Disk drive"; drive$
240 filename$ = drive$ + ":" + naym$
250 CLS : PRINT "Scan the "; naym$; " file on drive "; drive$
260 PRINT : PRINT "Press a key for next record": PRINT

300 REM ** Open a file for input as file #1 **
310 OPEN filename$ FOR INPUT AS #1

400 REM ** Scan the file, one record at a time **
405 ' Press a key to read next record and display on screen

410 WHILE EOF(1) = 0          'Loop while not end of file
420    LINE INPUT #1, record$  'Read 1 record from file #1
430    PRINT record$           'Print record to screen
440    akey$ = INPUT$(1)       'Wait for a key press
450 WEND

460 PRINT : BEEP: PRINT "*** End of file ***"

500 REM ** Print size, close the file and end the program **
510 PRINT : PRINT filename$; " has"; LOF(1); "bytes"
520 CLOSE #1
530 END
```

PROGRAM GWME1004   Scan an Unstructured Sequential File

The program begins with

```
Scan an unstructured sequential file

File name? _
```

Back in Chapter 3, you saved Program GWME0302 as an ASCII file under the filename GWME0302.ASC. To scan that file, type **GWME0302.ASC**, and press ENTER. Now the screen looks like this:

```
Scan an unstructured sequential file

File name? GWME0302.ASC

Disk drive? _
```

Type the disk drive letter and press ENTER. If you type **A** and press ENTER, you will see the following:

```
Scan the GWME0302.ASC file on drive A

Press a key for next record
```

Of course, if you ask for a file that is not on the disk drive you designate, instead of the above you will see a "File not found in 310" error message. However, if all goes well, you are now ready to scan the GWME0302.ASC file. Press a key to see the first record, as shown here:

```
Scan the GWME0302.ASC file on drive A

Press a key for next record

10 BEEP
```

The first record is the first line in the program. Continue pressing a key until the entire file is read and appears on the screen. When you have reached the end of the file, pressing a key causes the message, "*** End of file ***" to appear. The program then tells you the size of the file, and ends. Figure 10-4 shows a complete run of Program GWME1004.

```
Scan the GWME0302.ASC file on drive A

Press a key for next record

10 BEEP
15 CLS
20 PRINT DATE$
30 PRINT TIME$
40 PRINT "George Firedrake"
50 PRINT "Happy New Year!"

*** End of file ***

A:GWME0302.ASC has 107 bytes
```

FIGURE 10-4   Scanning an unstructured sequential file

Next use Program GWME1004 to scan the NotePad.Txt file, as shown in Figure 10-5. Note that the program reads the entire record, including quotation marks, exactly as the record was written by the WRITE # statement in Program GWME1001. The end-of-record characters, CR and LF, are discarded by BASIC as it reads each line.

After you supply the name of the file to be scanned and the letter of the disk drive on which the file resides, the program opens the file for input, as shown here:

```
310 OPEN filename$ FOR INPUT AS #1
```

A WHILE...WEND loop then acquires records from the file and prints them to the screen. This continues while end-of-file (EOF) has not been reached. Reaching EOF causes the WHILE...WEND loop to end. The WHILE...WEND loop is shown here:

```
410 WHILE EOF(1) = 0              'Loop while not end of file
420    LINE INPUT #1, record$     'Read 1 record from file #1
430    PRINT record$              'Print record to screen
440    akey$ = INPUT$(1)          'Wait for a key press
450 WEND
```

```
Scan the NotePad.Txt file on drive A

Press a key for next record

"This is the NotePad.Txt file."
"NotePad.Txt is an unstructured sequential file."
"Each record is one string, up to 255 characters."
"Use NotePad.Txt for notes of any kind."
"Meet Jester at noon on 4/1."
"Library books due 4/15 -- also mail tax return."
"Reality expands to fulfill the available fantasies."

*** End of file ***

A:Notepad.Txt has 316 bytes
```

FIGURE 10-5   A scan of the NotePad.Txt file by Program GWME1004

The statement

WHILE EOF(1) = 0

tells the computer to execute the lines inside the WHILE...WEND loop while the end-of-file has not been reached. When you open a nonempty file for input, the value of the EOF function for that file is set to zero (0). It remains zero until the end-of-file is reached, and then becomes −1. When this happens, the WHILE...WEND loop ends.

Each record is read by a LINE INPUT # statement (line 420). Therefore, all characters in the record, including the enclosing quotation marks, are read as one string. The LINE INPUT # statement reads everything up to the end-of-record characters, CR and LF.

If you don't want the quotation marks to be read as part of the string, use an INPUT # statement instead of a LINE INPUT # statement. The WHILE...WEND loop will then look like this:

```
410 WHILE EOF(1) = 0          'Loop while not end of file
420    INPUT #1, record$      'Read 1 record from file #1
430    PRINT record$          'Print record to screen
440    akey$ = INPUT$(1)      'Wait for a key press
450 WEND
```

Record Number	First Field (*Japanese$*)	Second Field (*English$*)
1	Nihon'go	Japanese language
2	Ohayoo gozaimasu	Good morning
3	Kon'nichi wa	Hello, Good day
4	Kon'ban wa	Good evening
5	Sayoonara	Goodbye

TABLE 10-1   Sample Records from Japanese.Txt, a Structured Sequential File

When the end-of-file (EOF) is reached, the WHILE...WEND loop ends. The program beeps, prints the message "*** End of file ***", and then prints the filename and the size of the file in bytes. The program ends.

Your turn. Use Program GWME1004 to scan some files. Try changing the LINE INPUT # statement to an INPUT # statement, and scan some files. Make changes to the program so that it becomes the program *you* want.

STRUCTURED SEQUENTIAL FILES

In a structured sequential file, each record consists of at least two fields. Each field in a record is a variable-length string; that is, a field can be any length, up to the maximum length allowed for a string, 255 characters.

For example, consider a file called Japanese.Txt, which contains Japanese words and phrases and their English equivalents. Each record in this file has two fields: *Japanese$* and *English$*. Sample records from this file are shown in Table 10-1. The spelling conventions in Table 10-1 are consistent with those in *Learn Japanese* by John Young and Kimiko Nakajima-Okano (Honolulu: University of Hawaii Press, 1984).

Another example of a structured sequential file is inspired by a catalog of

Page%	CatNum$	Item$	Price!	Ounces!
5	33-972	Backpack	129.95	72
10	47-865	Tent	199.95	96
19	50-336	Sleeping bag	99.95	53
25	40-027	Stove	41.95	13
27	40-115	Cooking kit	29.95	32
31	45-820	Compass	25.95	3
44	47-322	Swiss army knife	13.95	2

TABLE 10-2   Sample Records from Camping.Cat

camping equipment. In this file, each record has five fields, as follows:

Page%   : Page number, a numeric field

CatNum$: Catalog number, a string field

Item$: Brief description of item, a string field

Price!   : Price, a numeric field

Ounces!   : Weight in ounces, a numeric field

Table 10-2 shows sample records from the Camping.Cat file.

Creating a Structured Sequential File

Program GWME1005 (Create a Structured Sequential File) creates a sequential file in which each record consists of two fields. It is designed to create files used to study Japanese. In any file created by Program GWME1005, each record consists of two fields:

Japanese$ A Japanese word or phrase. This is a variable-length field. It is limited by the program to 38 characters maximum, so that this field and its English equivalent can fit side by side on one line of the screen.

English$ The English equivalent, or near-equivalent, of the Japanese
word or phrase. This variable-length field is also restricted
to 38 characters maximum.

```
1 REM ** Create a Structured Sequential File **
2 ' GW-BASIC Made Easy, Chapter 10.  File:GWME1005.BAS

100 REM ** Setup **
110 SCREEN 0: CLS : KEY OFF
120 DEFINT A-Z              'Undesignated variables are integer

200 REM ** Get name of the file & disk drive **
210 LOCATE 1, 1: PRINT "Create a structured sequential file"
220 LOCATE 3, 1: INPUT "File name"; naym$
230 LOCATE 5, 1: INPUT "Disk drive"; drive$
240 filename$ = drive$ + ":" + naym$
250 LOCATE 7, 1
260 PRINT "Create the "; naym$; " file on drive "; drive$
270 PRINT

300 REM ** Create the file **
310 OPEN filename$ FOR OUTPUT AS #1
320 GOSUB 1010                        'Enter records
330 PRINT
340 PRINT filename$; " has"; LOF(1); "bytes"
350 CLOSE #1
360 END

1000 REM ** SUBROUTINE: Enter records & write to file **
1005 ' Each record has 2 fields
1010 LINE INPUT "Japanese? "; Japanese$  'Get first field
1020 IF Japanese$ = "" THEN RETURN       'RETURN if empty string
1030 LINE INPUT "English ? "; English$   'Get second field
1040 Japanese$ = LEFT$(Japanese$, 38)    'Limit to 38 characters
1050 English$ = LEFT$(English$, 38)      'Limit to 38 characters
1060 WRITE #1, Japanese$, English$       'Write record to #1
1070 PRINT                               'Line space
1080 GOTO 1010                           'Go for more
```

PROGRAM GWME1005   Create a Structured Sequential File

The program uses a subroutine to acquire records entered from the keyboard and write them to the file. You can easily rewrite the subroutine to create files with a different structure, to be used for a different purpose. Here is the subroutine:

```
1000 REM ** SUBROUTINE: Enter records & write to file **
1005 ' Each record has 2 fields
1010 LINE INPUT "Japanese? "; Japanese$     'Get first field
1020 IF Japanese$ = ": THEN RETURN          'RETURN if empty string
1030 LINE INPUT "English ? "; English$      'Get second field
1040 Japanese$ = LEFT$(Japanese$, 38)       'Limit to 38 characters
1050 English$ = LEFT$(English$, 38)         'Limit to 38 characters
1060 WRITE #1, Japanese$, English$          'Write record to #1
1070 PRINT                                  'Line space
1080 GOTO 1010                              'Go for more
```

An alternative version of the subroutine is shown next. In this version, the first field is called *Question$* and the second field is called *Answer$*.

```
1000 REM ** SUBROUTINE: Enter records & write to file **
1005 ' Each record has 2 fields
1010 LINE INPUT "Question? "; Question$     'Get first field
1020 IF Question$ = "" THEN RETURN          'RETURN if empty string
1030 LINE INPUT "Answer  ? "; Answer$       'Get second field
1040 Question$ = LEFT$(Question$, 38)       'Limit to 38 characters
1050 Answer$ = LEFT$(Answer$, 38)           'Limit to 38 characters
1060 WRITE #1, Question$, Answer$           'Write record to #1
1070 PRINT                                  'Line space
1080 GOTO 1010                              'Go for more
```

Remember, you can write the subroutine your way.

In either subroutine, lines 1040 and 1050 limit the length of the strings being written to the file to 38 characters. This is done so that, when the file is used to study Japanese (or another subject you select), the first string (*Japanese$* or *Question$*) and the second string (*English$* or *Answer$*) will fit side by side on one line of the screen.

Line 1060 writes one record, consisting of two strings, to the file. The WRITE # statement encloses each string in quotation marks, and inserts a comma (,) between the two strings. Therefore, one record consists of the first string enclosed in quotation marks, a comma, the second string enclosed in quotation marks, and the usual two end-of-record characters, CR and LF.

```
Create a structured sequential file

File name? Japanese.Txt

Disk drive? A

Create the Japanese.Txt file on drive A

Japanese? Nihon'go
English ? Japanese language

Japanese? Ohayoo gozaimasu
English ? Good morning

Japanese? Kon'nichi wa
English ? Good day, Hello

Japanese? Kon'ban wa
English ? Good evening

Japanese? Sayoonara
English ? Goodbye

Japanese? _
```

FIGURE 10-6   Using Program GWME1005 to create a Japanese.Txt file

Figure 10-6 shows a sample run of Program GWME1005. The records previously shown in Table 10-1 have been entered, and the computer is waiting for the next Japanese word or phrase. Press ENTER to end the program and see the following end-of-program message:

```
A:Japanese.Txt has 153 bytes
```

To view the Japanese.Txt file, you can use Program GWME1004 or the MS-DOS TYPE command. Either method will display the five records as shown in the following.

"Nihon'go","Japanese language"

"Ohayoo gozaimasu","Good morning"

"Kon'nichi wa","Good day, Hello"

"Kon'ban wa","Good evening"

"Sayoonara","Goodbye"

Note that each record consists of two fields. Each field is enclosed in quotation marks. A comma separates the fields. For example:

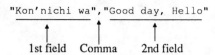

```
"Kon'nichi wa","Good day, Hello"
```

      1st field   Comma   2nd field

If you were studying Japanese, or some other language, you might create several files of this type, perhaps one called Nouns.Txt, another called Verbs.Txt, and so on. In order to append records to any of these files, change line 310 in Program GWME1005 to the following:

```
OPEN filename$ FOR APPEND AS #1
```

Remember: Opening a file for *output* erases an existing file, if any. Opening a file for *appending* does not erase an existing file. Instead, you may append new records to the end of the file, thus increasing the length of the file. If a file does not already exist, opening for *appending* creates a new file.

Use the Japanese.Txt File for Sequential Practice

Program GWME1006 (Use a File for Sequential Practice) scans the Japanese.Txt file one record at a time. You press a key to display the Japanese word or phrase, and then (when ready) press a key to display the English equivalent. Continue pressing keys to display the Japanese, then English, word or phrase. The Japanese and English words and phrases are placed side by side on the screen for your viewing convenience, as shown in Figure 10-7. In perusing the program, note that an INPUT # statement is used in line 3020 to read the two fields that comprise one record. Each field is assigned to a different string variable—the first field to *Japanese$,* the

```
1 REM ** Use a File for Sequential Practice **
2 '   GW-BASIC Made Easy, Chapter 10.  File:GWME1006.BAS

100 REM ** Setup **
110 SCREEN 0: CLS : KEY OFF
120 DEFINT A-Z                  'Undesignated variables are integer

300 REM ** Main program **
310 GOSUB 1010                           'Name of file & drive
320 GOSUB 2010                           'Tell what to do
330 OPEN filename$ FOR INPUT AS #1
340 GOSUB 3010                           'Scan the file
350 PRINT "That's all.  Press a key."
360 akey$ = INPUT$(1)                    'Wait for key press
370 CLOSE #1                             'Close the file
380 VIEW PRINT: CLS: END                 'End with normal screen

1000 REM ** SUBROUTINE: Get name of file & disk drive **
1010 LOCATE 1, 1: PRINT "Use a file for sequential practice"
1020 LOCATE 3, 1: INPUT "File name"; naym$
1030 LOCATE 5, 1: INPUT "Disk drive"; drive$
1040 filename$ = drive$ + ":" + naym$
1050 RETURN

2000 REM ** SUBROUTINE: Tell what to do & lock it in **
2010 CLS
2020 LOCATE 23, 1: PRINT STRING$(78, "*")
2030 PRINT "Practice with the "; naym$; " file on drive "; drive$
2040 PRINT "Press a key for next Japanese or English phrase";
2050 VIEW PRINT 1 TO 22
2060 RETURN

3000 REM ** SUBROUTINE: Scan file, one field at a time **
3005 ' Scans file with 2 fields
3010 WHILE EOF(1) = 0
3020    INPUT #1, Japanese$, English$    '1 record has 2 strings
3030    akey$ = INPUT$(1)                'Wait for key press
3040    PRINT Japanese$;                 'Print 1st field
3050    akey$ = INPUT$(1)                'Wait for key press
3060    PRINT TAB(40); English$          'Print 2nd field
3070    PRINT                            'Line space
3080 WEND
3090 RETURN                              'RETURN on EOF
```

PROGRAM GWME1006   Use a File for Sequential Practice

```
Nihon'go                         Japanese language

Ohayoo gozaimasu                 Good morning

Kon'nichi wa                     Good day, Hello

Kon'ban wa                       Good evening

Sayoonara                        Goodbye

That's all.  Press a key.
```

```
******************************************************************
Practice with the Japanese.Txt file on drive A
Press a key for next Japanese or English phrase
```

FIGURE 10-7   Sequential practice with the Japanese.Txt file

second field to *English$*. The INPUT # statement does not read the enclosing quotation marks, as the LINE INPUT # statement does. Therefore, as you can see in Figure 10-7, the information appearing on the screen is not enclosed in quotation marks.

Use the Japanese.Txt File for Random Practice

Program GWME1006 displayed the Japanese.Txt file sequentially, from the first record to the last. You can also use the file for practice in which records are selected randomly. To do this, first read the file into arrays, then select random array elements to print to the screen. Program GWME1007 (Use a File for Random Practice) provides this capability.

The program reads records from your selected file into the arrays *First$( )* and *Second$( )*. These arrays are dimensioned to store up to 200

```
1 REM ** Use a File for Random Practice **
2 ' GW-BASIC Made Easy, Chapter 10.  File:GWME1007.BAS

100 REM ** Setup **
110 SCREEN 0: CLS : KEY OFF
120 DEFINT A-Z
130 DIM First$(200), Second$(200)
140 RANDOMIZE TIMER

300 REM ** Main program **
310 GOSUB 1010                          'Name of file & drive
320 GOSUB 3010                          'Read file to arrays
330 GOSUB 2010                          'Tell what to do
340 GOSUB 4010                          'Random practice
350 PRINT "That's all.  Press a key."
360 akey$ = INPUT$(1)                   'Wait for key press
370 CLOSE #1                            'Close the file
380 VIEW PRINT: CLS: END                'End with normal screen

1000 REM ** SUBROUTINE: Get name of file & disk drive **
1010 LOCATE 1, 1: PRINT "Use a file for random practice"
1020 LOCATE 3, 1: INPUT "File name"; naym$
1030 LOCATE 5, 1: INPUT "Disk drive"; drive$
1040 filename$ = drive$ + ":" + naym$
1050 RETURN

2000 REM ** SUBROUTINE: Tell what to do & lock it in **
2010 CLS
2020 LOCATE 23, 1: PRINT STRING$(78, "*")
2030 PRINT "Practice with the "; naym$; " file on drive "; drive$
2040 PRINT "Press a key for next item, or press ESC to quit";
2050 VIEW PRINT 1 TO 21
2060 RETURN

3000 REM ** SUBROUTINE: Read file into arrays **
3010 OPEN filename$ FOR INPUT AS #1
3020 kk = 0
3030 WHILE EOF(1) = 0
3040   kk = kk + 1                        'Count records
3050   INPUT #1, First$(kk), Second$(kk)  '1 record, 2 strings
3080 WEND
3090 NmbrRecords = kk                     'Nmbr of records read
3100 RETURN                               'RETURN on EOF
```

PROGRAM GWME1007   Use a File for Random Practice

```
4000 REM ** SUBROUTINE: Random practice using arrays **
4010 RanSub = INT(NmbrRecords * RND) + 1  'Random subscript
4020 akey$ = INPUT$(1)                    'Wait for a key press
4030 IF akey$ = CHR$(27) THEN RETURN      'RETURN if ESC key
4040 PRINT First$(RanSub);                'Print first string
4050 akey$ = INPUT$(1)                     'Wait for a key press
4060 IF akey$ = CHR$(27) THEN RETURN      'RETURN if ESC key
4070 PRINT TAB(40); Second$(RanSub)       'Print second string
4080 PRINT : GOTO 4010                     'Go for another
```

PROGRAM GWME1007   Use a File for Random Practice (*continued*)

items each. The number of records actually read from the file is assigned to the variable *NmbrRecords*. Since the items printed are selected at random, it is possible to see a given item more than once. A sample run is shown in Figure 10-8. As before, the Japanese phrase is printed first on the left side of the screen, and the English phrase is printed on the right. You can easily modify the program so that it prints the English phrase first, on the left. There are several simple ways to do this. You can do it by changing only one line of the program.

Experiment with this program. For example, add more phrases in two languages (Spanish and English, for example) and combine them randomly to make complete sentences. Or, sort the arrays and print them sequentially. How would you sort the two arrays? (*Hint:* Sort *English$( )*, and for every *English$( )* element that is exchanged, also exchange that element in *Japanese$( )* .) In the next chapter you will learn to use random-access files, which are even more structured than structured sequential files.

SOME SUGGESTIONS ABOUT FILES

You now know how to create and scan sequential files. You also know how to append new information to the end of an existing file. This section describes additional file management tools, and suggests programs for you to write.

```
Sayoonara                          Goodbye

Nihon'go                           Japanese language

Kon'nichi wa                       Good day, Hello

Ohayoo gozaimasu                   Good morning

Sayoonara                          Goodbye

Kon'ban wa                         Good evening

Kon'nichi wa                       Good day, Hello

That's all.  Press a key.




****************************************************************
Practice with the Japanese.Txt file on drive A
Press a key for next item, or press ESC to quit
```

FIGURE 10-8   Random practice with the Japanese.Txt file

Creating a List of Your Files

Sometimes, especially when you have several different kinds of files on your
disks, you might wish to create a text file that lists each filename and a brief
description of the file's contents. You could use an unstructured sequential
file for this purpose, perhaps called FileNote.Txt. For example, FileNote.Txt
might include these records:

Record 1: This is the FileNote.Txt file

Record 2: NotePad.Txt contains notes of any type

Record 3: Japanese.Txt has Japanese and English words and phrases

Record 4: GWME1003.BAS, Append to Unstructured Sequential File

There is another way to keep track of your filenames and the contents of each file. You can write a GW-BASIC program that contains only REM statements and lines that begin with an apostrophe ('), as follows:

```
1 REM ** Notes on Files **
2 ' GW-BASIC Made Easy, Chapter 10.  File: FILENOTE.BAS
3 ' This "program" has only REM statements

10 ' NotePad.Txt contains notes of any kind
20 ' Japanese.Txt has Japanese and English words and phrases
30 ' GWME1003.BAS,  Append to an Unstructured Sequential File
```

Name this program FILENOTE.BAS and save it as an ASCII program, as follows:

```
SAVE "FILENOTE", A
```

Since FILENOTE.BAS is a program file with the .BAS extension, you can load it while in GW-BASIC and list all or part of it. As you create more files, load FILENOTE.BAS and add the filenames and descriptions of the new programs.

Since FILENOTE.BAS is saved in ASCII format, you can also use the MS-DOS TYPE command to view the file, as shown here:

```
A>TYPE FILENOTE.BAS
```

Changing a Filename

You can change the name of a file by using the MS-DOS RENAME command, or by using GW-BASIC's NAME statement. The NAME statement has the form

```
NAME "oldfilename" AS "newfilename"
```

where *oldfilename* is the current name of the file, and *newfilename* is the new name to be given to the file. Note that both filenames must be enclosed in quotation marks. For example, to change the name of the Japanese.Txt file to Nihongo.Txt, use the following statement:

```
NAME "Japanese.Txt" AS "Nihongo.Txt"
```

If the Japanese.Txt file is on disk drive B, change its name as follows:

```
NAME "B:Japanese.Txt" AS "B:Nihongo.Txt"
```

You can also change a file's name by using a NAME statement in which the filenames are the values of string variables, like this:

```
NAME oldname$ AS newname$
```

The current name of the file is the value of *oldname$*, and the new name is the value of *newname$*.

After a file's name has been changed, the file still exists on the same disk drive and in the same place on the disk as before; the only difference is that the file has a new name.

A Program for You to Write

Write a program to copy and edit a sequential file. It might begin like this:

```
Copy and Edit a Sequential File

Old file name  ? Japanese.Txt
Old file drive ? A
New file name  ? Nihongo.Txt
New file drive ? A
```

Remember: You can't copy a file onto itself on the same disk drive. You can't copy Japanese.Txt on drive A to Japanese.Txt on drive A. However, you can copy Japanese.Txt on drive A to another file on drive A, using a different filename. Then, after completion of the copying process, you can delete the old file and rename the new file.

Your program should read one record at a time from the old file, and then let you choose whether to copy it to the new file. This way you can copy only selected records from the old to the new file. If you wish, add an option to insert a new record from the keyboard at any time during the copy and edit process. Write your program as a main program and a set of subroutines to perform selected tasks. Start with a simple program, make it work, then expand it as you think of more ways to manage your files.

REVIEW

You now know how to create and use both program files and data files. Each program you create and save is a program file. If you save a program in ASCII format, it can also be used as a data file. There are two types of data files: sequential files and random-access files.

The records in a sequential file must be accessed in order: record 1, record 2, record 3, and so on. The records in a random-access file can be accessed in any order: record 344, record 3, record 11, record 102, and so on. This book presents both unstructured and structured sequential files. An unstructured sequential file is one in which each record is a single string. A structured sequential file contains records that have two or more fields.

To create a sequential file, the file is opened, records are written to it, and, finally, it is closed. To access the records in a sequential file, the file is opened and the records are read from the file. When all the records have been accessed, the file is closed.

Keep a list of your files and a brief description of each. You will find such a list especially useful as you create more and more files. Use the NAME statement to change the name of a file.

11

RANDOM-ACCESS FILES

In this chapter you will examine sequential and random-access files and how information is organized in each. You will also learn how to create and use random-access files. In particular, you will learn how to

- create a random-access file from a sequential file

- use the OPEN statement to open a random-access file for both input and output

- use the FIELD statement to define the record structure in a random-access file

- write (PUT) records to a random-access file

- read (GET) records from a random-access file

- use the MKI$ and MKS$ functions to convert numbers so they can be stored as special strings in a random-access file

- use the CVI and CVS functions to convert random-access file strings to numbers

SEQUENTIAL AND RANDOM-ACCESS FILE STORAGE

As you learned in the previous chapter, a sequential file is one in which the records must be accessed in the order in which they occur in the file. (To access record number 3, you must first access record number 1 and then record number 2.) A random-access file, in contrast, is one in which the records can be accessed in a random order. You can access record 5, then record 72, then record 1, then record 11, and so on. Any record can be obtained directly and quickly—without first reading any other record. If you wish to access record number 237, you can read it immediately, without first reading the previous 236 records in the file.

Random-access files are highly structured, fixed-length files, in which all records in a random file are the same length. When you open a random-access file, you set the record length of that file; if you do not specify a record length, GW-BASIC assigns a default record length of 128 characters.

Random-access file records are divided into fields. Each record has the same fields, in the same order; each field within a record has a fixed length. Corresponding fields in different records are the same length.

Random-access files have several advantages over sequential files: Any random-access file record can be accessed very quickly; a record can be modified without having to rewrite the entire file; records can be inserted or deleted more easily than in sequential files; and random-access files are easier to sort.

Random-access files also have some disadvantages: Their data is often stored inefficiently; since their files have fixed-length fields and fixed-length records, the same number of bytes is used regardless of the number of characters being stored. In addition, a random-access file must be designed in advance. The length of each field must allow enough space for any data that might possibly be stored in that field.

Sequential and random-access files store information somewhat differently. Though they both have fields, the fields in a sequential file may or may not be of fixed length, but the fields in a random-access file must be of fixed length. Also, numbers are stored differently in the two types of files.

Sequential File Storage

Sequential files are stored as ASCII text files. In a sequential file, each character in a string is stored as one character, and each digit in a number is stored as one character. Sequential files have variable-length records, and can be either unstructured or structured. In an unstructured sequential file, one string is one record. Structured sequential files have at least two variable-length fields. In Chapter 10, "Sequential Files," you created and used these two sequential files:

- NotePad.Txt is an unstructured sequential file. One record is one string of variable length. This is the simplest structure a file can have.

- Japanese.Txt is a structured sequential file with two fields, *Japanese$* and *English$*. Each field is of variable length, but is limited to 38 characters. This limit was imposed by the program that created the file.

The Japanese.Txt file, as it was created in Chapter 10, is shown here:

```
"Nihon'go","Japanese language"
"Ohayoo gozaimasu","Good morning"
"Kon'nichi wa","Good day, Hello"
"Kon'ban wa","Good evening"
"Sayoonara","Goodbye"
```

Each character in the file is shown, except for the two end-of-record characters that follow each record.

Notice that the fields in this file vary in length. Each field is enclosed in quotation marks, and the fields are separated by commas. In this file, a record can vary from a total of 7 to 83 characters in length, as follows:

First field enclosed in quotation marks:	2 to 40	
Comma separating the two fields:	1	1
Second field enclosed in quotation marks:	2 to 40	
End-of-record characters:	2	2
Character Total:	7 to 83	

The first record in the Japanese.Txt file is 32 bytes long—30 visible bytes, plus two end-of-record characters—as shown next:

```
"Nihon'go","Japanese language"  [Return] [Line feed]
```

End-of-record characters

The Japanese.Txt file just shown has five records. The shortest record is stored as 23 bytes, and the longest record as 35 bytes. There are 153 bytes in the entire file. Therefore, the average record length is 31 bytes (153 divided by 5, rounded to the nearest integer).

Random-Access File Storage

In a random-access file, all records are the same length; every record has the same fields, each of which is of fixed length. The first field is the same size in every record, the second field is the same size in every record, and so on. The record length and field lengths must be specified before any information is stored in the file.

There are two kinds of fields in a random-access file: string and numeric. Strings are stored in random-access files just as they are in sequential files; that is, one character in a string is stored as one character in a string field. However, unlike sequential files, if a string in a random-access file is shorter than the field length, spaces are added to fill out the field. If a string is longer than the field length, it is truncated to fit into the field.

Numbers are stored in a random-access file differently from how they're stored in a sequential file. In a random-access file, they are not stored as strings. Instead, they are stored in a compact binary form, as follows:

- Integers are stored in 2 bytes.

- Single precision numbers are stored in 4 bytes.

- Double precision numbers are stored in 8 bytes.

In this chapter, you will create and use two random-access files. Japanese.Ran is a random-access version of the Japanese.Txt file used in Chapter 10; this file has two string fields. Camping.Cat is a random-access file containing data about camping equipment; it has three string fields and three numeric fields.

CREATING A RANDOM-ACCESS FILE

In Chapter 10, you created files by entering records from the keyboard. You can use this method to create a random-access file, and you will do so later in this chapter. Now, however, you will create Japanese.Ran, a random-access file, in another way. Program GWME1101 (Create Japanese.Ran Random-Access File) reads the records from the Japanese.Txt sequential file

```
1 REM ** Create Japanese.Ran Random-Access File **
2 ' GW-BASIC Made Easy, Chapter 11.  File: GWME1101.BAS
3 ' Reads records from Japanese.Txt and writes to Japanese.Ran

100 REM ** Setup **
110 SCREEN 0: CLS : KEY OFF
120 DEFINT A-Z

200 REM ** Tell what to do **
210 PRINT "Use Japanese.Txt file to create Japanese.Ran file."
220 PRINT "Files read from and written to default disk drive."
230 PRINT
240 PRINT "Press a key to begin.": akey$ = INPUT$(1)

300 REM ** Open Japanese.Txt for input on default drive **
310 OPEN "Japanese.Txt" FOR INPUT AS #1
320 PRINT
330 PRINT "Japanese.Txt is open for input."

400 REM ** Open Japanese.Ran for random on default drive **
410 OPEN "Japanese.Ran" FOR RANDOM AS #2 LEN = 76
420 PRINT
430 PRINT "Japanese.Ran is open for random."

500 REM ** Define field structure for Japanese.Ran file **
510 FIELD #2, 38 AS Jfield$, 38 AS Efield$

600 REM ** No records yet, so set record number to zero **
610 RecordNmbr = 0

700 REM ** Copy records from Japanese.Txt to Japanese.Ran **
710 WHILE EOF(1) = 0
720    INPUT #1, Japanese$, English$     'Read one record
730    LSET Jfield$ = Japanese$          'Prepare fields to go to
740    LSET Efield$ = English$           'random-access file
750    RecordNmbr = RecordNmbr + 1       'Update record number
760    PUT #2, RecordNmbr                'Write record to file
770 WEND
```

PROGRAM GWME1101   Create Japanese.Ran Random-Access File

```
800 REM ** Print lengths of both files, close 'em, and end **
810 PRINT
820 PRINT "The Japanese.Txt file has"; LOF(1); "bytes."
830 PRINT "The Japanese.Ran file has"; LOF(2); "bytes."
840 CLOSE #1, #2
850 PRINT : PRINT "Both files are closed."
860 END
```

PROGRAM GWME1101   Create Japanese.Ran Random-Access File (*continued*)

and writes them to the Japanese.Ran file.

A run of the program begins like this:

```
Use Japanese.Txt file to create Japanese.Ran file.
Files read from and written to default disk drive.

Press a key to begin.
```

Press a key. The program opens both files and prints a message to tell you the files are open. It then reads the records from Japanese.Txt and writes them to Japanese.Ran. When all the records have been read from Japanese.Txt, the length of each file is printed, the files are closed, and the program ends. A complete run is shown here:

```
Use Japanese.Txt file to create Japanese.Ran file.
Files read from and written to default disk drive.

Press a key to begin.

Japanese.Txt is open for input.

Japanese.Ran is open for random.

The Japanese.Txt file has 153 bytes.
The Japanese.Ran file has 380 bytes.

Both files are closed.
```

The run shown here is for the Japanese.Txt file created in Chapter 10. Japanese.Txt has five records; therefore, the Japanese.Ran file also has five

```
            Length of field #1 (Jfield$) = 38
            Length of field #2 (Efield$) = 38
                                           ──
                                           76 bytes per record



                        Length of file    380
    Length of record = ──────────────── = ─── = 76 bytes per record
                       Number of records   5
```

FIGURE 11-1   Length of a record in Japanese.Ran file

records. Note, however, that the Japanese.Ran file is much larger than the Japanese.Txt file. This is because of their different file structures. Japanese.Txt is a sequential file with five variable-length records, and Japanese.Ran is a random-access file with five fixed-length records. Each record in Japanese.Ran is 76 characters long, as explained in Figure 11-1.

You can use the FILES command to verify that the Japanese.Ran file now exists on the disk in the default drive. If it is there, return to MS-DOS (use SYSTEM), and then use the MS-DOS TYPE command to display the Japanese.Ran file on the screen. It will appear as shown in Figure 11-2.

```
A>TYPE Japanese.Ran
Nihon'go                     Japanese language              Ohay
oo gozaimasu                   Good morning               Kon'nich
i wa                       Good day, Hello              Kon'ban wa
                          Good evening                 Sayoonara
                        Goodbye

A>
```

FIGURE 11-2   Japanese.Ran displayed by MS-DOS TYPE command

The strange appearance of the Japanese.Ran file in Figure 11-2 is because, in a random-access file, there are no end-of-record characters to cause a carriage return (CR) and line feed (LF). To the MS-DOS TYPE command, the Japanese.Ran file looks like one long string of ASCII characters. The TYPE command prints this long sequence of characters to the screen, 80 characters per line. Note that the first line contains the first record (76 characters), plus the first four characters of the second record. The second line contains the rest of the second record (72 characters), and the first eight characters of the third record. And so it goes to the end of the file.

The behavior will seem even more strange later in this chapter when you use the TYPE command to print a random-access file containing numeric fields.

Program GWME1101 Explained

GWME1101 first opens the Japanese.Txt file for input and prints a message to the screen. This is done by block 300, shown here:

```
300 REM ** Open Japanese.Txt for input on default drive **
310 OPEN "Japanese.Txt" FOR INPUT AS #1
320 PRINT
330 PRINT "Japanese.Txt is open for input."
```

Note that Japanese.Txt is opened as file #1. Therefore, another file number must be used to open the Japanese.Ran file. Block 400 opens the Japanese.Ran file for random access as file #2, this way:

```
400 REM ** Open Japanese.Ran for random on default drive **
410 OPEN "Japanese.Ran" FOR RANDOM AS #2 LEN = 76
420 PRINT
430 PRINT "Japanese.Ran is open for random."
```

You have learned that when a random-access file is opened, it is opened for both input and output. Records can be read from and written to a random-access file without your having to close and reopen it with a new access mode, as would be required with sequential files.

The OPEN statement in line 410 also defines the length of a record with a LEN clause (LEN = 76). If you do not specify the length of a record, GW-BASIC assigns a default record length of 128 bytes. In the case of the Japanese.Ran file, this would be wasteful.

When creating a random-access file, you must use a FIELD statement to define a field structure. The Japanese.Ran file consists of two fields, each exactly 38 characters long. Block 500 defines this structure, as follows:

```
500 REM ** Define field structure for Japanese.Ran file **
510 FIELD #2, 38 AS Jfield$, 38 AS Efield$
```

Line 510 defines two string fields, called *Jfield$* and *Efield$,* for file #2, the Japanese.Ran file. Each field string variable is defined to have a length of 38 characters.

Jfield$ is a string field variable with a length of 38 characters.
Efield$ is a string field variable with a length of 38 characters.

The names *Jfield$* and *Efield$* are chosen arbitrarily. It is a good idea to choose names that in some way indicate that they represent field variables for a random-access file. Another way to do this is to name them *JapaneseF$* and *EnglishF$,* where the *F* at the end of the name is a reminder that these are field variables.

Records in a random-access file are numbered 1, 2, 3, and so on. Record number 1 is the first record in the file, record number 2 is the second record, and so on. When a record is accessed in a random-access file, it is accessed by its record number. The next program block (600) sets the *RecordNmbr* variable to zero (0). *RecordNmbr* is then used within a WHILE...WEND loop that writes records to the random-access file by record number. Here is block 600:

```
600 REM ** No records yet, so set record number to zero **
610 RecordNmbr = 0
```

The following WHILE...WEND loop then reads the records from Japanese.Txt, converts them to the field structure required for Japanese.Ran, and writes (or PUTs) them to the Japanese.Ran file.

```
700 REM ** Copy records from Japanese.Txt to Japanese.Ran **
710 WHILE EOF(1) = 0
720    INPUT #1, Japanese$, English$    'Read one record
730    LSET Jfield$ = Japanese$         'Prepare fields to go to
740    LSET Efields$ = English$         'random-access file
750    RecordNmbr = RecordNmbr + 1      'Update record number
760    PUT #2, RecordNmbr               'Write record to file
770 WEND
```

Line 720 reads one record from Japanese.Txt. It assigns the first variable-length field to the string variable *Japanese$*, and the second variable-length field to the string variable *English$*. Lines 730 and 740 then convert these values to the structure required for the Japanese.Ran file. This structure was defined by the FIELD statement in line 510.

The statement

LSET Jfield$ = Japanese$

assigns the value of *Japanese$* to *Jfield$*. If the value of *Japanese$* has less than 38 characters, spaces are added to make a total of 38 characters in *Jfield$*. For example, the first field in the first record of Japanese.Txt (Nihon'go) appears as follows in *Jfield$:*

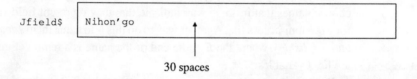

30 spaces

Note that the value of *Japanese$* is left justified in *Jfield$;* that is, it begins at the left end. Spaces, if required, are added on the right. You can use another statement, RSET, to right justify a string in a field variable.

If the value of *Japanese$* is exactly 38 characters long, then it exactly matches the length of *Jfield$* and no spaces are added. If the value of *Japanese$* has more than 38 characters, it is truncated. The first 38 characters (from the left) are assigned as the value of *Jfield$*.

The statement

RecordNmbr = RecordNmbr + 1

increases the value of *RecordNmbr* by 1. The first time through the WHILE...WEND loop, the value of *RecordNmbr* becomes 1 and is used to write the first record to Japanese.Ran. The second time through the loop, *RecordNmbr* is increased by 1 and is then used to write the second record to the file, and so on.

The statement

PUT #2, RecordNmbr

writes (PUTs) one record to file #2 as record number *RecordNmbr*. You must use a PUT statement to write records to a random-access file. The PUT statement writes a record as defined by a previously executed FIELD statement. Therefore, the PUT statement in this program writes a record consisting of two 38-character fields, the values of *Jfield$* and *Efield$*.

When the program reaches the end of the Japanese.Txt file, it exits from the WHILE…WEND loop, prints the length of both files, closes the files, and ends.

```
800 REM ** Print lengths of both files, close 'em, and end **
810 PRINT
820 PRINT "The Japanese.Txt file has"; LOF(1); "bytes."
830 PRINT "The Japanese.Ran file has"; LOF(2); "bytes."
840 CLOSE #1, #2
850 PRINT : PRINT "Both files are closed."
860 END
```

Add End-of-Record Characters to Japanese.Ran

You can add the end-of-record characters, CR and LF, to the Japanese.Ran file by changing the FIELD statement and creating a field string variable consisting of the two end-of-record characters. You must also increase the length of a record in the OPEN statement. Make these changes to Program GWME1101, as shown here:

```
410 OPEN "Japanese.Ran" FOR RANDOM AS #2 LEN = 78

510 FIELD #2, 38 AS Jfield$, 38 AS Efield$, 2 AS EORfield$
520 LSET EORfield$ = CHR$(13) + CHR$(10)
```

Line 410 now sets the length of each record at 78 characters (LEN = 78). Line 510 defines a record consisting of three fields—the two fields used previously (*Jfield$* and *Efield$)* and a two-character field called *EORfield$*. This name is chosen to remind you that it is an end-of-record field. Line 520 creates this field by assigning to it a two-character string consisting of the CR character (ASCII 13) and the LF character (ASCII 10).

Save this altered program under the filename GWME1102. Use Program GWME1102 (The New Create Japanese.RAN Random-Access File) to

```
1 REM ** Create Japanese.Ran Random-Access File **
2 ' GW-BASIC Made Easy, Chapter 11.  File: GWME1102.BAS
3 ' Reads records from Japanese.Txt and writes to Japanese.Ran
4 ' Attaches end-of-record characters CR and LF to each record

100 REM ** Setup **
110 SCREEN 0: CLS : KEY OFF
120 DEFINT A-Z

200 REM ** Tell what to do **
210 PRINT "Use Japanese.Txt file to create Japanese.Ran file."
220 PRINT "Files read from and written to default disk drive."
230 PRINT
240 PRINT "Press a key to begin.": akey$ = INPUT$(1)

300 REM ** Open Japanese.Txt for input on default drive **
310 OPEN "Japanese.Txt" FOR INPUT AS #1
320 PRINT
330 PRINT "Japanese.Txt is open for input."

400 REM ** Open Japanese.Ran for random on default drive **
410 OPEN "Japanese.Ran" FOR RANDOM AS #2 LEN = 78
420 PRINT
430 PRINT "Japanese.Ran is open for random."

500 REM ** Define field structure for Japanese.Ran file **
510 FIELD #2, 38 AS Jfield$, 38 AS Efield$, 2 AS EORfield$
520 LSET EORfield$ = CHR$(13) + CHR$(10)

600 REM ** No records yet, so set record number to zero **
610 RecordNmbr = 0

700 REM ** Copy records from Japanese.Txt to Japanese.Ran **
710 WHILE EOF(1) = 0
720    INPUT #1, Japanese$, English$      'Read one record
730    LSET Jfield$ = Japanese$           'Prepare fields to go to
740    LSET Efield$ = English$            'random-access file
750    RecordNmbr = RecordNmbr + 1        'Update record number
760    PUT #2, RecordNmbr                 'Write record to file
770 WEND
```

PROGRAM GWME1102   The New Create Japanese.Ran Random-Access File

```
800 REM ** Print lengths of both files, close 'em, and end **
810 PRINT
820 PRINT "The Japanese.Txt file has"; LOF(1); "bytes."
830 PRINT "The Japanese.Ran file has"; LOF(2); "bytes."
840 CLOSE #1, #2
850 PRINT : PRINT "Both files are closed."
860 END
```

PROGRAM GWME1102   The New Create Japanese.Ran Random-Access File
(*continued*)

create a new version of the Japanese.Ran file. A sample run is shown here:

```
Use Japanese.Txt file to create Japanese.Ran file.
Files read from and written to default disk drive.

Press a key to begin.

Japanese.Txt is open for input.

Japanese.Ran is open for random.

The Japanese.Txt file has 153 bytes.
The Japanese.Ran file has 390 bytes.

Both files are closed.
```

Note that the length of the Japanese.Ran file is 390 bytes, which is 10
bytes longer than before. The extra 10 bytes are the end-of-record characters
for the five records. Now return to MS-DOS and use the TYPE command to
display the file on the screen, as follows:

```
A>TYPE Japanese.Ran
Nihon'go                      Japanese language
Ohayoo gozaimasu              Good morning
Kon'nichi wa                  Good day, Hello
Kon'ban wa                    Good evening
Sayoonara                     Goodbye
```

Each record is displayed on a separate line. This happens because each
record now ends with the end-of-record characters, CR and LF, which cause

```
1 REM ** Enter Records from Keyboard to Japanese.Ran File **
2 ' GW-BASIC Made Easy, Chapter 11.  File: GWME1103.BAS

100 REM ** Setup **
110 SCREEN 0: CLS : KEY OFF
120 DEFINT A-Z

200 REM ** Tell what to do **
210 PRINT "Enter records from keyboard to Japanese.Ran file."
220 PRINT "To quit, enter zero (0) as the record number."
230 PRINT : PRINT "Press a key to begin.": akey$ = INPUT$(1)

300 REM ** Open Japanese.Ran for random on default drive **
310 OPEN "Japanese.Ran" FOR RANDOM AS #1 LEN = 78
320 PRINT : PRINT "Japanese.Ran is open for random."
340 PRINT

400 REM ** Define field structure for Japanese.Ran file **
410 FIELD #1, 38 AS Jfield$, 38 AS Efield$, 2 AS EORfield$
420 LSET EORfield$ = CHR$(13) + CHR$(10)

500 REM ** Enter records and put to the file **
510 INPUT "Record number (0 to quit)"; RecordNmbr
520 IF RecordNmbr = 0 THEN 610
530 LINE INPUT "Japanese? "; Japanese$
540 LINE INPUT "English ? "; English$
550 LSET Jfield$ = Japanese$
560 LSET Efield$ = English$
570 PUT #1, RecordNmbr
580 PRINT : GOTO 510

600 REM ** Print length of file, close it, and end **
610 PRINT : PRINT "The Japanese.Ran file has"; LOF(1); "bytes."
630 CLOSE #1: END
```

a carriage return and a line feed. This version of the Japanese.Ran file will be used in the next section.

ENTER RECORDS FROM THE KEYBOARD TO THE JAPANESE.RAN FILE

You can use Program GWME1103 (Enter Records from Keyboard to Japanese.Ran File) to change existing records in the Japanese.Ran file, or to enter new records to the end of the file.

First let's use GWME1103 to enter records to the Japanese.Ran file. Use the version of the file created by Program GWME1102, which has CR and LF characters at the end of each record. The existing file has five records numbered 1, 2, 3, 4, and 5. Each record is 78 bytes long; the length of the file is 390 bytes.

Figure 11-3 shows a sample run of Program GWME1103. Three records

```
Enter records from keyboard to Japanese.Ran file.
To quit, enter zero (0) as the record number.

Press a key to begin.

Japanese.Ran is open for random.

Record number (0 to quit)? 3
Japanese? san
English ? three

Record number (0 to quit)? 1
Japanese? ichi
English ? one

Record number (0 to quit)? 6
Japanese? roku
English ? six

Record number (0 to quit)? 0

The Japanese.Ran file has 468 bytes.
```

FIGURE 11-3   Enter records from the keyboard to the Japanese.Ran file

are entered. The first two (record number 3 and record number 1) change existing records. The third entry (record number 6) adds a new record to the end of the file. Note the length of the file at the end of the run. The file now contains six records with a total of 468 bytes.

If you return to MS-DOS and use the TYPE command to display the file, you will see the following:

```
A>TYPE Japanese.Ran
ichi                                one
Ohayoo gozaimasu                    Good morning
san                                 three
Kon'ban wa                          Good evening
Sayoonara                           Goodbye
roku                                six
```

You can see that the file now has six records, and that two of the original records have been changed to contain new information.

USE THE JAPANESE.RAN FILE FOR SEQUENTIAL PRACTICE

Use Program GWME1104 (Use Japanese.Ran for Sequential Practice) to scan the Japanese.Ran file one record at a time. You press a key to display the Japanese word or phrase, and then (when ready) press a key to display the English equivalent. Continue pressing keys to display the Japanese, then English, words or phrases. This program is similar to Program GWME1006,

---

```
1 REM ** Use Japanese.Ran for Sequential Practice **
2 ' GW-BASIC Made Easy, Chapter 11.  File:GWME1104.BAS

100 REM ** Setup **
110 SCREEN 0: CLS : KEY OFF
120 DEFINT A-Z              'Undesignated variables are integer
```

PROGRAM GWME1104   Use Japanese.Ran for Sequential Practice

```
300 REM ** Main program **
310 GOSUB 1010                          'Name of file & drive
320 GOSUB 2010                          'Tell what to do
330 GOSUB 4010                          'Open the file
340 GOSUB 3010                          'Scan the file
350 PRINT "That's all.  Press a key."
360 akey$ = INPUT$(1)                   'Wait for key press
370 VIEW PRINT: CLS : END               'End with normal screen

1000 REM ** SUBROUTINE: Get name of file & disk drive **
1010 LOCATE 1, 1: PRINT "Use a file for sequential practice."
1020 LOCATE 3, 1: INPUT "File name"; naym$
1030 LOCATE 5, 1: INPUT "Disk drive"; drive$
1040 filename$ = drive$ + ":" + naym$
1050 RETURN

2000 REM ** SUBROUTINE: Tell what to do & lock it in **
2010 CLS
2020 LOCATE 22, 1: PRINT STRING$(78, "*")
2030 PRINT "Practice with the "; naym$; " file on drive "; drive$
2040 PRINT "Press a key for next Japanese or English phrase.";
2050 VIEW PRINT 1 TO 21
2060 RETURN

3000 REM ** SUBROUTINE: Scan file, one field at a time **
3010 RecordNmbr = 0
3020 WHILE EOF(1) = 0
3030    RecordNmbr = RecordNmbr + 1      'Next record number
3040    GET #1, RecordNmbr               '1 record has 2 strings
3050    akey$ = INPUT$(1)                'Wait for key press
3060    PRINT Jfield$;                   'Print 1st field
3070    akey$ = INPUT$(1)                'Wait for key press
3080    PRINT TAB(40); Efield$           'Print 2nd field
3090    PRINT                            'Line space
3100 WEND
3110 RETURN                              'RETURN on EOF

4000 REM ** SUBROUTINE: Open file, define record structure **
4010 OPEN filename$ FOR RANDOM AS #1 LEN = 78
4020 FIELD #1, 38 AS Jfield$, 38 AS Efield$, 2 AS EORfield$
4030 RETURN
```

PROGRAM GWME1104   Use Japanese.Ran for Sequential Practice (*continued*)

shown in Chapter 10. It begins by asking for the name of the file and the disk
drive, as shown here:

```
Use a file for sequential practice

File name? Japanese.Ran

Disk drive? A_
```

Press ENTER, and the program is ready to display the first record. Figure 11-4
shows a sample run.

```
ichi                          one

Ohayoo gozaimasu              Good morning

san                           three

Kon'ban wa                    Good evening

Sayoonara                     Goodbye

roku                          six



That's all.  Press a key.




********************************************************************
Practice with the Japanese.Ran file on drive A
Press a key for next Japanese or English phrase
```

FIGURE 11-4   Sequential practice with the Japanese.Ran file

Program GWME1104 is written as a main program and four subroutines. Line 330 calls the subroutine that opens the file and defines the file structure. This subroutine is shown here:

```
4000 REM ** SUBROUTINE: Open file, define record structure **
4010 OPEN filename$ FOR RANDOM AS #1 LEN = 78
4020 FIELD #1, 38 AS Jfield$, 38 AS Efield$, 2 AS EORfield$
4030 RETURN
```

After the file has been opened and the file structure defined, the program calls the subroutine to scan the file, shown next:

```
3000 REM ** SUBROUTINE:  Scan file, one field at a time **
3010 RecordNmbr = 0
3020 WHILE EOF(1) = 0
3030    RecordNmbr = RecordNmbr + 1       'Next record number
3040    GET #1, RecordNmbr                '1 record has 2 strings
3050    akey$ = INPUT$(1)                 'Wait for key press
3060    PRINT Jfield$;                    'Print 1st field
3070    akey$ = INPUT$(1)                 'Wait for key press
3080    PRINT TAB(40); Efield$            'Print 2nd field
3090    PRINT                             'Line space
3100 WEND
3110 Return                               'Return of EOF
```

The statement

GET #1, RecordNmbr

gets one record from file #1. It gets the record specified by the value of *RecordNmbr*. The GET statement acquires information as defined by a previously executed FIELD statement. In this program, the GET statement will acquire the values of *Jfield$, Efifeld$,* and *EORfield$,* as defined by the FIELD statement in line 4020.

Use Program GWME1104 to scan any random-access file that has the structure defined by the FIELD statement in line 4020. You can also easily modify the program to scan a file that has a different structure. Just rewrite the subroutines in blocks 3000 and 4000, and make appropriate minor changes to the rest of the program.

```
1 REM ** Use Japanese.Ran for Random Practice **
2 ' GW-BASIC Made Easy, Chapter 11.  File:GWME1105.BAS

100 REM ** Setup **
110 SCREEN 0: CLS : KEY OFF
120 DEFINT A-Z
130 DEF FNran (n) = INT(n * RND) + 1     'Random integer function
140 RANDOMIZE TIMER

300 REM ** Main program **
310 GOSUB 1010                        'Name of file & drive
320 GOSUB 2010                        'Tell what to do
330 GOSUB 4010                        'Open the file
340 GOSUB 3010                        'Random practice
350 PRINT "That's all.  Press a key."
360 akey$ = INPUT$(1)                 'Wait for key press
370 VIEW PRINT: CLS : END             'End with normal screen

1000 REM ** SUBROUTINE: Get name of file & disk drive **
1010 LOCATE 1, 1: PRINT "Use a file for random practice"
1020 LOCATE 3, 1: INPUT "File name"; naym$
1030 LOCATE 5, 1: INPUT "Disk drive"; drive$
1040 filename$ = drive$ + ":" + naym$
1050 RETURN

2000 REM ** SUBROUTINE: Tell what to do & lock it in **
2010 CLS
2020 LOCATE 22, 1: PRINT STRING$(78, "*")
2030 PRINT "Practice with the "; naym$; " file on drive "; drive$
2040 PRINT "Press a key for next item, or ESC to quit.";
2050 VIEW PRINT 1 TO 21
2060 RETURN

3000 REM ** SUBROUTINE: Random practice with random file **
3010 RecordNmbr = FNran(NmbrRcrds)     'Random record number
3020 GET #1, RecordNmbr                'Get the random record
3030 akey$ = INPUT$(1)                 'Wait for key press
3040 IF akey$ = CHR$(27) THEN 3100     'Exit loop if ESC pressed
3050 PRINT Jfield$;                    'Print 1st field
3060 akey$ = INPUT$(1)                 'Wait for key press
3070 IF akey$ = CHR$(27) THEN 3100     'Exit loop if ESC pressed
3080 PRINT TAB(40); Efield$            'Print 2nd field
3090 PRINT : GOTO 3010                 'Go to top of loop
3100 RETURN                            'RETURN after ESC pressed
```

PROGRAM GWME1105   Use Japanese.Ran for Random Practice

```
4000 REM ** SUBROUTINE: Open file, define record structure **
4010 OPEN filename$ FOR RANDOM AS #1 LEN = 78
4020 FIELD #1, 38 AS Jfield$, 38 AS Efield$, 2 AS EORfield$
4030 NmbrRcrds = LOF(1) / 78            'Number of records in file
4040 RETURN
```

PROGRAM GWME1105   Use Japanese.Ran for Random Practice (*continued*)

USE JAPANESE.RAN FOR RANDOM PRACTICE

In Chapter 10, you used Program GWME1007 for random practice with the Japanese.Txt file. This program first read the file into string arrays in memory, because records in a sequential file cannot be randomly accessed.

You can use the Japanese.Ran file for random practice without first reading it into memory. Program GWME1105 (Use Japanese.Ran File for Random Practice) provides this capability. Figure 11-5 shows the end of a practice session, which exits appropriately with "Sayoonara" (Goodbye).

The subroutine that opens the Japanese.Ran file and defines the file structure is shown next. Note line 4030 of the subroutine.

```
4000 REM ** SUBROUTINE: Open file, define record structure **
4010 OPEN filename$ FOR RANDOM AS #1 LEN = 78
4020 FIELD #1, 38 AS Jfield$, 38 AS Efield$, 2 AS EORfield$
4030 NmbrRcrds = LOF(1) / 78            'Number of records in file
4040 RETURN
```

The statement

NmbrRcrds = LOF(1) / 78

computes the number of records in file #1 and assigns it as the value of *NmbrRcrds*. This is computed by dividing the length of the entire file (LOF) by the length of one record (78). The *NmbrRcrds* value is used in the random practice subroutine shown on the next page.

```
3000 REM ** SUBROUTINE: Random practice with random file **
3010 RecordNmbr = FNran(NmbrRcrds)    'Random record number
3020 GET #1, RecordNmbr               'Get the random record
3030 akey$ = INPUT$(1)                'Wait for key press
3040 IF akey$ = CHR$(27) THEN 3100    'Exit loop if ESC pressed
3050 PRINT Jfield$;                    'Print 1st field
3060 akey$ = INPUT$(1)                'Wait for key press
3070 IF akey$ = CHR$(27) THEN 3100    'Exit loop if ESC pressed
3080 PRINT TAB(40); Efield$            'Print 2nd field
3090 PRINT : GOTO 3010                'Go to top of loop
3100 RETURN                           'RETURN after ESC pressed
```

Line 3010 computes a random record number and assigns it as the value of
RecordNmbr. This value is a random integer in the range 1 to the number
represented in *NmbrRcrds*. The function *FNran* is defined in the setup block
of the program.

```
ichi                              one

Ohayoo gozaimasu                  Good morning

Ohayoo gozaimasu                  Good morning

Kon'ban wa                        Good evening

Ohayoo gozaimasu                  Good morning

ichi                              one

roku                              six

ichi                              one

Sayoonara                         Goodbye

That's all.  Press a key

*****************************************************************
Practice with the Japanese.Ran file on drive A
Press a key for next item, or ESC to quit.
```

FIGURE 11-5   End of a practice session using the Japanese.Ran file

Line 3020 gets a random record from the file consisting of the values of *Jfield$*, *Efield$*, and *EORfield$*, defined by the FIELD statement in line 4020. You can press the ESC key to exit the GOTO loop and return to the main program, or another key to display the values of *Jfield$* and *Efield$*.

Things to Try

The Japanese.Ran file shown here is very short. The authors have several long files used for studying Japanese and other subjects. Here are some suggestions for programming projects you can do.

Write a program to use a file for sequential practice, with an option to save for later review any item for which your response is incorrect.

Write a program to use a file for random practice. Initially, each record has the same probability of being chosen as any other record. After making your mental response, then viewing the correct response, press the C key to indicate "correct," or the N key to indicate "not correct." Your program then increases the probability of choosing any record on which you make an incorrect response.

Write a program to retrieve a record by means of a substring search. For example, if you want to know what "ohayoo" means, you enter **ohayoo** as the search string, and your program produces the record.

```
Ohayoo gozaimasu              Good morning
```

A PERSONAL CAMPING EQUIPMENT CATALOG

If you are a catalog browser, you might find the next two programs useful. They are designed to store and retrieve information from various camping equipment catalogs. If you aren't interested in camping, you can use these programs to store information on other topics, by making minor changes to the program.

Use Program GWME1106 (Enter Records into Camping.Cat Random-Access File) to create a new file or to append records to the end of an existing file. The program computes the number of records in the file and adjusts the record number, so that a record you enter from the keyboard is appended to the end of the file.

```
1 REM ** Enter Records into Camping.Cat Random-Access File **
2 ' GW-BASIC Made Easy, Chapter 11.  File:GWME1106.BAS

100 REM ** Setup **
110 SCREEN 0: CLS : KEY OFF
120 DEFINT A-Z

300 REM ** Main program **
310 GOSUB 1010                        'Name of file & drive
320 GOSUB 2010                        'Tell what to do
330 GOSUB 3010                        'Open file, def record

340 GOSUB 4010                        'Enter record
350 IF quit$ = "yes" THEN 400         'No more records
360 GOSUB 5010                        'Save this record (y/n)
370 IF INSTR("nN", keep$) <> 0 THEN 340 'If no, try again
380 GOSUB 6010                        'Put record to file
390 GOTO 340                          'Go for another record

400 CLOSE : VIEW PRINT: CLS : END     'Close all files & end

1000 REM ** SUBROUTINE: Get name of file & disk drive **
1010 PRINT "Enter records into a random-access file."
1020 PRINT : INPUT "File name"; naym$
1030 PRINT : INPUT "Disk drive"; drive$
1040 filename$ = drive$ + ":" + naym$
1050 RETURN

2000 REM ** SUBROUTINE: Tell what to do & lock it in **
2010 CLS
2020 LOCATE 22, 1: PRINT STRING$(78, "*")
2030 PRINT "Enter records into "; naym$; " file on drive "; drive$
2050 VIEW PRINT 1 TO 21
2060 RETURN

3000 REM ** SUBROUTINE: Open file & define record structure **
3010 OPEN filename$ FOR RANDOM AS #1 LEN = 120
3020 FIELD #1, 20 AS CatalogF$, 2 AS PageF$, 78 AS ItemF$
3030 FIELD #1, 100 AS PreviousF$, 12 AS CatNumF$, 4 AS PriceF$
3040 FIELD #1, 116 AS PreviousF$, 4 AS OuncesF$
3050 RETURN
```

PROGRAM GWME1106   Enter Records into Camping.Cat Random-Access File

```
4000 REM ** SUBROUTINE: Enter record **
4010 CLS
4020 RecordNmbr = LOF(1) / 120
4030 PRINT "File has"; RecordNmbr; "record(s),"; LOF(1); "bytes."
4040 PRINT : PRINT "Press a key to enter a record (ESC to quit)"
4050 quit$ = INPUT$(1)
4060 IF quit$ = CHR$(27) THEN quit$ = "yes": RETURN
4070 PRINT : LINE INPUT "Name of catalog? "; Catalog$
4080 PRINT : INPUT "Page number"; Page%
4090 PRINT : LINE INPUT "Description of item? "; Item$
4100 PRINT : LINE INPUT "Catalog number? "; CatNum$
4110 PRINT : INPUT "Price, each"; Price!
4120 PRINT : INPUT "Weight, ounces"; Ounces!
4130 RETURN

5000 REM ** SUBROUTINE: Save record (y/n)? **
5010 PRINT : PRINT "Save this record (y/n)?"
5020 keep$ = "?"                       'Make sure not empty
5030 WHILE INSTR("yYnN", keep$) = 0    'cause empty string
5040    BEEP: keep$ = INPUT$(1)        'satisfies condition
5050 WEND                              'in WHILE statement
5060 RETURN

6000 REM ** SUBROUTINE: Put record to file **
6010 LSET CatalogF$ = Catalog$
6020 LSET PageF$ = MKI$(Page%)
6030 LSET ItemF$ = Item$
6040 LSET CatNumF$ = CatNum$           'Assign values to fields
6050 LSET PriceF$ = MKS$(Price!)
6060 LSET OuncesF$ = MKS$(Ounces!)
6070 RecordNmbr = RecordNmbr + 1       'Next record number
6080 PUT #1, RecordNmbr
6090 RETURN
```

PROGRAM GWME1106 Enter Records into Camping.Cat Random-Access File
(continued)

The file is opened and the record structure defined by the following subroutine:

```
3000 REM ** SUBROUTINE: Open file & define record structure **
3010 OPEN filename$ FOR RANDOM AS #1 LEN = 120
3020 FIELD #1, 20 AS CatalogF$, 2 AS PageF$, 78 AS ItemF$
3030 FIELD #1, 100 AS PreviousF$, 12 AS CatNumF$, 4 AS PriceF$
3040 FIELD #1, 116 AS PreviousF$, 4 AS OuncesF$
3050 RETURN
```

Lines 3020, 3030, and 3040 define the record structure. Line 3020 reserves 100 bytes of memory space for the field string variables *CatalogF$, PageF$,* and *ItemF$.* The second FIELD statement, in line 3030, first reserves 100 bytes for the previously defined field variables (100 AS *PreviousF$*), then reserves 12 bytes for *CatNumF$* and 4 bytes for *PriceF$.* So far, 116 bytes have been reserved. The third FIELD statement, in line 3040, first reserves 116 bytes for the previously defined field variables (116 AS *PreviousF$*), then reserves 4 bytes for *OuncesF$.* Together, the three FIELD statements reserve 120 bytes, the length of a record, as defined in the OPEN statement (LEN = 120).

The variables *PageF$, PriceF$,* and *OuncesF$* are string field variables whose values represent numbers converted to strings by functions called MKI$ and MKS$. You will see these functions used later in the subroutine that PUTs a record to the file. The field variable names all end with the letter *F* to indicate that they are field variables. These variables should not be used in INPUT, LINE INPUT, or assignment statements. They may be used with LSET, RSET, and PRINT statements.

The program next calls the subroutine to enter a record from the keyboard, as shown here:

```
4000 REM ** SUBROUTINE: Enter record **
4010 CLS
4020 RecordNmbr = LOF(1) / 120
4030 PRINT "File has"; RecordNmbr; "record(s),"; LOF(1); "bytes."
4040 PRINT : PRINT "Press a key to enter a record (ESC to quit)"
4050 quit$ = INPUT$(1)
4060 IF quit$ = CHR$(27) THEN quit$ = "yes": RETURN
4070 PRINT : LINE INPUT "Name of catalog? "; Catalog$
4080 PRINT : INPUT "Page number"; Page%
4090 PRINT : LINE INPUT "Description of item? "; Item$
```

```
4100 PRINT : LINE INPUT "Catalog number? "; CatNum$
4110 PRINT : INPUT "Price, each"; Price!
4120 PRINT : INPUT "Weight, ounces"; Ounces!
4130 RETURN
```

The subroutine clears the view port (lines 1 to 21), then computes and prints the number of records (if any) in the file. It also prints the total length of the file. If you are creating a new file, both these values will be zero (0). This information will appear again after you enter a new record. You can now press ESC to quit, or another key to enter a record. If you press ESC, the subroutine sets the value of *quit$* to "yes" and returns to the main program. Line 370 will detect your decision to quit. If you press a key other than ESC, the program continues with the subroutine shown next.

```
5000 REM ** SUBROUTINE: Save record (y/n)? **
5010 PRINT : PRINT "Save this record (y/n)?"
5020 keep$ = "?"                        'Make sure not empty
5030 WHILE INSTR("yYnN", keep$) = 0     'cause empty string
5040   BEEP: keep$ = INPUT$(1)          'satisfies condition
5050 WEND                               'in WHILE statement
5060 RETURN
```

Records for this file are quite long and somewhat complex. So it is likely that you might occasionally make an error in entering data. If you do, just say no when the computer asks if you want to save this record (press the **N** key). If the record is correct and you want to save it, press the **Y** key. Your response is assigned as the value of *keep$* and used in the main program (line 370) to decide what to do next. If you decide to save the record, your decision is carried out by the following subroutine:

```
6000 REM ** SUBROUTINE: Put record to file **
6010 LSET CatalogF$ = Catalog$
6020 LSET PageF$ = MKI$(Page%)
6030 LSET ItemF$ = Item$
6040 LSET CatNumF$ = CatNum$           'Assign values to fields
6050 LSET PriceF$ = MKS$(Price!)
6060 LSET OuncesF$ = MKS$(Ounces!)
6070 RecordNmbr = RecordNmbr + 1       'Next record number
6080 PUT #1, RecordNmbr
6090 RETURN
```

Line 6010 converts the values entered from the keyboard to proper field string variables. In line 6020, the MKI$ function converts the value of the integer variable *Page%* to a 2-byte string and assigns it to the field string variable *PageF$*. In line 6050, the MKS$ function converts the value of the single precision variable *Price!* to a 4-byte string and assigns it to the field string variable *PriceF$*. In line 6060, the MKS$ function converts the value of the single precision variable *Ounces!* to a 4-byte string and assigns it as the value of the field string variable *OuncesF$*.

MKI$ converts an integer to a 2-byte field string. MKS$ converts a single precision number to a 4-byte field string. (There is a third function called MKD$ that converts a double precision number to an 8-byte field string. MKD$ is not used in this program.)

When this subroutine is called, the value of *RecordNmbr* is the number of the last record in the current file. Line 6070 increases this number by one; then line 6080 puts the record to the file.

The Camping.Cat file consists of six fixed-length fields. The storage requirements for these fields are shown in Table 11-1, along with the corresponding FIELD statement clauses used in lines 3020 and 3030.

Run Program GWME1106. It begins by asking for the filename and disk drive. Enter these, and the program continues as follows (assuming that no file previously existed):

```
File has 0 record(s), 0 bytes

Press a key to enter a record (ESC to quit).
```

Name of Field	Bytes Required	FIELD Statement Clause
CatalogF$	20	20 AS CatalogF$
ItemF$	78	78 AS ItemF$
CatNumF$	12	12 AS CatNumF$
PageF$	2	2 AS PageF$
PriceF$	4	4 AS PriceF$
OuncesF$	4	4 AS OuncesF$
Total	120	

TABLE 11-1   Camping.Cat Field and Record Sizes

```
File has 0 record(s), 0 bytes.

Press a key to enter a record (ESC to quit)

Name of catalog? Real Good Gear

Page number? 37

Description of item? Slobbovian army knife

Catalog number? SAK-1234

Price, each? 9.95

Weight, ounces? 3

Save this record (y/n)?
```

FIGURE 11-6   First record entered into Camping.Cat file

You can see that Camping.Cat is now empty, since it has zero records and 0 bytes. Press a key to enter a record. Figure 11-6 shows a sample record selected from the Fall '89 catalog of the Real Good Gear company.

Note that you are asked if this record should be saved. If you made a mistake while entering the record, answer **N**, and you can try again. If the information is correct, press **Y**, and the record will be written to the file. You will next see the following information:

```
File has 1 record(s), 120 bytes.

Press a key to enter a record (ESC to quit).
```

The file is no longer empty. It now contains one record, and is 120 bytes long. Press a key and add another record. The second record, shown in Figure 11-7, is selected from the Vagabond Outfitters catalog. Press **Y** to enter the record and you will see the new status of the file, as shown here:

```
File has 2 record(s), 240 bytes.

Press a key to enter a record (ESC to quit).
```

```
File has 1 record(s), 120 bytes.

Press a key to enter a record (ESC to quit)

Name of catalog? Vagabond Outfitters

Page number? 6

Description of item? Slumberbum sleeping bag

Catalog number? zzzzz007

Price, each? 69.95

Weight, ounces? 48

Save this record (y/n)?
```

FIGURE 11-7   Second record entered into Camping.Cat file

Be sure to enter the records shown in Figures 11-6 and 11-7. You will need them in the next section. Enter additional records if you wish, or press ESC to quit.

```
1 REM ** Scan Camping.Cat Random-Access File **
2 ' GW-BASIC Made Easy, Chapter 11.  File:GWME1107.BAS

100 REM ** Setup **
110 SCREEN 0: CLS : KEY OFF
120 DEFINT A-Z

300 REM ** Main program **
310 GOSUB 1010                      'Name of file & drive
320 GOSUB 2010                      'Open file, def record
330 NmbrRecords = LOF(1) / LenRcrd  'Number of records in file
340 GOSUB 3010                      'Tell what to do

350 RecordNmbr = 1
```

PROGRAM GWME1107   Scan the Camping.Cat File

```
360 WHILE RecordNmbr <= NmbrRecords
370    GOSUB 4010                          'Get & display record
380    RecordNmbr = RecordNmbr + 1
390 WEND

400 CLOSE #1: VIEW PRINT: CLS : END  'Close file & end

1000 REM ** SUBROUTINE: Get name of file & disk drive **
1010 PRINT "Get records from a random-access file."
1020 PRINT : INPUT "File name"; naym$
1030 PRINT : INPUT "Disk drive"; drive$
1040 filename$ = drive$ + ":" + naym$
1050 RETURN

2000 REM ** SUBROUTINE: Open file & define record structure **
2010 OPEN filename$ FOR RANDOM AS #1 LEN = 120
2020 FIELD #1, 20 AS CatalogF$, 2 AS PageF$, 78 AS ItemF$
2030 FIELD #1, 100 AS PreviousF$, 12 AS CatNumF$, 4 AS PriceF$
2040 FIELD #1, 116 AS PreviousF$, 4 AS OuncesF$
2050 LenRcrd = 120                                'Length of record
2060 RETURN

3000 REM ** SUBROUTINE: Tell what to do & lock it in **
3010 CLS
3020 LOCATE 22, 1: PRINT STRING$(78, "*")
3030 PRINT "Scan "; naym$; " file on drive "; drive$
3040 PRINT "File has"; NmbrRecords; "records.";
3050 VIEW PRINT 1 TO 21
3060 RETURN

4000 REM ** SUBROUTINE: Get a record and display it **
4010 GET #1, RecordNmbr
4020 CLS
4030 PRINT "Record number"; RecordNmbr; ":"
4040 PRINT : PRINT "Name of catalog: "; CatalogF$
4050 PRINT : PRINT "Page number: "; CVI(PageF$)
4060 PRINT : PRINT "Description of item:"
4070 PRINT ItemF$
4080 PRINT : PRINT "Catalog number: "; CatNumF$
4190 PRINT : PRINT "Price each: "; CVS(PriceF$)
4100 PRINT : PRINT "Weight, ounces: "; CVS(OuncesF$)
4110 PRINT : PRINT "Press a key to continue"
4120 akey$ = INPUT$(1)
4130 RETURN
```

PROGRAM GWME1107   Scan the Camping.Cat File (*continued*)

SCAN THE CAMPING.CAT CATALOG

Now that you have created the Camping.Cat file, you can use Program GWME1107 (Scan the Camping.Cat File) to browse through the file. In the discussion that follows, it is assumed that the file has only the two records shown in the previous section. Run Program GWME1107. After you supply the filename and disk drive designation, the computer displays the first record, as shown here:

```
Record number 1 :

Name of catalog: Real Good Gear

Page number:  37

Description of item:
Slobbovian army knife

Catalog number: SAK-1234

Price each:  9.95

Weight, ounces:  3

Press a key to continue
```

Press a key to get the next record.

```
Record number 2 :

Name of catalog: Vagabond Outfitters

Page number:  6

Description of item:
Slumberbum sleeping bag

Catalog number: zzzzz007

Price each:  69.95

Weight, ounces:  48

Press a key to continue
```

Press a key. Since there are no more records, the program ends.

The subroutine to get and display a record is shown here:

```
4000 REM ** SUBROUTINE: Get a record and display it **
4010 GET #1, RecordNmbr
4020 CLS
4030 PRINT "Record number"; RecordNmbr; ":"
4040 PRINT : PRINT "Name of catalog: "; CatalogF$
4050 PRINT : PRINT "Page number: "; CVI(PageF$)
4060 PRINT : PRINT "Description of item:"
4070 PRINT ItemF$
4080 PRINT : PRINT "Catalog number: "; CatNumF$
4090 PRINT : PRINT "Price each: "; CVS(PriceF$)
4100 PRINT : PRINT "Weight, ounces: "; CVS(OuncesF$)
4110 PRINT : PRINT "Press a key to continue"
4120 akey$ = INPUT$(1)
4130 RETURN
```

Lines 4050, 4090, and 4100 use functions to convert values of field string variables to numbers. Remember, the values of the field string variables *PageF$, PriceF$,* and *OuncesF$* represent numbers converted to strings by the MKI$ and MKS$ functions. The CVI and CVS functions perform the opposite operation and convert these special strings back to numbers.

In line 4050, the CVI function converts the value of *PageF$* to an integer. In lines 4090 and 4100, the CVS function converts the values of *PriceF$* and *OuncesF$* to single precision numbers. (A third function, called CVD, converts a field string representing a double precision number to a double precision number. The CVD function is not used in this program.)

Program GWME1106 used numeric variables *Page%, Price!,* and *Ounces!*. The values of these variables were converted to special strings and assigned to field string variables, as follows:

```
LSET PageF$ = MKI(Page%)        PageF$ is a 2-byte string
LSET PriceF$ = MKS(Price!)      PriceF$ is a 4-byte string
LSET OuncesF$ = MKS(Ounces!)    OuncesF$ is a 4-byte string
```

Program GWME1107 uses the CVI and CVS functions to convert the values of *PageF$, PriceF$,* and *OuncesF$* back to standard GW-BASIC integers and single precision numbers.

CVI(*PageF$*) is an integer

CVS(*PriceF$*) is a single precision number

CVS(OuncesF$) is a single precision number

REVIEW

Random-access files are files in which any record can be directly and immediately accessed. In a random-access file, every record is the same size. That is, every record has exactly the same number of bytes.

A record consists of one or more fields. Fields are of fixed length, and the sum of the lengths of the fields is the length of the record. Every record in a random-access file has the same field structure. Use FIELD statements to define the record structure.

When you open a random-access file, it is open for both input and output. You can use a PUT statement to write a record to the file, or a GET statement to retrieve a record from the file. You use a record number to immediately access any record in the file.

12

GRAPHICS

Simple graphic shapes can be drawn using the default GW-BASIC mode, SCREEN 0 (called the text mode). However, you can make more detailed and pleasing graphics in either the high-resolution graphics mode, SCREEN 2, or the medium-resolution graphics mode, SCREEN 1.

The high-resolution graphics mode is described in the first part of this chapter. The last part of the chapter is devoted to the medium-resolution mode. You will learn to use both screens. In particular, you will learn

- the advantages and disadvantages of each graphics mode

- how to locate graphic positions (column and row) using both graphics modes

- how to draw lines, rectangles, and other shapes with the LINE statement

- how to draw circles, sectors of circles, and arcs with the CIRCLE statement

- how to color the interior of closed shapes with the PAINT statement

- how to use LINE, CIRCLE, and PAINT statements to draw various kinds of graphs and charts

- to use graphics in useful and entertaining ways

This chapter makes extensive use of subroutines that are useful in many programs.

SOME FACTS ABOUT HIGH-RESOLUTION (SCREEN 2)

The high-resolution graphics mode is invoked by the execution of a SCREEN 2 statement. You can access twice as many points per line (640) in this mode as you can in the medium-resolution graphics mode (320). You can access the same number of graphic lines (200) in both modes.

You have access to only two colors in the high-resolution graphics mode: black and white. On some monitors, white may appear as amber or green.

The text you enter in SCREEN 2 is the same as in SCREEN 0 with WIDTH 80, that is, 80 characters per line, and 25 lines. This character size is half as wide as that printed on SCREEN 1 (which is the same as SCREEN 0, WIDTH 40). Therefore, SCREEN 2 is more suited to labeling graphs and charts.

DRAWING LINES

The quickest way to draw a line from one point on the screen to another is to use a LINE statement. The basic form for this statement is

```
LINE (ColOne, RowOne) — (ColTwo, RowTwo)
```

The pairs of values (column, row) are often referred to as coordinates of a point, or position. The column and row values of the LINE statement are separated by a comma and enclosed in parentheses. The point represented by the values (*ColOne, RowOne*) is one end of the line. The point (*ColTwo, RowTwo*) is the other end of the line.

Notice that the order of the column and row values for the LINE statement is the reverse of that for the LOCATE statement used for text as described in Chapter 6.

Enter and run Program GWME1201 (Diagonals on SCREEN 2) to see how lines are drawn from one corner of the screen to the opposite corner.

```
1 REM ** Diagonals on SCREEN 2 **
2 ' GW-BASIC Made Easy, Chapter 12.  File: GWME1201.BAS

100 REM ** Set screen **
110 SCREEN 2: CLS : KEY OFF                'Set screen

120 REM ** Draw diagonal & label **
130 ColOne = 0: RowOne = 0                 'First coordinates
140 ColTwo = 639: RowTwo = 199             'Second coordinates
150 GOSUB 60010                            'Go draw line
160 LOCATE 1, 4: PRINT "(0, 0)";           'Print labels
170 LOCATE 1, 70: PRINT "(639, 0)";

180 REM ** Draw diagonal & label **
190 ColOne = 0: RowOne = 199               'First coordinates
200 ColTwo = 639: RowTwo = 0               'Second coordinates
210 GOSUB 60010                            'Go draw line
220 LOCATE 25, 4: PRINT "(0, 199)";        'Print labels
230 LOCATE 25, 68: PRINT "(639, 199)";

240 REM ** Pause for ESC key press **
250 LOCATE 2, 28: PRINT "Press the ESC key to quit";
260 WHILE INKEY$ <> CHR$(27): WEND         'Wait
270 CLS : END                              'Clear and end

60000 REM ** SUBROUTINE: Draw a Line **
60010 LINE (ColOne, RowOne) - (ColTwo, RowTwo)
60020 RETURN
```

PROGRAM GWME1201   Diagonals on SCREEN 2

The coordinates of the beginning and end of each line are labeled on the screen by the PRINT statements.

First, the screen is cleared; then the coordinates of one end point of the line are assigned to the variables *ColOne* and *RowOne*.

```
130 ColOne = 0: RowOne = 0
```

Next, the coordinates of the second point are assigned to the variables *ColTwo* and *RowTwo*.

```
140 ColTwo = 639: RowTwo = 199
```

The GOSUB statement calls the subroutine to draw the line, as shown here:

```
210 GOSUB 60010
   .
   .
   .
60000 REM ** SUBROUTINE: Draw a Line **
60010 LINE (ColOne, RowOne)-(ColTwo, RowTwo)
60020 RETURN
```

Since variables are used in the subroutine, the subroutine can be used more than once in the same program.

The first line is drawn using the coordinates assigned in the main program. The line is drawn from the upper-left corner of the screen (0, 0) to the lower-right corner (639, 199). Then the end points are labeled so that you can see their relative location on the screen. Here are the lines that accomplish this:

```
160 LOCATE 1, 4: PRINT "(0, 0)";           'Print labels
170 LOCATE 25, 68: PRINT "(639, 199)";
```

Note: Graphics screen numbering begins in the upper-left corner. Column numbers and row numbers start with zero (0). (This is another difference between graphics and text numbering. Row and column numbers for text begin with row 1 and column 1.) Thus, in SCREEN 2

Text: first row = 1, first column = 1

           last row = 25, last column = 80

Graphics: first row = 0, first column = 0

           last row = 199, last column = 639

After the first line is drawn, the subroutine returns to the main program. New values are assigned to the end points.

```
190 ColOne = 0: RowOne = 199           'First coordinates
200 ColTwo = 639: RowTwo = 0           'Second coordinates
```

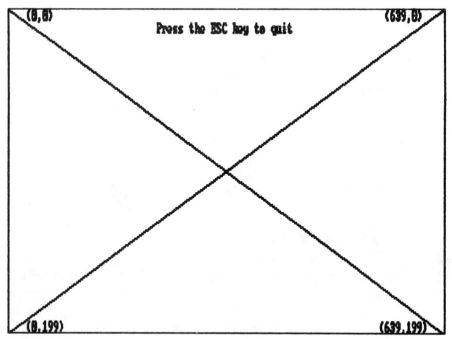

FIGURE 12-1   Output of Program GWME1201

The same subroutine is then called, but when it draws the line, it uses the new coordinates. New labels are printed for this line. The program then waits in a WHILE…WEND loop while you study the screen. When you have seen enough, press the ESC key as suggested by the prompt. The screen clears, and the program ends.

As you can see in Figure 12-1, the coordinates of the upper-left corner of the screen are (0, 0). The lower-right corner of the screen is 639 columns to the right and 199 rows down from the upper-left corner of the screen. Therefore, the coordinates of the lower-right corner are (639, 199). The first line is drawn between these two points, as follows:

```
LINE (0, 0) - (639, 199)
```

Also labeled in Figure 12-1 are the coordinates of the end points of the second diagonal: (0, 199) and (639, 0). The lower-left corner of the screen is at (0, 199), and the upper-right corner of the screen is at (639, 0). The second line is drawn between these points as follows.

```
LINE (0, 199) — (639, 0)
```

The "Draw a Line" subroutine can be saved as a separate file and merged with other programs, as described in Chapter 8. If you do this, you should include remarks that remind you to assign values to the variables *before* executing the GOSUB statement that references the subroutine. For example:

```
60000 REM ** SUBROUTINE: Draw a Line **
60010 ' Assign values to ColOne, RowOne
60020 ' ColTwo, and RowTwo before calling
```

Tiny Pixels Make a Line

The single *pixels* (picture elements) on SCREEN 2 are hard to see and impossible to measure. When the computer draws a line, it places a string of pixels adjacent to each other. You can measure such a line and calculate the size of a pixel. The next short program draws the boundaries of the graphics area for SCREEN 2. It uses an abbreviated form of the LINE statement.

You first used the LINE statement in this form:

```
LINE (ColOne, RowOne)-(ColTwo, RowTwo)
```

Note that both end points are specified.

Once a line is drawn using this form of the LINE statement, the computer remembers the last point that was referenced: (*ColTwo, RowTwo*). Therefore, if you want to draw a line that is connected to (*ColTwo, RowTwo*), you can use the following shortened form:

```
LINE -(ColThree, RowThree)
```

The new line is drawn to (*ColThree, RowThree*) from (*ColTwo, RowTwo*).

To calculate pixel size, first enter and run the following short program. Leave the result on the screen.

```
100 SCREEN 2: CLS : KEY OFF

110 LINE (0, 0) — (639, 0)                          —— Top line
120 LINE -(639, 199): LINE -(0, 199): LINE -(0, 0)

130 ky$ = INPUT$(1)
```

Connecting lines

All text and graphics in SCREEN 2 are printed with the displayed boundaries as screen limits. Let's measure these boundaries and calculate the pixels' size, as follows:

1. Measure the length of the top (or bottom) boundary line.
2. Measure the length of the left (or right) boundary line.
3. Divide the length of the top boundary line by 640. The result is the width of one pixel.
4. Divide the length of the left boundary line by 200. The result is the height of one pixel.

For example, here are the measurements on a Tandy CM-ll color monitor. If you are using a different monitor, your measurements may be different. (*Note:* Measurements and calculations are approximate.)

1. Length of top: 9.75 inches or 24.765 centimeters
2. Length of side: 6.625 inches or 16.8275 centimeters
3. Width of a pixel: $9.75 \; / \; 640 \; = .015$ inches
$24.765 \; / \; 640 \; = .039$ centimeters
4. Height of a pixel: $6.625 \; / \; 200 \; = .033$ inches
$16.8275 \; / \; 200 \; = .084$ centimeters

From the calculations, you can see that a pixel is very small. To get a visual indication of pixel size, enter and run Program GWME1202 (Pixel Hunt on SCREEN 2). This is an extended variation of the short program listed previously that drew the screen boundaries you measured. Note that the subroutine from Program GWME1201 is used again. If you saved that subroutine separately, you can simply merge it into this program.

In addition, GWME1202 contains a subroutine that draws connecting lines, and a subroutine that sets a point (explained below). You may want to save the last two subroutines separately so that they can also be used with other programs.

After column and row positions are selected in the main program, the "Connect a line" subroutine draws the connecting line. Here is line 60110:

```
60110 LINE -(col, row)
```

```
1 REM ** Pixel Hunt on SCREEN 2 **
2 ' GW-BASIC Made Easy, Chapter 12.  File: GWME1202.BAS

100 REM ** Setup **
110 SCREEN 2: CLS : KEY OFF                       'Set screen

120 REM ** Draw boundaries, set points **
130 WHILE ky$ <> CHR$(27)                         'Look for ESC
140    ColOne = 0: RowOne = 0: ColTwo = 639: RowTwo = 0
150    GOSUB 60010                                'First line
160    col = 639: row = 199: GOSUB 60110          'Connect line
170    col = 0: row = 199: GOSUB 60110            'Connect line
180    col = 0: row = 0: GOSUB 60110              'Connect line

190    REM ** Set a random point **
200    col = INT(638 * RND) + 1: row = INT(198 * RND) + 1
210    GOSUB 60210                                'Set point

220    REM ** Wait, then label; wait, then repeat **
230    ky$ = INPUT$(1)
240    LOCATE 2, 2: PRINT col, row
250    ky$ = INPUT$(1): LOCATE 2, 2: PRINT SPACE$(18);
260 WEND
270 CLS:END

60000 REM ** SUBROUTINE: Draw a line **
60010 LINE (ColOne, RowOne)-(ColTwo, RowTwo)
60020 RETURN

60100 REM ** SUBROUTINE: Connect a line **
60110 LINE -(col, row)
60120 RETURN

60200 REM ** SUBROUTINE: Set a point **
60210 PSET (col, row)
60310 RETURN
```

PROGRAM GWME1202   Pixel Hunt on SCREEN 2

A pixel position is randomly picked in the main program so that the pixel will be placed within the boundaries, as shown here:

```
200 col = INT(638 * RND) + 1: row = INT(198 * RND) + 1
```

The range for columns is 1 through 638, and the range for rows is 1 through 198. Pixels are printed in the "Set a point" subroutine by the PSET statement:

```
60210 PSET (col, row)          'Set a pixel at this point
```

After the subroutine turns on (sets) a randomly placed pixel, the computer returns to the main program and waits for you to scan the screen and find the pixel. When you find it, press a key, and the coordinates of the point are printed at the top of the screen.

Press a key again, and a new pixel is turned on. Again, the computer waits for you to scan the screen. The first point is still in its place, but the new pixel is also in its place. Unless the computer picked the same random number (almost impossible), or the first pixel was erased when its coordinates were printed (possible), you should be able to see both pixels. Press a key, and the coordinates of the second point are printed at the top of the screen.

This process continues until you press the ESC key. Good hunting!

Using Real-World Coordinates

If you are going to do any serious graphics work, such as making charts and graphs, you will find it difficult working with the coordinate system just discussed. That system, called the Screen Coordinate System, is topsy-turvy. Everything is measured from the top of the screen. In the real world, things grow from the bottom upward. Measurements make more sense when made from left to right, and bottom to top.

GW-BASIC has a statement that will transform these coordinates according to a new system, known as the World Coordinate System. This WINDOW statement will let you specify the boundaries of the display:

```
WINDOW (ColLeft, RowLow)-(ColRight, RowHigh)
```

The lower-left corner of the screen is assigned the coordinates (*ColLeft, RowLow*), and the upper-right corner is assigned the coordinates (*ColRight, RowHigh*).

The statement

```
WINDOW (0, 0)-(639, 199)
```

redefines the graphics area to be (0, 0) for the lower-left corner, and (639,

199) for the upper-left corner. These are "real-world" coordinates.

One of the important uses of the LINE statement is in making line graphs that display changing information. Program GWME1203 (Simple Line Graph) uses the LINE statement to connect points of data for such a presentation.

The program first uses a WINDOW statement (line 110) to define the screen in real-world coordinates. The vertical boundary of the graph is marked at ten-unit intervals, as follows:

```
170 FOR num = 10 TO 100 STEP 10                          'Scale
180    ColOne = 118: RowOne = 50 + num
190    ColTwo = 122: RowTwo = RowOne: GOSUB 60010
200 NEXT num
```

You will also see two familiar subroutines that draw the lines necessary for the graph.

```
1 REM ** Simple Line Graph **
2 ' GW-BASIC Made Easy, Chapter 12.  File: GWME1203.BAS

100 REM ** Setup **
110 SCREEN 2: CLS : KEY OFF: WINDOW (0, 0)-(639, 199)

120 REM ** Draw labels and title **
130 LOCATE 20, 20                              'Print labels
140 PRINT "J    F    M    A    M    J    J    A    S    O    N    D";
150 LOCATE 22, 33: PRINT "Simple line graph";
160 LOCATE 10, 10: PRINT "Temp";
170 FOR num = 10 TO 100 STEP 10                'Scale
180    ColOne = 118: RowOne = 50 + num:
190    ColTwo = 122: RowTwo = RowOne: GOSUB 60010
200 NEXT num

210 REM ** Draw graph boundaries **
220 ColOne = 580: RowOne = 50: ColTwo = 120: RowTwo = 50
230 GOSUB 60010                                'Horizontal
240 col = 120: row = 160: GOSUB 60110
```

PROGRAM GWME1203   Simple Line Graph

```
250 REM ** Get data for points **
260 DIM row(12): num = 12: GOSUB 60210              'Vertical

270 REM ** Draw lines **
280 pnt = 1: col = 235: ColOne = 155: RowOne = row(pnt)
290 ColTwo = 195: RowTwo = row(pnt + 1): GOSUB 60010  'First
300 FOR pnt = 3 TO 12
310   row = row(pnt): GOSUB 60110                   'Connect
320   col = col + 30                                'New point
330 NEXT pnt

340 REM ** Wait, then end **
350 ky$ = INPUT$(1): CLS:END

60000 REM ** SUBROUTINE: Draw a line **
60010 LINE (ColOne, RowOne)-(ColTwo, RowTwo)
60020 RETURN

60100 REM ** SUBROUTINE: Connect a line **
60110 LINE -(col, row)
60120 RETURN

60200 REM ** SUBROUTINE: Read data points **
60210 FOR num = 1 TO 12
60220   READ row(num)
60230 NEXT num
60240 DATA 105, 104, 116, 118, 122, 134
60250 DATA 146, 153, 137, 125, 110, 116
60260 RETURN
```

PROGRAM GWME1203   Simple Line Graph (*continued*)

An array is used in this program and is dimensioned in line 260 with this DIM statement:

```
DIM row(12)
```

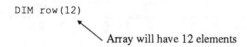
Array will have 12 elements

In the subroutine, Read data points, the data for the row coordinates of the points of the graph are read into an array called row(pnt).

```
60210 FOR num = 1 TO 12
60220    READ row(num)
60230 NEXT num
```

These values are used when the subroutines are called to draw the lines of the bar graph.

Figure 12-2 shows the output of the program.

Drawing Rectangular Shapes

As you know, rectangles can be drawn using four separate LINE statements. However, there is another LINE option—the B option—that draws rectangles with only one statement. Enter and run this short program to see how it's done.

```
100 SCREEN 2: CLS : KEY OFF: WINDOW (0, 0)-(639, 199)
110 LOCATE 9, 16
120 PRINT "This rectangle is drawn by the line statement:"
130 LOCATE 11, 25: PRINT "LINE (50, 68)-(570, 152),,B"
```

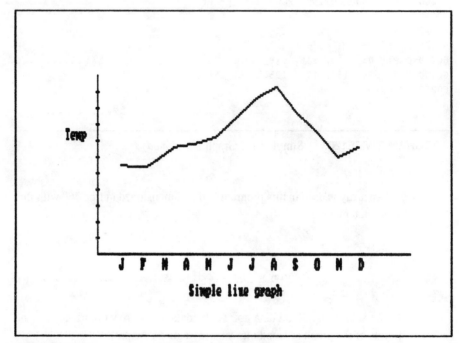

FIGURE 12-2   Output of Program GWME1203

```
140 LOCATE 13, 22: PRINT "(50, 68) is the upper-left corner"
150 LOCATE 14, 22: PRINT "(570, 152) is the lower-right corner"
160 LOCATE 15, 24: PRINT "The B option says, 'Draw a box'";
170 LINE (50, 68)-(570, 152), , B
180 ky$ = INPUT$(1)
```

Figure 12-3 shows the output of the program.

When you use the B option, the LINE statement interprets the two coordinate pairs as opposite corners, as shown here:

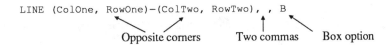

In Figure 12-3, the rectangle encloses text. This technique is useful when you want to put emphasis on important ideas in reports, charts, or graphs, so that the enclosed information is not likely to be overlooked.

Another use of the rectangle is in drawing bar graphs for business purposes or home use. You may even want to color or shade the interior of the bars. This can be quickly done by using the F option in the LINE statement.

This rectangle is drawn by the line statement:

LINE (50, 68)-(570, 152),,B

(50, 68) is the lower-left corner
(570, 152) is the upper-right corner
The B option says, 'Draw a box'

FIGURE 12-3   LINE with B option

```
1 REM ** Simple Bar Graph **
2 ' GW-BASIC Made Easy, Chapter 12.  File: GWME1204.BAS

100 REM ** Setup **
110 SCREEN 2: CLS : KEY OFF: WINDOW (0, 0)-(639, 199)

120 REM ** Draw labels and title **
130 LOCATE 20, 20
140 PRINT "1     2     3     4     5     6     7";      'Labels
150 LOCATE 22, 30: PRINT "Simple bar graph";

160 REM ** Draw graph boundaries; then bars **
170 ColOne = 100: RowOne = 50: ColTwo = 500: RowTwo = 148
180 GOSUB 60010                                    'Boundaries
190 GOSUB 60210                                    'Bars

200 REM ** Wait, then end **
210 ky$ = INPUT$(1)
220 END

60000 REM ** SUBROUTINE: Draw a rectangle **
60010 LINE (ColOne, RowOne)-(ColTwo, RowTwo), , B
60020 RETURN

60100 REM ** SUBROUTINE: Draw filled rectangle **
60110 LINE (ColOne, RowOne)-(ColTwo, RowTwo), , BF
60120 RETURN

60200 REM ** SUBROUTINE: Draw bars **
60210 FOR bar = 1 TO 7
60220    READ ColOne, RowOne, ColTwo, RowTwo
60230    IF bar / 2 = INT(bar / 2) THEN GOSUB 60010
60240    IF bar / 2 <> INT(bar / 2) THEN GOSUB 60110
60250 NEXT bar
60260 DATA 148,50,164,81, 196,50,212,91, 244,50,260,87
60270 DATA 292,50,308,109, 340,50,356,115, 388,50,404,105
60280 DATA 436,50,452,123
60290 RETURN
```

PROGRAM GWME1204   Simple Bar Graph

The F option is used along with the B option to Fill a **Box**, this way:

```
LINE (ColOne, RowOne)-(ColTwo, RowTwo), , BF
```

Box   Fill

Program GWME1204 (Simple Bar Graph) uses the B and the BF options to draw a bar graph. Odd-numbered bars are drawn using the BF option. Even-numbered bars are drawn using only the B option. The entire graph is enclosed in a large rectangle using the B option.

Real-world coordinates are then used to draw the bars from top to bottom.

```
WINDOW (0, 0)-(639, 199)
```

Once again, subroutines are used to draw the graphics. You should save the subroutines separately if you are building a tool kit of useful graphic subroutines. READ and DATA statements are used to access the coordinates used to draw the bars. The title and labels are displayed by PRINT statements.

Figure 12-4 shows the bar graph drawn by the program.

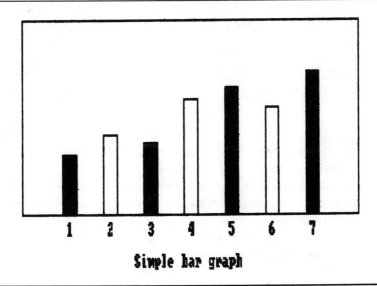

FIGURE 12-4   Output of Program GWME1204

ROUNDISH SHAPES

You can draw a roundish shape in SCREEN 2 with a CIRCLE statement. Enter and run this two-line program:

```
100 SCREEN 2: CLS
110 CIRCLE (320, 100), 70
```

Even though the statement says CIRCLE, you can see that the figure drawn is not a circle. It is an ellipse that is taller than it is wide.

The CIRCLE statement has many options. The keyword CIRCLE is followed by the coordinates of its center in parentheses. Then the radius is specified.

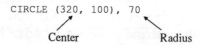

If you want the shape to look round (like a circle) on the screen, you must specify the eccentricity (ratio of height to width) of the shape. In SCREEN 2, an eccentricity of about .45 is satisfactory on the screen used in this book. You may have to experiment to find the right eccentricity for your monitor. Here is a modified CIRCLE statement with the eccentricity specified:

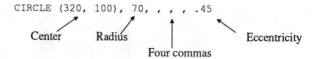

The commas are necessary as placeholders for three other options that will be discussed later.

Here is a short program that draws randomly placed and sized circles on the screen. The column and row of each circle's center, and its radius, are printed also. Each time you press a key, a new circle is drawn, and its characteristics printed. Enter and run the program. Look at several different circles. Press the ESC key to quit.

```
100 SCREEN 2: CLS : KEY OFF: RANDOMIZE TIMER
110 WHILE ky$ <> CHR$(27)
120   col = INT(640 * RND): row = INT(200 * RND)
```

```
130    radius = INT(100 * RND) + 2
140    CIRCLE (col, row), radius, , , , .45
150    LOCATE 2, 2: PRINT "column"; col; "   row"; row;
160    PRINT " radius"; radius
170    ky$ = INPUT$(1): CLS
180 WEND
```

Each time you press a key, the screen is cleared and a new circle drawn. Notice the coordinates of the circle's center and the circle's radius. Sometimes, all of the circle cannot fit on the screen. This doesn't bother the computer. It draws the part of the circle that will fit on the screen, and ignores the rest of the circle. Keep this in mind when you use the CIRCLE statement. Size your circle so it will fit on the screen.

Circle Sectors

Two options are available to draw *arcs* and *sectors* (parts of circles). One option specifies the starting point for the arc in *radians*. The other option specifies the end point of the arc. A complete circle contains approximately 6.28 radians.

The following CIRCLE statement draws an arc whose length is one-fourth of the *circumference* of a circle. The circumference is the distance around the circle.

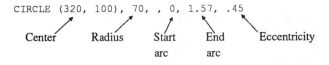

```
CIRCLE (320, 100), 70, , 0, 1.57, .45
```
Center   Radius   Start   End   Eccentricity
                    arc   arc

The arc is drawn from the starting point (3 o'clock) counterclockwise, as shown here:

End

Start

A sector is drawn by specifying the start and end points of the arc as negative quantities, this way:

```
CIRCLE (320, 100), 70, , -.0001, -1.57, .45
```
Negative end points

The computer doesn't recognize a negative zero, so a tiny negative amount is used (–.0001). The statement draws the sector shown here:

Circle sectors are very useful in drawing circle graphs. Program GWME1205 (Circle Graph) uses circle sectors to draw a circle graph that shows the total sales by a company, in percentages by geographic area. Each

```
1 REM ** Circle Graph **
2 ' GW-BASIC Made Easy, Chapter 12.  File: GWME1205

100 REM ** Set screen and define variables **
110 SCREEN 2: CLS : KEY OFF
120 col = 320: row = 100: radius = 120
130 Tile1$ = CHR$(128) + CHR$(32) + CHR$(8) + CHR$(2)
140 Tile2$ = CHR$(2) + CHR$(8) + CHR$(32) + CHR$(128)
150 Tile3$ = CHR$(16) + CHR$(16) + CHR$(16) + CHR$(16)
160 one = -.3: two = -.25: start = -.01
170 sec1 = one * 6.28: sec2 = sec1 + two * 6.28

180 REM ** Draw circle sectors **
190 CIRCLE (col, row), radius, 1, start, sec1
200 CIRCLE (col, row), radius, 1, sec1, sec2
210 CIRCLE (col, row), radius, 1, sec2, start

220 REM ** Shade circle sectors **
230 PAINT (col + 35, row + 15), Tile1$
240 PAINT (col + 35, row - 15), Tile2$
250 PAINT (col - 35, row - 15), Tile3$

260 REM ** Label and Title **
270 LOCATE 5, 29: PRINT "Sales by Geographic Area"
280 LOCATE 12, 29: PRINT " Area 2 ";
290 LOCATE 11, 43: PRINT " Area 1 ";
300 LOCATE 16, 38: PRINT " Area 3 ";

310 REM ** Wait, clear screen and end **
320 ky$ = INPUT$(1): CLS
330 END
```

PROGRAM GWME1205   Circle Graph

sector of the circle is shaded for contrast.

Since only two colors are available in SCREEN 2, shading is used instead of coloring. The shading patterns are accomplished by painting with tiles instead of colors. For example:

CHR$(128) =
CHR$(32) =
CHR$(8)   =
CHR$(2)   =

The shaded pixels are turned on according to the bits that comprise each byte of the file string. When the tiles are concatenated, a pattern such as the one shown here is painted within the figure's boundaries.

```
130 Tile1$ = CHR$(128) + CHR$(32) + CHR$(8) + CHR$(2)
```

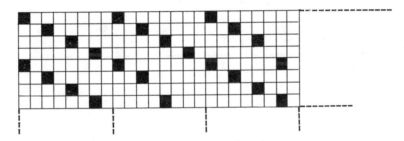

Figure 12-5 shows the output of Program GWME1205. Text could be "wrapped around" this graph to create a company report, for distribution within the sales force or for other business purposes. Graphs such as this one and the bar graph of Program GWME1204 are often referred to as *presentation graphics*, as they are presented as slides or handouts at business conferences.

SOME FACTS ABOUT COLOR GRAPHICS (SCREEN 1)

The balance of this chapter demonstrates the color graphics of the medium-resolution mode. This mode is invoked by the execution of a SCREEN 1 statement. You can access four colors in this mode; therefore, the screens will be more vivid. Color greatly enhances graphics used for business or entertainment.

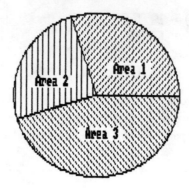

FIGURE 12-5   Simple circle graph

In gaining added color, this screen mode gives up some horizontal resolution. The size of a pixel is twice as wide as a pixel in SCREEN 2. Therefore, only 320 pixels will fit on a row in the medium-resolution mode. However, both SCREEN 1 and SCREEN 2 have the same number of pixel rows (200).

Any text entered in this mode is the same as in SCREEN 0 when you use WIDTH 40. The character size is then twice as wide as in SCREEN 2. Therefore, SCREEN 1 is not as well suited for labeling graphs and charts as SCREEN 2.

SELECTING COLORS

You may select a background color from one of eight background colors. The other three colors on your screen depend on the *palette* you select in a COLOR statement.

```
COLOR Back, Pal
```
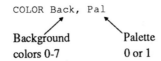
Background   Palette
colors 0-7   0 or 1

Colors available are shown in Table 12-1.

The drawing color is specified in the graphics statements that you use. For example, these two statements used together draw a green circle on a black background:

```
COLOR 0, 0                    'Selects black background,
                              'and palette 0

CIRCLE (160, 100), 7, 1       'Selects color 1 in the palette
                              'which is green
```

The following two statements used together draw a magenta rectangle on a cyan background:

```
COLOR 3, 1                    'Selects cyan background,
                              'and palette 1

LINE (0, 0)-(10, 20), 2, B    'Selects color 2 in the
                              'palette which is magenta
```

Background	Foreground	
	Palette 0	Palette 1
0 black		
1 blue		
2 green	0 background	0 background
3 cyan	1 green	1 cyan
4 red	2 red	2 magenta
5 magenta	3 brown	3 white
6 brown		
7 white		

TABLE 12-1   Colors for SCREEN 1

PSET IN SCREEN 1

Since only 320 pixels will fit on a row in this mode, the columns used when locating a pixel are numbered from 0 through 319. The rows are the same as in SCREEN 2, and are numbered from 0 through 199. Enter and run the following short program to see the four corners and approximate center of the screen.

```
100 SCREEN 1: COLOR 0, 1    'Black background, palette 1
110 CLS: KEY OFF
120 PSET (0, 0), 3          'Upper-left corner, white
130 PSET (319, 0), 3        'Upper-right corner, white
140 PSET (0, 199), 1        'Lower-left corner, cyan
150 PSET (319, 199), 1      'Lower-right corner, cyan
160 PSET (160, 100), 2      'Center, magenta
```

Notice that the COLOR statement selects the background color and palette to be used. The PSET statement selects the color used to set (turn on) a point.

Color 3 is white in palette 1

As noted in the comments of the program, the upper corners are colored white (3), the lower corners are colored cyan (1), and the center is colored magenta (2). You can also use the background color with color number 0. The background color can be laid over a previously colored point to erase the color.

Using PSET

Zappy Artist stopped by recently. Zappy likes to zap around the screen, drawing random shapes in SCREEN 1. He left a disk with two programs that draw wavy lines with the PSET statement. If you remember your high school algebra classes, you may recognize the sine curves drawn in Program GWME1206 (Sine Wave by PSET). Don't worry if you don't remember what a sine curve is. Just enter the program and run it. Then sit back, relax, and enjoy the output as the computer draws complete sine curve cycles in random colors.

```
1 REM ** Sine Wave by PSET **
2 ' GW-BASIC Made Easy, Chapter 12.  File: GWME1206

100 REM ** Set black background, palette 1, variables **
110 SCREEN 1: COLOR 0, 1: CLS
120 KEY OFF: WINDOW (0, -2)-(6.28, 2)
130 RANDOMIZE TIMER

140 REM ** Define variables **
150 DEFINT A-Z
160 hght! = 2 * RND: kolor = INT(3 * RND) + 1
170 GOSUB 60010

180 REM ** Do some more or quit **
190 LOCATE 23, 2: PRINT "Press ESC to quit,";
200 LOCATE 24, 2: PRINT "another key for more";
210 ky$ = INPUT$(1)
220 LOCATE 23, 2: PRINT SPACE$(20);
230 LOCATE 24, 2: PRINT SPACE$(20);
240 IF ky$ <> CHR$(27) THEN 160
250 CLS: SCREEN 0: WIDTH 80: END

60000 REM ** SUBROUTINE: Draw the wave **
60010 FOR col! = 0 TO 6.28 STEP .05
60020   PSET (col!, hght! * SIN(col!)), kolor
60030 NEXT col!
60040 RETURN
```

PROGRAM GWME1206   Sine Wave by PSET

The WINDOW statement in line 120 sizes the display to show one complete cycle of a sine curve (0 to 6.28 radians). The height of the window allows the magnitude of the curve to range from −2 to +2.

```
WINDOW (0, -2)-(6.28, 2)
```

Since the maximum magnitude of a sine wave is 1, a multiplier for the sine wave is randomly selected so that the curves will vary in height, as shown here:

```
hght! = 2 * RND        'Greater than 0, but less than 2
```

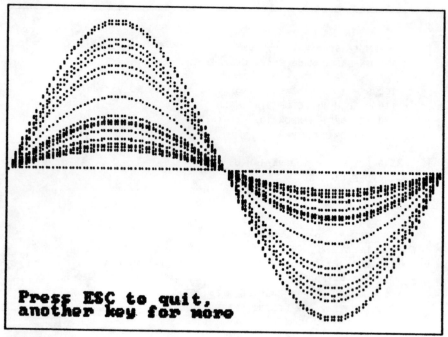

FIGURE 12-6   Sine curves

The PSET statement in the subroutine multiplies *hght!* times the value of the sine (SIN(col!)) to obtain the row coordinate for each column (*col*) value.

```
60010 FOR col! = 0 TO 6.28 STEP .05
60020    PSET (col!, hght! * SIN(col!)), kolor
60030 NEXT col!
```

After a sine curve is drawn, the computer pauses to let you draw another curve or to quit. Figure 12-6 shows a typical display after several sine curves have been drawn. The curves will appear on your screen in the color specified in the PSET statement, and randomly selected by

```
kolor = INT(3 * RND) + 1
```
1 added to avoid black as a drawing color

Zappy's second program uses the SIN function in a more subtle way. Program GWME1207 (Flower by PSET) changes the size of the window so that the sine curves will appear smaller on the display. It also draws a negative sine curve to form a symmetrical shape. Sine curves are added along a vertical axis to form a flower shape.

Enter the program and run it several times. Figure 12-7 shows a flower drawn by the program.

Palette 1 was used for both Program GWME1206 and Program GWME1207. Try them both with Palette 0, or modify the programs to switch palettes after each sine curve is drawn.

LINE IN SCREEN 1

You can draw colorful lines, rectangles, and other shapes formed by the LINE statement when you are using SCREEN 1. The LINE statement has

---

```
1 REM ** Flower by PSET **
2 ' GW-BASIC Made Easy, Chapter 12.  File: GWME1207

100 REM ** Set black background, palette 1, window **
110 SCREEN 1: COLOR 0, 1: CLS
120 KEY OFF: WINDOW (-8, -8)-(8, 8)
130 RANDOMIZE TIMER: DEFINT A-Z

140 REM ** Draw flower with PSET **
150 FOR num = 1 TO 15
160    hght! = 1.5 * RND                       'Height factor
170    kolor = INT(3 * RND) + 1                 'Drawing color
180    FOR col! = 0 TO 6.3 STEP .1
190      PSET (col! - 3.1, hght! * SIN(col!) + .2), kolor
200      PSET (col! - 3.1, -hght! * SIN(col!) + .2), kolor
210      PSET (hght! * SIN(col!) / 2, 1.2 * col! - 3.7), kolor
220      PSET (-hght! * SIN(col!) / 2, 1.2 * col! - 3.7), kolor
230    NEXT col!
240 NEXT num

250 REM ** Do some more or quit **
260 PRINT "Press space bar for another, ESC to quit";
270 ky$ = INPUT$(1): LOCATE 2, 2
280 IF ky$ <> CHR$(27) THEN CLS : GOTO 150
290 CLS: SCREEN 0: WIDTH 80: CLS END
```

PROGRAM GWME1207   Flower by PSET

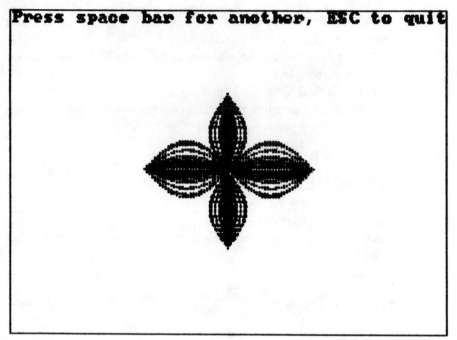

FIGURE 12-7   Flower

an option to draw the line in any of the colors available in palette 0 and palette 1. The COLOR statement works for LINE statements as well as PSET statements. The LINE statement specifies the color number of the palette in use in this way:

```
LINE (ColStart, RowStart)-(ColEnd, RowEnd), kolor
```

Here is a short program that draws randomly selected colored lines:

```
100 SCREEN 1: COLOR 0, 1: CLS: KEY OFF
110 WINDOW (0, 0)-(319, 199): DEFINT A-Z

120 WHILE ky$ <> CHR$(27)
130 kolor = INT(3 * RND) + 1
140 Col1 = INT(160 * RND): Row1 = INT(100 * RND)
150 ColAdd = 160-INT(160 * RND)
160 RowAdd = 100-INT(100 * RND)
170 LINE (Col1, Row1)-(Col1 + ColAdd, (Row1 + RowAdd), kolor
180 ky$ = INPUT$(1)
190 WEND
200 CLS: SCREEN 0: WIDTH 80: END
```

Enter the program and run it. A random colored line is drawn at a random place on the screen. Press any key but ESC to draw another line. Hold the key down, and lines are drawn without a hesitation. Release the key to pause. Press ESC when you have seen enough. The output after many lines have been drawn may remind you of the game, Pick-up Sticks.

In Screen 1, lines are drawn just as they were in SCREEN 2. However, now you can add color to the lines. Line length is restricted by the upper limit of the column number (319).

Nested Rectangles

The colors in SCREEN 1 allow you to display some startling effects. Zappy Artist has supplied two programs that draw rectangles in ever-increasing sizes, so that they seem to grow from the center of the screen.

Program GWME1208 (Growing Boxes) draws a series of nested boxes in one color. Then it repeats the process with a different color, cycling through all four colors in palette 1.

```
1 REM ** Growing Boxes **
2 ' GW-BASIC Made Easy, Chapter 12.  File: GWME1208.BAS

100 REM ** Set screen and randomize **
110 SCREEN 1: COLOR 0, 1: CLS : KEY OFF
120 RANDOMIZE TIMER: DEFINT A-Z

130 REM ** Draw boxes **
140 FOR kolor = 3 TO 0 STEP -1               'A range of colors
150   col = 150                              'Starting column
160   FOR row = 90 TO 10 STEP -2             'Move row up
170     LINE (col, row)-(320 - col, 200 - row), kolor, B
180     delay! = .125: start! = TIMER
190     WHILE TIMER < start! + delay!: WEND  'Pause a bit
200     col = col - 2                        'Move column left
210   NEXT row
220 NEXT kolor
230 CLS: SCREEN 0: WIDTH 80: END
```

PROGRAM GWME1208   Growing Boxes

First, the program draws a small white box at the center of the screen, using column 150 and row 90 as one corner. The other corner is defined so that the rectangle will be symmetrical around the center of the screen. Here is the LINE statement:

```
LINE (col, row)-(320 - col, 200 - row), kolor, B
```

Thus if one corner is (150, 90), the opposite corner of the box will be at (320-150, 200-90) or (170, 110).

After the first box is drawn, the starting column is moved left and the starting row is moved up. (See lines 160-210.) A new white box is drawn. This process repeats until 41 boxes are displayed.

Next, the color is changed to magenta, and the process repeats. This time, the magenta boxes are drawn over white boxes, one by one, from the center of the screen outward. When the cycle is completed, the color is changed to cyan, and the process repeats, with cyan boxes replacing the magenta boxes.

The last cycle uses black as the drawing color. Of course, the existing boxes are erased one by one from the center of the screen outward. When all are gone, the program ends.

```
1 REM ** Box Color Varied **
2 ' GW-BASIC Made Easy, Chapter 12.  File: GWME1209.BAS

100 REM ** Setup **
110 SCREEN 1: COLOR 0, 1: CLS : KEY OFF
120 RANDOMIZE TIMER: DEFINT A-Z

130 REM ** Draw Boxes in any of 4 colors **
140 WHILE INKEY$ <> CHR$(27)
150    col = 150
160    FOR row = 90 TO 10 STEP -2
170       kolor = INT(4 * RND)
180       LINE (col, row)-(320 - col, 200 - row), kolor, B
190       delay! = .125: start! = TIMER
200       WHILE TIMER < start! + delay!: WEND
210       col = col - 2
220    NEXT row
230 WEND
240 CLS: SCREEN 0: WIDTH 80: END
```

PROGRAM GWME1209   Box Color Varied

Changing Patterns

Program GWME1209 (Box Color Varied) is a variation of Program GWME1209. Instead of drawing the boxes in cycles of color, a random color is selected each time a box is drawn.

These two lines of the program:

```
kolor = INT(4 * RND)
LINE (col, row)-(320 - col, 200 - row), kolor, B
```

produce randomly varied designs in varying colors. Since black is included in the random color selection, some boxes cannot be seen—blank spaces appear to exist between some boxes. Drawing continues until one series of 41 boxes have been drawn. Figure 12-8 shows a typical screen after the drawing cycle has been completed.

A very interesting variation results if you switch lines 140 and 150 so that they look like this:

```
140    col = 150
150 WHILE INKEY$ <> CHR$(27)
```

FIGURE 12-8   Nested rectangles

Make this change and run the program again. What does it look like? Use your imagination...you might call it Dream Rooms....

Nonrectangular Shapes

You can use the LINE statement to draw any figure with straight lines—not just rectangles. Zappy Artist gave us Program GWME1210 (A Diamond of Triangles) which draws a series of triangles grouped in a diamond pattern. The interior of the triangles blink back and forth in alternating colors. Enter the program and run it.

The triangles are drawn using white. The first line is drawn using both end points. Then the other two sides of the triangle are drawn using the abbreviated form of LINE to connect to the last point referenced, as follows:

```
160    LINE (Col1, Row2)-(Col2, Row2), 3
170    LINE -(Col3, Row3), 3: LINE -(Col1, Row1), 3
```

Next, a point is calculated that will lie within each triangle:

```
180    ColP(num) = (Col1 + Col2) / 2
190    RowP(num) = (Row1 + Row3) / 2
```

The triangle is painted from this point to its white boundary, as shown next, using the paint color (kolor) that has been read in at line 150 from a DATA statement.

```
200    PAINT (ColP(num), RowP(num)), kolor, 3
```

Paint from here   Use this   Paint to
                       paint color   this color

When all eight triangles have been drawn and filled with color, a WHILE...WEND loop is used to determine the interior color of each triangle.

When used as follows, the POINT function reads the color number of the specified location:

```
270 WHILE INKEY$ <> CHR$(27)
280    FOR num = 1 TO 8
290       z = POINT(ColP(num), RowP(num))
```

```
1 REM ** A Diamond of Triangles **
2 ' GW-BASIC Made Easy, Chapter 12.  File: GWME1210.BAS

100 REM ** Setup **
110 SCREEN 1: COLOR 0, 1: KEY OFF: CLS: DEFINT A-Z
120 DIM ColP(8), RowP(8)

130 REM ** Colored triangles **
140 FOR num = 1 TO 8
150    READ Col1, Row1, Col2, Row2, Col3, Row3, kolor
160    LINE (Col1, Row2)-(Col2, Row2), 3
170    LINE -(Col3, Row3), 3: LINE -(Col1, Row1), 3
180    ColP(num) = (Col1 + Col2) / 2
190    RowP(num) = (Row1 + Row3) / 2
200    PAINT (ColP(num), RowP(num)), kolor, 3
210 NEXT num
220 DATA 120,45,200,45,160,10,2,  72,85,152,85,112,50,2
230 DATA 120,50,200,50,160,85,1,  168,85,248,85,208,50,2
240 DATA 72,90,152,90,112,125,2,  120,125,200,125,160,90,1
250 DATA 168,90,248,90,208,125,2,  120,130,200,130,160,165,2

260 REM ** Change partners **
270 WHILE INKEY$ <> CHR$(27)
280    FOR num = 1 TO 8
290       z = POINT(ColP(num), RowP(num))
300       IF z = 1 THEN z = 2 ELSE z = 1
310       PAINT (ColP(num), RowP(num)), z, 3
320    NEXT num
330    delay! = .5: start! = TIMER
340    WHILE TIMER < start! + delay!: WEND
350 WEND
360 CLS: SCREEN 0: WIDTH 80: END
```

PROGRAM GWME1210   A Diamond of Triangles

When the color number is found, the color numbers are switched. If the color number is 1, it is changed to 2. If the color number is 2, it is changed to 1. The triangle is then repainted with the new color. Here are the lines that accomplish this:

```
300       IF z = 1 THEN z = 2 ELSE z = 1
310       PAINT (ColP(num), RowP(num)), z, 3
320    NEXT num
```

New color

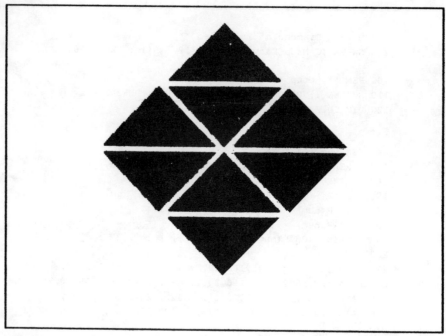

FIGURE 12-9   Triangle group

A time delay of one-half second is used after all triangles have been repainted (line 330). Then another repainting cycle is executed.

Press ESC to end the program. Figure 12-9 shows the pattern of triangles.

CIRCLES IN SCREEN 1

SCREEN 1 permits more colorful circles than SCREEN 2. The circles can be empty (background color), or they can be filled with any one of three colors chosen from the selected palette.

This chapter concludes with another demonstration from Zappy Artist's portfolio of entertaining programs. Program GWME1211 (Ever-Changing Mandala) places circles of randomly selected colors and sizes in a symmetric pattern on the screen. Such a pattern is called a *mandala*.

A small circle, painted white, is drawn first; then a WHILE...WEND loop begins at line 150. On each pass through the loop, four circles are drawn— one in each quadrant of the screen. This forms a symmetrical pattern around the circle in the center of the screen.

```
1 REM ** Ever-Changing Mandala **
2 ' GW-BASIC Made Easy, Chapter 12.  File: GWME1211.BAS

100 REM ** Setup **
110 SCREEN 1: COLOR 0, 1: CLS : KEY OFF
120 RANDOMIZE TIMER: DEFINT A-Z

130 REM ** Draw mandala until ESC key is pressed **
140 CIRCLE (160, 100), 2, 3: PAINT (160, 100), 3, 3    'Center
150 WHILE INKEY$ <> CHR$(27)
160 ' Assign random values to variables
170    radius = INT(8 * RND) + 3
180    OneKolor = INT(3 * RND) + 1: TwoKolor = INT(4 * RND)
190    DelH = INT(155 * RND) + 10              'Horizontal offset
200    DelV = INT(95 * RND) + 10               'Vertical offset

210 ' Draw and paint circles
220    CIRCLE (160 + DelH, 100 + DelV), radius, OneKolor
230    PAINT (160 + DelH, 100 + DelV), TwoKolor, OneKolor
240    CIRCLE (159 - DelH, 100 + DelV), radius, OneKolor
250    PAINT (159 - DelH, 100 + DelV), TwoKolor, OneKolor
260    CIRCLE (159 - DelH, 99 - DelV), radius, OneKolor
270    PAINT (159 - DelH, 99 - DelV), TwoKolor, OneKolor
280    CIRCLE (160 + DelH, 99 - DelV), radius, OneKolor
290    PAINT (160 + DelH, 99 - DelV), TwoKolor, OneKolor
300    delay! = .5: start! = TIMER
310    WHILE TIMER < start! + delay!: WEND         'Pause
320 WEND

330 REM ** Check to see if more or quit **
340 ky$ = INPUT$(1): IF ky$ <> CHR$(27) THEN 150   'More or quit
350 CLS: SCREEN 0: WIDTH 80: END
```

PROGRAM GWME1211   Ever-Changing Mandala

On each pass through the loop, the computer randomly selects a radius, a drawing color (*OneKolor*), a painting color (*TwoKolor*), and the column and row offsets for drawing new circles, as follows:

```
170    radius = INT(8 * RND) + 3
180    OneKolor = INT(3 * RND) + 1: TwoKolor = INT(4 * RND)
190    DelH = INT(155 * RND) + 10              'Horizontal offset
200    DelV = INT(95 * RND) + 10               'Vertical offset
```

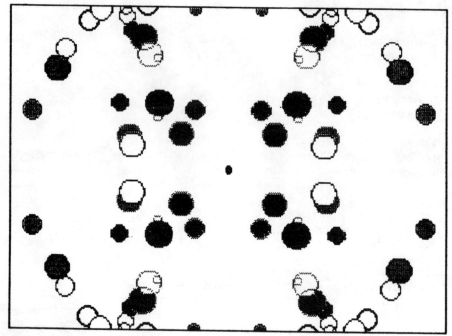

FIGURE 12-10   Dynamic mandala

A typical pattern is shown in Figure 12-10.

The number of circles on the screen increases until you press the ESC key. The computer then pauses while you scan the screen. At this point, you can press the ESC key again to quit, or press any other key to continue drawing circles.

Place a ruler on Figure 12-10. Measure the distance from any circle (call it Circle One) to the small circle in the center of the figure. With the ruler still in place, move along it to a point the same distance on the other side of the small circle. You should find the mirror image of Circle One at that point. That's why the pattern is said to be symmetrical around the center of the screen. Try the same thing for several circles.

REVIEW

The basic tools used to create a point, line, or graphics shape are PSET, LINE, and CIRCLE. You use PSET to draw very small individual pixels.

The LINE statement quickly places pixels adjacent to each other to draw lines. You can form curves with the CIRCLE statement. In addition, you can use auxiliary tools such as PAINT and POINT. There are also options that can be used with these tools to draw geometric shapes such as an arc, a circle sector, or an ellipse.

You used two graphics screens in this chapter. SCREEN 2 has only two colors, foreground and background. Graphics pixels (picture elements) in this mode are arranged as 200 rows of 640 pixels per row. Pixel numbering for the screen normally begins in the upper-left corner of the screen, with column 0 and row 0. However, with a WINDOW statement, you can reverse the vertical pixel numbering and change the number limits. The size of text printed in SCREEN 2 allows 80 characters per line, and 25 lines.

In SCREEN 1, you can use four colors at one time. Three colors are selected from one of two color palettes. The background color is specified in a COLOR statement, along with the palette desired. Drawing and painting colors are specified in each graphics statement (PSET, LINE, CIRCLE, and so on). The pixels of SCREEN 1 are twice as wide as those in SCREEN 2. Therefore, only one-half as many (320) will fit in any given row. Pixels are numbered the same way for both modes. Only the column maximum value is different.

SCREEN 2 is well suited to serious, detailed work. SCREEN 1 is livelier with its colors, and is often used when you want fun and entertainment. However, SCREEN 1 is also useful in dressing up business reports with colorful graphs and charts.

TRADEMARKS

Dungeons and Dragons™	TSR Hobbies
GW-BASIC®	Microsoft Corporation
IBM®	International Business Machines Corporation
IBM® PC	International Business Machines Corporation
Microsoft® BASIC	Microsoft Corporation
Microsoft® QuickBASIC	Microsoft Corporation
MS-DOS®	Microsoft Corporation
Tandy®	Tandy Corporation
Tandy® BASIC	Tandy Corporation
Tandy® CM-11	Tandy Corporation
Tandy® 1000	Tandy Corporation
Land of Ninja	© Chaosium
RuneQuest	© Chaosium

INDEX

' , as REM, 94, 118

*

    as arithmetic operator, 37, 71
    .BAS, 57

^ , as arithmetic operator, 71

:

    after disk-drive letter, 57
    as statement separator, 150, 166

,

    in PRINT statement, 86, 118, 138
    in PRINT USING format string, 102

. , in PRINT USING format string, 102

$

    in PRINT USING format string, 102
    as string designator, 137

= , in IF statement, 147

! , as single precision designator, 84

> , in IF statement, 147

< , in IF statement, 147

− , arithmetic operator, 37, 71

< > , in IF statement, 147

#

    as double precision designator, 84
    in PRINT USING format string, 98

% , as integer designator, 84

+

    as arithmetic operator, 37, 71
    as string concatenation operator,
    138, 210

?

    as abbreviation for PRINT, 39
    during INPUT, 91

" " , empty string, 177

" " , null string, 209

" , to enclose a string, 32, 136, 140

; , in PRINT statement, 138

/ , as arithmetic operator, 37, 71

/S option, in FORMAT command, 6, 10

A

A Colorful FOR...NEXT Loop
    (GWME0607), 169

A Diamond of Triangles (GWME1210),
    401

A> (MS-DOS), 4, 21, 40

AD & D (Advanced Dungeons &
Dragons), 217

Adding a program line, 61

Addition (+), 38, 71

Advanced Dungeons & Dragons
(AD & D), 217

ALT+P shortcut for PRINT, 39

ALTAIR 8800 computer, 3

ALTAIR BASIC, 3

Apostrophe (') as REM, 94, 118

Append to an Unstructured Sequential File
    (GWME1003), 317

APPEND, in OPEN statement, 308

Arc, of a circle, 387

Argument of a function, 197, 212, 219

Arithmetic, 36, 71

Array, 262

    dimension, 262
    double precision, 262, 279
    element, 262
    integer, 262
    numeric, 262
    single precision, 262, 279
    string, 262
    variable, 262

AS, in NAME statement, 333

AS, in OPEN statement, 308
ASC function, 206
ASCII, 63, 178, 201, 205, 306, 338
ASCII Codes and Characters
   (GWME0707), 204
Asterisk (*) as a wild card, 57

B

B:, disk drive designation, 58
B option, in LINE statement, 382
Bad command or filename message, 46
Bar graph, 383
.BAS, file extension, 56
BASIC, 1-2
BASIC.EXE file, 5, 22
BASICA, 1, 3
BASICA.EXE file, 5, 22
BEEP statement, 25, 47, 172
Beep with Time Delay Subroutine
   (GWME0801), 230
Beep with Variable Time Delay
   Subroutine (GWME0803), 236
Box (B) option, in LINE statement, 382
Box Color Varied (GWME1209), 398
Boxes, drawing, 382
Break in line...message, 115
Bubble Sort, 294
Built-in function, 192, 212

C

C> (MS-DOS), 5
Camping.Cat file, 323, 359
Concatenate strings, 210
Changing a filename, 333
CHR$ function, 178, 203
Circle Graph (GWME1205), 388
CIRCLE statement, 386, 403
Circumference of a circle, 387
Clearing the screen, 24
CLOSE statement, 309
Closing a file, 309
CLS statement, 27, 61
Coin Flipper (GWME0714), 220
Colon (:)
   after disk-drive letter, 57
   as statement separator, 150, 166
Color numbers, 170, 199

COLOR statement, 168, 390
Colors, in SCREEN 1, 391
Colors, random, 199
Columns on screen, 166
Comma (,) in PRINT statement, 86,
   118, 138
COMMAND.COM file (MS-DOS), 5
Command, direct, 19
Command, immediate, 19
Command line (MS-DOS), 21, 40
Comparisons, 147
Compound interest programs, 105-111,
   124-136
Compressed binary format, 63
Condition, in IF statement, 147, 180
Condition, in WHILE statement, 156, 157
Control structures, 145
Coordinates of a graphic point, 372
Coordinates, center of a circle, 386
Coordinates, real-world, 379
COPY command (MS-DOS), 4, 8, 11
Correcting a typing error, 51
Count to Ten Method #1 (GWME0603),
   160
Count to Ten Method #2 (GWME0604),
   160
Count Down...Blast Off! with Spaceship
   Liftoff (GWME0606), 164
Count Down...Blast Off! with Time Delay
   Subroutine (GWME0804), 237
CR (carriage return), end-of-record
   character, 316
Create a Structured Sequential File
   (GWME1005), 324
Create an Unstructured Sequential File
   (GWME1002), 314
Create Japanese.Ran Random-Access File
   (GWME1101), 341
Create Japanese.Ran Random-Access File
   (GWME1102), 348
Create the NotePad.Txt File
   (GWME1001), 311
Creative Computing, 3
CTRL+BREAK, 114, 156
CTRL+L, 24
Cursor, GW-BASIC, 24
Cursor, MS-DOS, 4, 20

CVC function, 370
CVI function, 370

D

D, in double precision floating point
    number, 82
Dartmouth BASIC, 2
Data file, 304
DATA statement, 217
DATE$ function, 30, 47, 194
Date, in MS-DOS, 20
Date, setting the, 32
DEF FN statement, 212
Default disk drive, 4
DEFINT statement, 270
Deleting a program from disk, 252
Deleting a program line, 64
Demonstrate ASC Numeric Function
    (GWME0708), 206
Demonstrate CHR$ String Function
    (GWME0706), 203
Demonstrate FIX and INT Numeric
    Functions (GWME0703), 198
Demonstrate INPUT$ String Function
    (GWME0705), 201
Demonstrate TIMER and INKEY$
    Functions (GWME0701), 192
Diagonals on SCREEN (GWME1201),
    2, 373
Dice-rolling program, 213
DIM statement, 264
DIR command, MS-DOS, 4, 7, 11, 66
Direct command, 19, 70
Direct statement, 19, 70
Disk drive A, 4, 6
Disk drive B, 9
DISKCOPY command, MS-DOS, 4,
    14, 17
Division (/), 38
Dollar sign ($), string variable designator,
    137
Dot Product of Two Arrays
    (GWME0903), 280
Dot Product with Line Item Printout
    (GWME0904), 282
Double precision array, 262
Double precision number, 79, 81
Double precision variable, 84

Drawing
    bar graphs, 383
    circles, 386, 403
    ellipses, 386
    line graphs, 380
    lines, 372
    rectangles (boxes), 382
    triangles, 400
Dungeons & Dragons, 214
Duration, in SOUND statement, 172, 196

E

E, in floating point number, 77
Eccentricity of an ellipse, 386
Element of an array, 262
Ellipse, drawing an, 386
ELSE clause, in IF statement, 180
Empty file, 316
Empty string (" "), 177
End of file (EOF), 320
End-of-record characters (CR and LF),
    316, 339, 347
ENTER key, 20, 25
Enter Records from Keyboard to
    Japanese.Ran File (GWME1103), 350
Enter Records Into Camping.Cat
    Random-Access File (GWME1106), 360
Entering a program, 49
EOF function, 320
Equals sign (=), in IF statement, 147
Erasing a program line, 64
ESC key, 178
Ever-Changing Mandala (GWME1211),
    403
.EXE file extension, 24, 44
Exit from GOTO loop, 150
Expanded Sales Tax Program
    (GWME0404), 97
Expanded Sales Tax Program with PRINT
    USING (GWME0405), 98
Exponent, 77
Exponentiation operator (^), 73

F

F option in LINE statement, 383
F1 function key (LIST), 49
F2 function key (RUN), 50, 53

F3 function key (LOAD"), 58
F4 function key (SAVE"), 56
F7 function key (TRON), 231
F8 function key (TROFF), 231
F9 function key (KEY), 29, 39
Field, in random-access file, 345, 362
Field, in sequential file, 306, 322, 327
FIELD statement, 345, 362
File not found in...message, 319
File
    closing a, 309
    data, 304
    empty, 316
    extension, 24, 44, 56
    number, 308
    opening a, 308
    program, 304
    random-access, 305
    record, 304, 327, 343
    sequential, 304, 322
Filename, 55, 306
FILENOTE.BAS file, 333
FileNote.Txt file, 332
FILES statement, 56
Fill (F) option, in LINE statement, 383
FIX function, 186, 197
Fixing a mistake, 51
Floating point number, 76, 79
Flower by PSET (GWME1207), 395
FNran function, 220
FNranchar$ function, 222
FNroll2D6 function, 213
FNroll3D6 function, 215
FNrollD6 function, 212
FOR statement, 167
FOR, in OPEN statement, 308
FOR...NEXT loop, 166
Format command, MS-DOS, 4, 6, 9
Format string in PRINT USING, 99, 102
Formatting a disk, 6
FORTRAN, 2
Freezing the screen, 117
Frequency, in SOUND statement, 172, 196
Function keys (F1, F2, F3, ...), 24, 29, 68
Functions, 192, 197, 212, 219
Future Value — Compound Interest with
    Counting Loop (GWME0505), 130, 132

Future Value — Compound Interest with
    GOTO Loop (GWME0503), 125
Future Value — Compound Interest with
    Modified GOTO Loop (GWME0506),
    134
Future Value of Money — Compound
    Interest (GWME0409), 104
Future Value of Money — Compound
    Interest #2 (GWME0410), 107
Future Value of Money — Compound
    Interest #3 (GWME0411), 109

G

Gates, Bill, 2
GET statement, 355
GOSUB statement, 230
GOTO loop, 114
GOTO statement, 114
Graph
    bar, 383
    circle, 388
    line, 380
Graphics, 371
    circles, 386, 403
    high resolution (SCREEN 2), 372
    lines, 372
    medium resolution (SCREEN 1), 389
    pixel, 376
    presentation, 389
    rectangles (boxes), 382
    screen coordinate system, 379
    triangles, 400
    world coordinate system, 379
Greater than sign (>), in IF statement, 147
Growing Boxes (GWME1208), 397
GW-BASIC, 1, 3
    arithmetic operations, 71
    cursor, 24
    keyword, 25
    opening screen, 23, 45
    program, 43, 47
    prompt (Ok), 24
    work disk, 5
GWBASIC.EXE file, 5, 22
GWME0301 program, 55-56
GWME0302 program, 63-64
GWME0302.ASC program, 64

GWME0401, Sales Tax with INPUT Statement, 94

GWME0402, Sales Tax with Enhanced INPUT Statement, 94

GWME0403, Sales Tax with Enhanced INPUT & PRINT Statements, 96

GWME0404, Expanded Sales Tax Program, 97

GWME0405, Expanded Sales Tax Program with PRINT USING, 98

GWME0406, Sales Tax with Double Precision Variables, 100

GWME0407, Sales Tax with Dollars and Commas in Printout, 102

GWME0408, Value of Stocks, 103

GWME0409, Future Value of Money — Compound Interest, 104

GWME0410, Future Value of Money — Compound Interest #2, 107

GWME0411, Future Value of Money — Compound Interest #3, 109

GWME0501, Sales Tax with GOTO Loop, 122

GWME0502, Value of Stocks with GOTO Loop, 124

GWME0503, Future Value — Compound Interest with GOTO Loop, 125

GWME0504, Modified Future Value — Compound Interest Program, 128

GWME0505, Future Value — Compound Interest with Counting Loop, 132

GWME0506, Future Value — Compound Interest with Modified GOTO Loop, 134

GWME0601, Negative, Zero, or Positive #1, 148

GWME0602, Value of Stocks with Total Value of All Stocks, 153

GWME0603, Count to Ten Method #1, 160

GWME0604, Count to Ten Method #2, 160

GWME0605, Time Delay Using a WHILE...WEND Loop, 163

GWME0606, Count Down...Blast Off! with Spaceship Liftoff, 164

GWME0607, A Colorful FOR...NEXT Loop, 169

GWME0608, SOUND Demonstrator, 174

GWME0609, Siren Song, 176

GWME0610, INKEY$ Demonstrator, 177

GWME0611, Sound Effects Experimenter, 179

GWME0612, Negative, Zero, or Positive #2, 182

GWME0613, The People's Poll #1, 185

GWME0614, The People's Poll #2, 187

GWME0701, Demonstrate TIMER and INKEY$ Functions, 192

GWME0702, Random music, 196

GWME0703, Demonstrate FIX and INT Numeric Functions, 198

GWME0704, Print a Name in Random Colors, 199

GWME0705, Demonstrate INPUT$ String Function, 201

GWME0706, Demonstrate CHR$ String Function, 203

GWME0707, ASCII Codes and Characters, 204

GWME0708, Demonstrate ASC Numeric Function, 206

GWME0709, Word Maker, 210

GWME0710, Roll Two Six-Sided Dice (Roll 2D6), 213

GWME0711, Roll a Character Using the Trust-to-Luck Method, 214

GWME0712, Roll a Character Using the Trust-to-Luck Method #2, 216

GWME0713, Roll a Character Using the Trust-to-Luck Method #3, 219

GWME0714, Coin Flipper, 220

GWME0715, Word Maker with Random Character Function, 222

GWME0716, Wordsworth, 224

GWME0801, Beep with Time Delay Subroutine, 230

GWME0802, Information About Trace, 232

GWME0803, Beep with Variable Time Delay Subroutine, 236

GWME0804, Count Down...Blast Off! with Time Delay Subroutine, 237

GWME0805, Word Maker with Subroutines, 239

GWME0806, Negative, Zero, or Positive #3, 242

GWME0807, The People's Poll #3, 244

GWME0901, High, Low, and Average Temperature for One Week, 267

GWME0902, High, Low, and Average Temperatures, 274

GWME0903, Dot Product of Two Arrays, 280

GWME0904, Dot Product with Line Item Printout, 282

GWME0905, Scramble an Array of Numbers, 286

GWME0906, Scramble and Sort an Array of Numbers, 289

GWME0907, Sort a String Array, 295

GWME0908, Sort a String Array with LOCASE Subroutine, 298

GWME1001, Create the NotePad.Txt File, 311

GWME1002, Create an Unstructured Sequential File, 314

GWME1003, Append to an Unstructured Sequential File, 317

GWME1004, Scan an Unstructured Sequential File, 318

GWME1005, Create a Structured Sequential File, 324

GWME1006, Use a File for Sequential Practice, 328

GWME1007, Use a File for Random Practice, 330

GWME1101, Create Japanese.Ran Random-Access File, 341

GWME1102, Create Japanese.Ran Random-Access File, 348

GWME1103, Enter Records from Keyboard to Japanese.Ran File, 350

GWME1104, Use Japanese.Ran for Sequential Practice, 352

GWME1105, Use Japanese.Ran for Random Practice, 356

GWME1106, Enter Records Into Camping.Cat Random-Access File, 360

GWME1107, Scan Camping.Cat Random-Access File, 366

GWME1201, Diagonals on SCREEN 2, 373

GWME1202, Pixel Hunt on SCREEN 2, 378

GWME1203, Simple Line Graph, 380

GWME1204, Simple Bar Graph, 384

GWME1205, Circle Graph, 388

GWME1206, Sine Wave by PSET, 393

GWME1207, Flower by PSET, 395

GWME1208, Growing Boxes, 397

GWME1209, Box Color Varied, 398

GWME1210, A Diamond of Triangles, 401

GWME1211, Ever-Changing Mandala, 403

H

High, Low, and Average Temperature for One Week (GWME0901), 267

High, Low, and Average Temperatures (GWME0902), 274

High-resolution graphics mode, 372

HOLD key (Tandy 1000), 118, 130

I

IBM PC compatible computers, 3

IF statement, 146

IF...THEN statement, 146

IF...THEN...ELSE statement, 180

Immediate command, 19

Immediate statement, 19

Information About Trace (GWME0802), 232

INKEY$ Demonstrator (GWME0610), 177

INKEY$ function, 177, 192

INPUT, in OPEN statement, 309

INPUT statement, 90, 94, 95, 96, 139

INPUT # statement, 321, 322, 327, 329

INPUT$ function, 141, 200

Inserting a program line, 61

INSTR function, 223

INT function, 197

Integer, 79
    array, 262
    type designator (%), 84
    variable, 84

Interrupting a program, 114

J

Japanese.Ran file, 340

Japanese.Txt file, 322, 339

K

Kemeny, John G., 2
Key line, 24, 28
KEY OFF statement, 28
KEY ON statement, 28
Keyword, GW-BASIC, 25
KILL statement, 252
Kurtz, Thomas E., 2

L

Labeling a disk, 13, 16
Land of Ninja, 214
Learn Japanese, 322
Leaving GW-BASIC, 40
LEFT$ function, 284
LEN keyword, in OPEN statement, 344
Less than sign (<), in IF statement, 147
LF (line feed), end-of-record character, 316
Line graph, drawing a, 380
LINE INPUT statement, 311, 320, 329
LINE INPUT # statement, 311, 321-322, 329
Line number, 47
LINE statement, 372
    B option, 382
    F option, 383
Lines on screen, 166
LIST statement, 49
Listing a program on the printer, 60
Listing a program on the screen, 49
LLIST statement, 60
LOAD statement, 58
Loading a program, 58
Loading from drive B, 59
Loading GW-BASIC, 22
Loading MS-DOS, 20
Local variable, 220
LOCASE subroutine, 257, 298
LOCATE statement, 165
LOF function, 357
Loop
    FOR...NEXT, 166
    GOTO, 114
    time delay, 161
    WHILE...WEND, 156
LPRINT statement, 109

LPRINT USING statement, 109
LSET statement, 346, 363, 369

M

Main program, 230, 243
Making music, 172
Mandala, 402
Mantissa, 77
Megabyte, 76
MERGE statement, 253
Microsoft, 1, 3, 4
    MID$ function, 208
Mistakes, fixing, 51
MKD$ function, 364
MKI$ function, 364, 369
MKS$ function, 364, 369
MOD arithmetic operator, 206
Modified Future Value — Compound
    Interest Program (GWME0504), 128
MS-DOS, 1, 4
    A>, 4
    C>, 5
    COMMAND.COM file, 5
    command line, 21
    cursor, 4, 21
    DIR command, 66
    DISKCOPY command, 4, 14
    FORMAT command, 4, 6, 9
    opening screen, 22
    prompt, 4, 21
    TYPE command, 66, 314, 326, 343, 349
Multiplication (*), 38
Musical note frequencies, 173

N

NAME statement, 333
Negative number, 39
Negative, Zero, or Positive #1
    (GWME0601), 148
Negative, Zero, or Positive #2
    (GWME0612), 182
Negative, Zero, or Positive #3
    (GWME0806), 242
NEW statement, 48
NEXT statement, 167
Not equal sign (< >), in IF statement, 147
NotePad.Txt file, 306

Null string (" "), 193, 209
Number
    double precision, 79, 81
    floating point, 76, 79
    integer, 79
    negative, 39
    positive, 39
    pseudorandom, 194
    random, 194
    in random-access file, 340
    single precision, 79
Numeric
    array, 262
    expression, 38, 70
    function, 192, 212
    variable, 83

O

Ok (GW-BASIC prompt), 24
ON...GOSUB statement, 242
ON...GOTO statement, 181
OPEN statement, 308
Opening a file, 308
OUTPUT, in OPEN statement, 308

P

PAINT statement, 400
Palette, 390
PC-DOS, 4
People's Computer Company, 3
People's Poll #1 (GWME0613), 185
People's Poll #2 (GWME0614), 187
People's Poll #3 (GWME0807), 244
Pitch, in SOUND statement, 172
Pixel (picture element), 376, 390
Pixel Hunt on SCREEN (GWME1202),
    2, 378
Plus sign (+), string concatenation
    operator, 138, 210
Positive number, 39
Prefabricated programs, 253
Presentation graphics, 389
Print a Name in Random Colors
    (GWME0704), 199
PRINT statement, 30-32, 37-39, 47
PRINT # statement, 310
PRINT USING statement, 98, 102

Printer, 60
Printing to the printer, 109
Program, 47
    entering a, 49
    file, 304
    filename, 55
    GW-BASIC, 43, 47
    line, deleting a, 64
    line, erasing a, 64
    line, inserting a, 61
    listing a, 49
    loading a, 58
    saving a, 55
    tracing a, 231
Prompt, MS-DOS (>), 4, 21
Prompt, GW-BASIC (Ok), 24
PSET statement, 379, 392
Pseudorandom number, 194
PUT statement, 345

Q

QuickBASIC, 4, 46
Quotation mark ("), to enclose a string, 32,
    136, 140

R

Random-access file, 305, 338
Random-access file, record length, 338,
    343
Random colored lines, 396
Random colors, 199
RANDOM keyword, in OPEN statement,
    344
Random music (GWME0702), 196
Random number, 194
RANDOMIZE statement, 194
READ statement, 217
Real-world coordinates, 379
Record length, random-access file,
    338, 343
Record, in a file, 304, 327
Rectangles, drawing, 382
Redo from start message, 140
REM outline, 105
REM statement, 93
RENUM command, 254, 256
RESTORE statement, 217

RETURN statement, 230
Returning to MS-DOS, 40, 65
RND function, 194
Roberts, Ed, 3
Roll a Character Using the Trust-to-Luck
    Method (GWME0711), 214
Roll a Character Using the Trust-to-Luck
    Method #2 (GWME0712), 216
Roll a Character Using the Trust-to-Luck
    Method #3 (GWME0713), 219
Roll Two Six-Sided Dice (Roll 2D6)
    (GWME0710), 213
Rows on screen, 166
RSET statement, 346
RUN statement, 50
RuneQuest, 214

S

Sales Tax with Dollars and Commas in
    Printout (GWME0407), 102
Sales Tax with Double Precision Variables
    (GWME0406), 100
Sales Tax with Enhanced INPUT &
    PRINT Statements (GWME0403), 96
Sales Tax with Enhanced INPUT
    Statement (GWME0402), 94
Sales Tax with GOTO Loop
    (GWME0501), 122
Sales Tax with INPUT Statement
    (GWME0401), 94
SAVE statement, 56, 63
Saving a program, 55
    in ASCII, 63
    to drive B, 57
Scan an Unstructured Sequential File
    (GWME1004), 318
Scan Camping.Cat Random-Access File
    (GWME1107), 366
Scientific notation, 77, 79
Scramble an Array of Numbers
    (GWME0905), 286
Scramble and Sort an Array of Numbers
    (GWME0906), 289
Screen
    colors, 170, 391
    columns, 166
    coordinate system, 379
    freezing the, 117

rows (lines), 166
    unfreezing the, 117
SCREEN statement, 372, 389
    SCREEN 0 (text mode), 371
    SCREEN 1 (medium resolution), 389
    SCREEN 2 (high resolution), 372
SCROLL LOCK key, 118, 130
Sector, of a circle, 387
Semicolon (;) in PRINT statement, 99, 138
Sequential file, 304, 305, 322
Setting the date, 32
Setting the time, 34
SGN function, 183
Shortcuts for typing keywords, 39, 68
Simple Bar Graph (GWME1204), 384
Simple Line Graph (GWME1203), 380
SIN function, 394
Sine Wave by PSET (GWME1206), 393
Single precision
    array, 262
    number, 79
    type designator (!), 84
    variable, 84
Siren Song (GWME0609), 176
Sort a String Array (GWME0907), 295
Sort a String Array with LOCASE
    Subroutine (GWME0908), 298
Sort an array of numbers, 289
SOUND Demonstrator (GWME0608), 174
Sound Effects Experimenter
    (GWME0611), 179
SOUND statement, 172, 196
SPACE$ function, 205
statement, direct, 19, 70
statement, immediate, 19
STEP clause, in FOR statement, 171
Stopping a program, 114
String, 32, 136
    array, 262
    field variable, 345, 362
    function, 192, 212
    type designator ($), 137
    variable, 136
Structured sequential file, 322
Subroutine, 229
Subroutine, variable time delay, 235, 254
Subscript, 262
Substring, 208

Subtraction (−), 38, 71
SWAP statement, 288
Syntax, 47
Syntax error, 27, 51
Syntax error in...message, 51
SYSTEM statement, 40, 65

T

TAB function, 97
Tandy BASIC, 1, 3
Text file, ASCII, 338
Ticks, in SOUND statement, 172
Tiles, 389
Time, 221
Time delay loop, 161
Time delay subroutine, 230
Time Delay Using a WHILE...WEND
  Loop (GWME0605), 163
Time delay, variable, 235
Time, setting the, 34
TIME$ function, 30, 34, 47, 194
TIMER function, 117, 161, 192
Trace off (TROFF), 233
Trace on (TRON), 233
Tracing a program, 231
Triangle, drawing a, 400
TROFF statement, 233
TRON statement, 233
Trust-to-Luck Method, 214, 216, 219
TYPE command, MS-DOS, 66, 304, 326,
  343, 349

U

Unfreezing the screen, 117
Unstructured sequential file, 305
Use a File for Random Practice
  (GWME1007), 330
Use a File for Sequential Practice
  (GWME1006), 328
Use Japanese.Ran for Random Practice
  (GWME1105), 356
Use Japanese.Ran for Sequential Practice
  (GWME1104), 352
User-defined function, 212

V

VAL function, 249
Value
  of a function, 192
  of a string variable, 137
  of a variable, 83
Value of Stocks (GWME0408), 103
Value of Stocks with GOTO Loop
  (GWME0502), 124
Value of Stocks with Total Value of All
  Stocks (GWME0602), 153
Variable, 83
  array, 262
  double precision, 84
  integer, 84
  name, 83
  numeric, 83
  single precision, 84
  string, 136
  string field, 345, 362
  time delay subroutine, 235, 254
  value of a, 83
View port, 247
VIEW PRINT statement, 247

W

WEND statement, 156
WHILE statement, 156
WHILE...WEND loop, 156
WIDTH statement, 199
Wild card (*), 57
WINDOW statement, 379, 393
Word maker (GWME0709), 210
Word Maker with Subroutines
  (GWME0805), 239
Wordsworth (GWME0716), 224
Work disk, GW-BASIC, 5
World Coordinate System, 379
WRITE # statement, 310, 325
Write-protect notch, 12, 13

Z

Zappy Artist, 392